T0419811

SPORTS AND ATHLETICS PREPARATION, PERFORMANCE, AND PSYCHOLOGY

ESSENTIAL TOPICS IN BASEBALL

FROM PERFORMANCE ANALYSIS TO INJURY PREVENTION

SPORTS AND ATHLETICS PREPARATION, PERFORMANCE, AND PSYCHOLOGY

Additional books and e-books in this series can be found on Nova's website under the Series tab.

ESSENTIAL TOPICS IN BASEBALL

FROM PERFORMANCE ANALYSIS TO INJURY PREVENTION

ERIK WELCH
EDITOR

nova
science publishers
New York

NOTICE TO THE READER

Library of Congress Cataloging-in-Publication Data

Names: Welch, Erik, editor.
Title: Essential topics in baseball: from performance analysis to injury
Identifiers: LCCN 2019044614 (print) | LCCN 2019044615 (ebook) | ISBN
    9781536165333 (hardcover) | ISBN 9781536165340 (adobe pdf)
Subjects: LCSH: Baseball--Physiological aspects. | Baseball players--Health and hygiene. | Baseball injuries--
    Prevention. | Batting (Baseball)
Classification: LCC RC1220.B3 E77 2020 (print) | LCC RC1220.B3 (ebook) | DDC 617.1/0276357--dc23
LC record available at https://lccn.loc.gov/2019044614
LC ebook record available at https://lccn.loc.gov/2019044615

Published by Nova Science Publishers, Inc. † New York

CONTENTS

PREFACE

Baseball is a game of tabulation and tracking. While baseball has a long and storied history of analyzing performance, it was not until recent history that analytical approaches have been applied to the medical and physical aspects of baseball. In today's game, at every level, baseball players are tracked for factors beyond wins and losses, to help maintain player health, or in an attempt to improve performance. Essential Topics in Baseball: From Performance Analysis to Injury Prevention explores the future of baseball monitoring in the context of being able to handle, interpret, and extrapolate predictions from the masses of data being collected.

In baseball, the throwing motion consists of a sequence of movements from the lower limbs to the upper limbs through the trunk. Failures in the sequence of movements can place an excess load on the upper arm and causes various disorders, the main causes being a high number of throws and inadequate throwing form. Too many throws will cause medial collateral ligament injury of the elbow and rotator cuff tear and periarthritis of the shoulder.

As such, the authors aim to determine whether upper extremity strength is predictive of injury, how upper extremity strength can be reliably and practically tested in the clinic, and whether or not strengthening programs will have an effect on upper extremity strength ratios, as well as compare and contrast current throwing programs found in the literature.

Additionally, ten right-handed college baseball batters participated in an experiment. They swung a bat towards five imaginary impact locations of different heights and lateral positions in the strike zone. They also hit a ball mounted on a tee stand placed in the strike zone which corresponded to the same five locations. The process was repeated seven times for each location, all of which were randomly assigned. Movements of the bat and ball were captured by an optical motion capture system at 250 Hz and 3-dimensional coordinates of the bat and ball were calculated.

The freely available Statcast Trackman data provides continuous location coordinates for individual pitches using Doppler radar. This detailed spatial information can be employed to visualize a batter's ability across regions in and around the strike zone. As such, the authors summarize classical geostatistical methodology and show how it can be applied to real data.

In another study, the authors explore hitting a stable ball mounted on a tee stand, rather than hitting a flying ball, to focus on the importance of vision in executing a batter's prepared or preplanned hitting movement for an impact location. This is achieved by eliminating the necessity of processing visual information regarding the ball's flight to predict the time and location of the pitch's arrival and modulate the movement with respect to the flight of the pitch.

The closing chapter examines the long history of tobacco use in baseball that dates back to the 19th century and the creation of the sport. Athletes and coaches initially used spit tobacco as a way to keep their mouths moist during dusty games and to alter the baseball to improve grip and break.

Chapter 1 - Baseball is a game of tabulation and tracking. While baseball has a long and storied history of analyzing performance, it has not been until recent history that analytical approaches have been applied to the medical, health, and physical aspects of baseball. In today's game, at every level, baseball players are tracked for factors beyond wins and losses, to help maintain player health, or in an attempt to improve performance. The term used to describe this tracking is player monitoring. Baseball player monitoring can be stratified into three factors: medical, physical, and performance. Medical player monitoring involves examining factors associated with baseball players' health, specifically injuries or clinical information. Physical player monitoring entails observing factors associated with physiology or physical loading (i.e., forces or torque). Physical factors include heart rate, endocrine levels, internal and external training load, and neurological efficiency. Finally, performance monitoring involves tracking factors that have a direct effect upon baseball performance, including pitch velocity, spin rate, bat speed, and launch angle. The advent and rapid growth in baseball player monitoring has allowed increased precision in evaluating player health, and advances in understanding and implementing factors affecting individual and team performance.

Baseball monitoring will evolve as clinicians, coaches, and players continue to pursue a deeper understanding of the data being outputted by current baseball monitoring technologies. As more and more data is tabulated and analysed, greater robust inferences can be made, continuing to change how the game is interpreted and played. The future of baseball monitoring is being able to handle, interpret, and extrapolate predictions from the masses of data being collected.

Chapter 2 - The throwing motion consists of a sequence of movements from the lower limbs to the upper limbs through the trunk. Failures in the sequence of movements place excess load on the upper arm and causes various disorders. The main causes of disability are a high number of throws and inadequate throwing form. Too many throws will cause medial collateral ligament injury of the elbow and rotator cuff tear and periarthritis of the shoulder.

In the wind-up phase of the throwing motion, it is necessary to save throwing energy by turning the body so that the buttocks face home plate. In the early cocking phase, the little finger side of the throwing hand should be raised upward.

Throwing energy decreases if the pelvis and trunk turn too early when the foot of the non-throwing side is in contact with the ground. To compensate for the loss of energy, pitchers use the upper extremities; however, this places a burden on the elbow and shoulder of the throwing arm. In the acceleration phase, the area between the waist and hip joint on the non-throwing side becomes the axis of rotation, and the straight line connecting both shoulders and upper limbs rotate quickly around this axis. In the follow-through phase, the mound tilt is used to shift the weight of the entire body forward and transmit the force to the throwing arm. If the trunk and legs do not move properly, less energy is transferred to the ball.

Therefore, a form that relies too much on the strength of the upper limbs will inevitably lead to injuries of the shoulder and elbow, and subsequent inability to throw a ball with speed. Checking and improving the throwing form is very important, so the authors will explain the correct pitching form that achieves high pitching performance and reduces the risk of injury.

Chapter 3 - Overhead throwing athletes, such as baseball players, have a high incidence of upper extremity pathology. The incidence of elbow pain in high school, college, and professional baseball players is reported to be over 50%. Approximately 20% of baseball players report shoulder pain. Injuries associated with throwing are most common in the elbow and shoulder due to the extreme forces that the inherently violent motion places on each of these joints. To counteract these forces, these athletes must be able to effectively control their upper extremity throughout the throwing motion. The high injury rates call for effective and proven prevention programs. There are few evidence based programs for upper extremity injury prevention; most of the current literature relies on expert opinion.

Upper extremity strengthening is often a component of injuries prevention programs. There is some mixed evidence that upper extremity strength, particularly of the rotator cuff, may be a predictor of injury. Most recently, strength ratios of the upper extremity have been the focus of prevention programs. This literature review aims to determine whether upper extremity strength is predictive of injury, how upper extremity strength can be reliably and practically tested in the clinic, and whether or not strengthening programs will have an effect on upper extremity strength ratios as well as compare and contrast current throwing programs found in the literature.

Chapter 4 - Baseball batters practice swinging their bat to assess their movements, build a mechanically effective swing style, and improve the consistency of swing trajectory. To achieve this aim, they swing the bat to different locations in the air by imagining the flights of different pitches.

These different trajectories of the bat pass through different locations in the strike zone, and are considered to be a mental representation of the movements of the bat and ball. If this mental representation deviates from the actual strike zone (defined by the rule of baseball), the pitch may be missed, or the ball-bat impact may be inaccurate. Therefore, the authors investigated the difference between striking a real ball at various heights and lateral positions, and swinging a bat to imaginary locations in the strike zone. If the trajectory of the bat to an imaginary location (e.g., an inside-high pitch) deviates from the trajectory of the actual ball, the possibility of failing to correctly estimating the pitch will increase. Through the identification and correction of such a deviance the chance of failure can be reduced. Therefore, the aim of this study was to explore the association between mental representation and the actual event. Ten right-handed college baseball batters participated in the experiment. They swung a bat to five imaginary impact locations of different heights and lateral positions in the strike zone. They also hit a ball mounted on a tee stand placed in the strike zone which corresponded to the same five locations. The process was repeated seven times for each location, all of which were randomly assigned. Movements of the bat and ball were captured by an optical motion capture system at 250 Hz and 3-dimensional coordinates of the bat and ball were calculated. The focus of analysis was the difference between the bat top positions at the moment of the imaginary impact in the bat swinging task, and at the moment of impact in the tee-batting. When the batter swung a bat toward the imaginary impact location, the bat top position deviated from the location of the ball in the tee-batting task (i.e., by shifting to the outer edge in the lateral direction). In the pitcher-catcher orientation, the bat top position shifted forward when swinging the bat to the inside impact location, while the swing trajectories to the outside and middle lateral positions were consistent with the impact location in the tee-batting task. The vertical deviation was either upward or downward, depending on the participant. However, variability relative to mean bat top position in the swinging tasks was consistent with the tee-batting. These results suggest that the mental representation of swinging a bat to each location in the strike zone did not correspond to the actual strike zone, but was consistent for the bat swing movement to be reproducible across trials. In summary, using this method to assess the mental representation of bat movements to the strike zone will facilitate the identification of inaccurate practice swings and thereby lead to improvements in batting performance.

Chapter 5 - Baseball is a game of stats, more so in recent years with the advent of "big data" and the emerging field of data science. Extensive statistical literature has been devoted to baseball data. However, comparatively less is known about the utility of geostatistical techniques to produce accurate and comprehensive heat maps. The freely available Statcast Trackman data provides continuous location coordinates for individual pitches using Doppler radar. This detailed spatial information can be employed to visualize a batter's ability across regions in and around the strike zone.

This chapter summarizes classical geostatistical methodology, shows how it can be applied to real data, and presents comprehensive heat maps based on Major League Baseball pitches from 2006 to 2018.

The stochastic process underlying batting ability is assumed to be a spatial Gaussian field with isotropic covariance that is estimated from the forementioned data. The authors then use the Kriging Residuals approach introduced in Cross and Sylvan (2015) to obtain best estimates of heat maps of batting ability for individual players. The authors also assess uncertainty in these estimates by using Monte Carlo simulations and resampling and show confidence regions for visualization.

Chapter 6 - Visual information on the trajectory of an oncoming pitch is critically important for a successful baseball hitting. However, the time available for batters to process this information and make a decision about swinging the bat is very limited, given the pitch's flight time of approximately 450 ms, as opposed to a batter's reaction time of 200 ms and bat-swinging movement time of 200 ms. Furthermore, the time available for the vision to be utilized is limited, given the time required for the visual feedback mechanism to work. Within this limited time window for baseball hitting, how long a batter can use the visual information, before the ball arrives to the home plate, to predict the time and location of the pitch's arrival and prepare and produce a bat-swinging movement? To address this issue, the authors investigated the effect of occluding the vision of the batter during the bat-swinging movement on the accuracy of the ball–bat impact to obtain evidence regarding the utilization of visual information for accurate hitting. The authors examined hitting a stable ball mounted on a tee stand rather than hitting a flying ball to focus on the importance of vision in executing a batter's prepared or preplanned hitting movement for an impact location (predetermined by the tee position) by eliminating the necessity of processing visual information regarding the ball's flight to predict the time and location of the pitch's arrival and modulate the movement with respect to the flight of the pitch. For this purpose, 10 college baseball batters performed tee stand-batting with five different ball locations, which were set within the strike zone. They wore liquid crystal shutter goggles, and their vision was occluded approximately at the moment of different movement phases: initiation of stepping with a front foot toward the pitcher, the stepped foot touching the ground, initiation of the bat swing, and right before the moment of the ball–bat contact. Batting performance under these vision conditions was compared with that observed in the absence of visual occlusion. Movements of hitting motion and batted ball were recorded using an optical motion capture system at 250 Hz, and three-dimensional coordinates of the body landmarks and ball were calculated. The duration of the bat-swinging movement did not differ between the full-vision and occlusion conditions immediately prior to the ball–bat contact. However, when the vision was occluded at the step foot touchdown and swing initiation phases, the duration was significantly longer than that reported under the full-vision condition. The velocity of the bat movement did not differ between the full-vision and occlusion conditions. However, the velocity of the batted ball decreased when the full-visual occlusion was initiated at approximately 250 ms prior to the ball–bat impact. These velocity results indicate the reduced accuracy of the ball–bat contact due to the occluded vision. This finding suggests that the hitting movement is modulated for an accurate ball–bat contact on the basis of the visual information available until approximately 150 ms prior to impact.

Chapter 7 - There is a long history of tobacco use in baseball that goes back to the 19th century and the creation of the sport. Athletes and coaches initially used spit tobacco (ST) as a way to both keep their mouths moist during dusty games and to alter the baseball to improve grip and break. However, there are significant health risks associated with the use of ST, including: oral diseases; systemic illnesses, such as cardiovascular disease; and various forms of cancer. The use of ST during games by collegiate and professional athletes and coaches, who are role models for the younger generations of baseball players, legitimizes the practice and relationship that ST has developed with the sport and enforces behavior that is detrimental to the health of all. It is important for baseball players and coaches to understand their role in the modeling of proper behaviors for younger athletes to protect their health and permanently sever the connection between baseball and ST.

In: Essential Topics in Baseball
Editor: Erik Welch

ISBN: 978-1-53616-533-3
© 2019 Nova Science Publishers, Inc.

Chapter 1

BASEBALL PLAYER MONITORING: FROM INJURY TO PERFORMANCE

Garrett S. Bullock[1,2,*], DPT Jenna Gourlay,[3] DPT and Robert J. Butler[4], DPT, PhD

[1]Centre for Sport, Exercise and Osteoarthritis Research
Versus Arthritis, University of Oxford, UK
[2]Nuffield Department of Orthopaedics, Rheumatology,
and Musculoskeletal Sciences, University of Oxford, Oxford, UK
[3]ProRehab, Evansville, Indiana, US
[4]St. Louis Cardinals Baseball Club, St. Louis, MO, US

ABSTRACT

Baseball is a game of tabulation and tracking. While baseball has a long and storied history of analyzing performance, it has not been until recent history that analytical approaches have been applied to the medical, health, and physical aspects of baseball. In today's game, at every level, baseball players are tracked for factors beyond wins and losses, to help maintain player health, or in an attempt to improve performance. The term

* Corresponding Author's E-mail: garrett.bullock@ndorms.ox.ac.uk; garrettbullock@gmail.com.

used to describe this tracking is player monitoring. Baseball player monitoring can be stratified into three factors: medical, physical, and performance. Medical player monitoring involves examining factors associated with baseball players' health, specifically injuries or clinical information. Physical player monitoring entails observing factors associated with physiology or physical loading (i.e., forces or torque). Physical factors include heart rate, endocrine levels, internal and external training load, and neurological efficiency. Finally, performance monitoring involves tracking factors that have a direct effect upon baseball performance, including pitch velocity, spin rate, bat speed, and launch angle. The advent and rapid growth in baseball player monitoring has allowed increased precision in evaluating player health, and advances in understanding and implementing factors affecting individual and team performance.

Baseball monitoring will evolve as clinicians, coaches, and players continue to pursue a deeper understanding of the data being outputted by current baseball monitoring technologies. As more and more data is tabulated and analysed, greater robust inferences can be made, continuing to change how the game is interpreted and played. The future of baseball monitoring is being able to handle, interpret, and extrapolate predictions from the masses of data being collected.

INTRODUCTION

Baseball is a game of tabulation and tracking. (James 2010) Since the inception of Major League Baseball in the late 19th century, baseball players' worth and performance have been calculated and scrutinized. (Rader 2008) Every action (or inaction) is registered, calculated, and analyzed. These measures range from the traditional batting average, runs batted in (RBI), and earned run average (ERA), to the new age metrics of fielding independent pitching (FIP) and wins above replacement (WAR) (James, Albert, and Stern 1993; James and Solutions 2018; James 2010).

While baseball has a long and storied history of analyzing performance, it has not been until recent history that analytical approaches have been applied to the medical, health, and physical aspects of the game (James and Solutions 2018; Pollack et al. 2016; Lapinski et al. 2009). In today's game, at every level, baseball players are tracked for factors beyond pure wins and losses, to help maintain player health, or in an attempt to improve performance (Lapinski et al. 2009; James and Solutions 2018). The term used to describe this tracking is termed player monitoring (Suchomel and Bailey 2014). Monitoring is defined as "A device used for observing, checking, or keeping a continuous record of something, or to maintain regular surveillance over" (J.A. Murray et al. 1933). Player monitoring can be used in many facets of baseball, (Pollack et al. 2016; Lapinski et al. 2009; Jinji and Sakurai 2006) and continues to rise in importance (Mills 2017).

Baseball player monitoring can be stratified into three factors: medical, physical, and performance (Pollack et al. 2016; Lapinski et al. 2009; Jinji and Sakurai 2006). Medical player monitoring involves examining factors associated with baseball players' health, specifically injuries or clinical information (Pollack et al. 2016). Physical player monitoring entails observing factors associated with physiology or physical loading (i.e., forces or torque). Physical factors include heart rate, endocrine levels, internal and external training load, and neurological efficiency (Lapinski et al. 2009; Aubert, Seps, and Beckers 2003; Healy et al. 2014; Day et al. 2004; Chambers et al. 2015). Finally, performance monitoring involves tracking factors that have a direct effect upon baseball performance, including pitch velocity, spin rate, bat speed, and launch angle (Jinji and Sakurai 2006; Garrett S Bullock, Schmitt, et al. 2018; Sawicki, Hubbard, and Stronge 2003).

The advent and rapid growth in baseball player monitoring has allowed increased precision in evaluating player health, (Pollack et al. 2016) and advances in understanding and implementing factors affecting individual and team performance (Lewis 2004). However, this rapid growth can cause confusion and an inability to decipher what are the right tools and systems to use for baseball player monitoring (Rowen 2018). Therefore, there is a need to elucidate the reasoning behind modern baseball monitoring methods, and to assist clinicians, coaches, and players in choosing the right monitoring devices and systems for their specific needs.

The purpose of this chapter is to describe the underlying principles behind baseball player monitoring; to summarize and clarify devices and systems used for medical, physical and baseball performance monitoring; and to give practical guidance on best practices and applications for baseball player monitoring. This chapter is split into three different sections: Medical player monitoring, physical player monitoring, and performance player monitoring. Medical player monitoring will cover topics that can help sports medicine providers track injury and medical needs of baseball players. Physical player monitoring will cover topics that track physical measures (e.g., heart rate variability, internal player load, external player load, forces on joints, etc.) that sports medicine and performance professionals can use to help maintain player health. Performance monitoring will cover themes that specifically monitor baseball performance measures (e.g., pitch velocity, spin rate, bat speed, etc.). Each section gives the reasoning behind why certain factors are monitored, overviews the main systems and devices used, and how current clinicians and coaches use the data in their own practice and coaching. There are also case studies implemented into the chapter. Each case study is a baseball professional's account on how they use a player monitoring device in their own practice. The case studies give practical advice on the baseball professional's personal reasoning for using a certain monitoring method, how they use the monitoring in their own practice, and how this specific monitoring method has changed how they treat, train, or coach baseball players.

MEDICAL MONITORING

Injuries in baseball players are a significant problem, at all competition levels (S. Conte, Camp, and Dines 2016a; Posner et al. 2011; Wilk et al. 2011; Wilk et al. 2014). The greatest incidence of acute and chronic injury is attributed to the shoulder, (Wilk et al. 2011; Posner et al. 2011) elbow, (Wilk et al. 2014; Posner et al. 2011; Garrison, Johnston, and Conway 2015) and trunk, (Posner et al. 2011) with throwing overuse injuries being the most common (Collins and Comstock 2008; Petty et al. 2004). Injury incidence has been reported as high as 3.6, 5.8, and 4.0 injuries per 1000 athletic exposures in professional, college, and in high school baseball players, respectively (Shanley et al. 2011; Hootman, Dick, and Agel 2007; Posner et al. 2011). Baseball player injuries are rising, (S. Conte, Camp, and Dines

2016a; Pytiak et al. 2018) with orthopaedic surgeries, such as ulnar collateral ligament reconstruction or 'Tommy John Surgery', increasing (Justin L. Hodgins et al. 2016; Mahure et al. 2016). The burden from baseball injury is high, with increased health care costs, (S. B. Knowles et al. 2007a) workplace time loss, (S. Conte, Camp, and Dines 2016a) and a substantial overall economic loss (S. B. Knowles et al. 2007a; Pollack et al. 2016).

Baseball injuries can be better understood, and ultimately prevented, through a stepwise process that enables the identification of injury type, injury risk factors, etiology, and injury mechanisms (Finch 2006). The 'Translating Research into Injury Prevention Practice' (TRIPP) framework is a six-step framework, established for injury surveillance in sports (Figure 1) (Finch 2006). Step 1 establish the extent of the problem, typically using incidence and severity of injuries; Step 2 establish causes and injury mechanisms through epidemiological research; Step 3 develop preventative measures; Step 4 scientific evaluation of preventative measure under ideal conditions; Step 5 develop implementation strategies and Step 6 evaluate effectiveness of preventative measures in implementation context (Finch 2006).

Model Stage	TRIPP Framework
1	Injury surveillance
2	Establish aetiology and mechanisms of injury
3	Develop preventative measures
4	Study under ideal conditions
5	Describe intervention context to inform implementation strategy
6	Evaluate effectiveness of preventive measures in implementation context

Figure 1. Translating Research into Injury Prevention Practice' (TRIPP) framework.

Understanding the factors that contribute to injury is the first step in developing injury prevention programs and policies. (Finch 2006) Baseball injury surveillance, is, "the ongoing systematic collection, analysis, and interpretation of health data, essential to the planning, implementation, and evaluation of health practice, closely integrated with the timely dissemination of these data to those who need to know" (Thacker, Qualters, and Lee 2012). Injury surveillance facilitates injury trends detection, and factors that help increase injury risk (Thacker, Qualters, and Lee 2012;

Thacker and Berkelman 1988). Further, continued injury surveillance helps in analyzing the impact of specific policy rule changes on injury, allowing for direct analysis of specific interventions (And their success and/or failure at mitigating risk) (Pollack et al. 2016).

Professional Baseball Injury Surveillance

Baseball injury surveillance has been occurring since the inception of the Major League Baseball disabled list in the 19th century (Neft, Cohen, and Neft 2004). The disabled list, now termed the injured list, tabulates illness, injuries, and time loss from collisions (Pollack et al. 2016; Posner et al. 2011; S. Conte, Requa, and Garrick 2001). However, the injured list does not require professional baseball clubs to list reasons for placing players on the injured list (Pollack et al. 2016). This allows baseball clubs to leverage the injured list as a way to increase the number of players on a roster, in order to try to improve overall team performance (Pollack et al. 2016). The injured list also does not allow for single game entries. Players must be placed on a seven, ten, or sixty-day injured list, further decreasing the reliability and ability for Major League Baseball to effectively monitor professional baseball player injuries (Pollack et al. 2016).

To counteract the inadequacies of the Major League Baseball injured list, an electronic medical record (EMR) was established (Pollack et al. 2016). The EMR was designed to create a more standardized and efficient method to enter and evaluate professional baseball injuries (Pollack et al. 2016). The EMR is a web-based database that consists of all professional baseball medical records (Major and Minor League: >7500 players and >230 teams). To gain access, a password and secure identification token code are needed (Pollack et al. 2016). Certified athletic trainers, physical therapists, and physicians enter all player medical data, consisting of injuries and illnesses on baseball and non-baseball related events (Pollack et al. 2016).

The EMR is linked to the professional baseball Health and Injury Tracking System (HITS). HITS is a centralized database that de-identifies patients from the EMR system, and is connected to all 30 Major League

Baseball clubs and the Office of the Commissioner. Having the HITS database linked to all clubs and the Major League Baseball governing body allows for the transfer of medical records, and roster transactions. This system describes injuries (diagnosis, body part, activity, date of injury, etc.), performance (wins, losses, batting average, etc.), and athletic exposures (number of games played, innings, etc.) (Pollack et al. 2016). The HITS database also allows for video, imaging, and medical notes to be included in a player's profile, creating a comprehensive database (Pollack et al. 2016).

Since the inception of the Major League Baseball EMR in 2010, an average of 30,000 records are inputted each year (Pollack et al. 2016). Numerable studies have been published due to the EMR (Dahm et al. 2016; G.A. Green et al. 2015; B. J. Erickson et al. 2017; Justin L. Hodgins et al. 2016; J. L. Hodgins et al. 2018). Besides publications, the baseball EMR has been important in changing Major League Baseball policy. Specifically, HITS was integral in understanding the recovery period of baseball players following concussions (Pollack et al. 2016; G.A. Green et al. 2015) Concussion recovery in professional baseball players was found to typically require less than 15 days. Due to these findings, a specific 7-day concussion injured list was instituted (G.A. Green et al. 2015). Prior to this policy change, players with concussions were either listed day to day, potentially being pressured to return to play prior to recovery, or placed on the 15-day injured list, allowing for unnecessary prolonged time loss from competition (Pollack et al. 2016). Other policy changes include rule changes to player collisions, catchers protecting home plate, and identifying potential injury risk factors for arm injuries (Pollack et al. 2016). While EMR ramifications are still not fully understood, creating a more precise and reliable injury surveillance system has allowed Major League baseball to create more data driven decisions, and have a greater understanding of the underlying factors affecting injury and recovery time in this specific population (Pollack et al. 2016).

Although there are great advantages and insights gained from the EMR, (Dahm et al. 2016; G.A. Green et al. 2015; B. J. Erickson et al. 2017; Justin L. Hodgins et al. 2016; J. L. Hodgins et al. 2018) challenges and limitations still exist. Currently exposures are not well defined. The epidemiological definition of exposure is any factor that is related to an outcome. (Velentgas et al. 2013) In the case of baseball injury surveillance, an exposure can be defined as a game, an inning, or a pitch. The outcome is defined as an injury (Posner et al. 2011). Within the current EMR, a player that pinch hits in the bottom of the ninth is considered to have the same level of exposure as a player that participates in the entire game (Pollack et al. 2016). Quantifying exposures is important in understanding injury risk (Posner et al. 2011). Without precise exposure assessment, clinicians and researchers cannot understand if certain risk factors are cumulative, nor the importance of practice and training sessions (Pollack et al. 2016). Further EMR limitations include the great burden of data input on athletic trainers, physical therapists, and medical doctors. Having to give refined detail on each injury, and on each individual player, requires further time demands on the medical professionals (Department 2019). Increased burden from data input, can lead to burnout and job drop out (Kania, Meyer, and Ebersole 2009; Pitney 2006). While data input has improved, the time and detail required for injury input is still high (Pollack et al. 2016). Possible solutions that have been proposed to help counteract this burden include increasing sports medicine clinician staff and hiring ancillary staff for data entry (Kania, Meyer, and Ebersole 2009; Mclaine 2005). However, all of these proposed solutions require resources, which are in short supply at many institutions.

Collegiate Baseball Injury Surveillance

The National Collegiate Athletic Association (NCAA) has instituted an injury surveillance system since 1982. All divisions and major sports were encouraged to participate. Originally a pen and paper system, two page reports were written for each individual athlete injury (Dick, Agel, and Marshall 2007). Weekly, total exposure of overall training, practice, and competition time were written and sent by mail or fax to NCAA headquarters. Athletic trainers had to document twice all injuries, once for internal records and the other for the NCAA injury surveillance program.

This system increased athletic trainer burden, due to double documentation, and also had poor data quality (Kerr et al. 2014).

With the advent of ubiquitous computer and internet technology, a piloted electronic injury surveillance system was instituted in 2004 (Kerr et al. 2014). The first electronic system allowed for the cessation of double documentation, and was considered a functional EMR. Data was also encrypted and protected. While this was an improvement from the original pen and paper surveillance program, there were still issues. Issues included, the system was not flexible to multiple electronic platforms, and did not allow full input of pertinent clinical and health information. Due to these flaws, a second internet-based platform was piloted in 2009 (Kerr et al. 2014). Renamed the Injury Surveillance Program, the new system allowed multiple electronic platforms to be instituted including The Athletic Trainer System (Keffer development services, Grove City, PA), The Injury Surveillance Tool (Datalys Center, Indianapolis, IN), and The Sports Injury Monitoring System (Flan Tech Computer Services, Iowa City, IA). The new electronic based platform allowed for athletic trainers to input all clinical notes and information, not just specific injury data. New allowable information included skin infection, heat injury, and illness. Other improvements included improved encryption and verification (Kerr et al. 2014).

There are 450,000 NCAA student athletes competing at all divisions, (Dick, Agel, and Marshall 2007) and almost 35,000 baseball players playing at the collegiate level (Association 2019). The current NCAA Injury Surveillance Program releases new data every five years, allowing for updated research to be commenced. Multiple studies have been published from The Injury Surveillance Program, (Hootman, Dick, and Agel 2007; Dick, Agel, and Marshall 2007; Kerr et al. 2015; Kerr et al. 2017) gaining insight into specific injury risk specific to collegiate baseball. For example, college baseball practice injury incidence is low compared to other collegiate sports; but there is a large increase in injury risk during competition (Hootman, Dick, and Agel 2007). College baseball players were found to have high incidence of non-contact injuries, compared to other sports, with shoulder and elbow having the largest injury incidence (Kerr et al. 2014).

Even with the reengineering of the NCAA Injury Surveillance Program, there are still issues. Not all institutions take part in the Injury Surveillance Program (Kerr et al. 2014). This may due to the perceived burden of participating in The Injury Surveillance Program, or that many NCAA programs still use paper based notes (Michael Sola ATC 2019). Many programs still use paper based notes due to the cost barrier to creating an EMR. Many NCAA programs do not have the monetary funds, or are not affiliated with a health care system, which inhibits the creation of an EMR (McDonald 1997). These limitations create bias in injury reporting, specifically with poorer athletic programs, decreasing the generalizability of the findings to all NCAA athletes.

High School Baseball Injury Surveillance

Professional and collegiate baseball has specific governing bodies that allow for a comprehensive and effective injury surveillance system (Pollack et al. 2016; Dick, Agel, and Marshall 2007). Within high school athletics, while there is a national body, (National Federation of State High School Association, 2019) high school sport governing power is delegated through each state. Due to this dispersion of governance, there is not one specific high school baseball or sport injury surveillance system. This does not allow for ubiquitous surveillance or a full understanding of high school baseball injury risk.

Although there is not one overarching injury surveillance system, there are multiple smaller systems that capture pertinent high school baseball injury data (Schroeder et al. 2015; Comission 2019). The National electronic injury surveillance system (NEISS) is a national injury surveillance system that reports on accidents and emergency situations that are reported to emergency departments in a national sample of United States Hospitals (Comission 2019). While the main objective is to report on consumer product injuries and poisonings, since 2000, NEISS has also reported on sport and recreational injuries (Comission 2019).

Each May, NEISS provides an annual report on the most pertinent injuries. Data sets can be accessed for a full year (January 1 through December 31). There are specific NEISS codes for particular injuries, while each injury incident is also accompanied by a 'narrative' which gives further injury description (Comission 2019). From this information, it is possible to understand emergency injury data. Multiple baseball studies have been published from these data (Buzas, Jacobson, and Morawa 2014; Coronado et al. 2015; Carniol et al. 2015; Sarah B Knowles et al. 2007b). While understanding emergency department injury is important, the majority of baseball injuries are overuse in nature (Posner et al. 2011; Hootman, Dick, and Agel 2007; Shanley et al. 2011). Overuse injuries typically are gradual, with pain, and performance detriments continuing over a period of time (Clarsen, Myklebust, and Bahr 2013; Young 1993) Overuse injuries are typically non-traumatic, (Clarsen, Myklebust, and Bahr 2013; Young 1993) and are not usually reported to the emergency department (Adirim and Cheng 2003). Furthermore, NEISS does account for exposure data, decreasing the utility of the data. This only allows NEISS data to gain a small perspective on injury risk in baseball players.

Another injury surveillance system is the National High School Sports-Related Injury Surveillance System (The Research Institute at Nationwide Children's Hospital, Columbus, OH) (Control and Prevention 2006). This system has an online portal, the High School Reporting Information Online (RIO), which allows high school athletic trainers to report data involved with high school injury and exposures. (Control and Prevention 2006) The High School RIO only incorporates data from specific boys (football, soccer, basketball, wrestling, and baseball) and girls (soccer, volleyball, basketball, and softball) high school sports (Rechel, Collins, and Comstock 2011). Athletic trainers must also be affiliated with the National Athletic Trainers Association (NATA). Using the High School RIO is voluntary, and requires double documentation of all notes (Rechel, Collins, and Comstock 2011; Control and Prevention 2006).

The High School RIO allows for the delineation of acute and overuse injuries, and also the incorporation of athletic exposures (Rechel, Collins, and Comstock 2011). However, due to the limitations within high school sport statistics and monitoring, most exposure data is limited to accounting a practice or a game as one exposure (Rechel, Collins, and Comstock 2011). This is in contrast to other injury surveillance systems in which exposures can be calculated per pitch or innings counts, (Dick, Agel, and Marshall 2007; Shanley et al. 2011) decreasing the specificity and precision of the data. Nevertheless of these limitations, the High School RIO allows for a more robust monitoring and surveillance of high school baseball injury (Control and Prevention 2006; Rechel, Collins, and Comstock 2011; Saper et al. 2018). Multiple publications have stemmed from this surveillance system, (Saper et al. 2018; Swenson et al. 2010; Schroeder et al. 2015; Marar et al. 2012; Rechel, Collins, and Comstock 2011) and have been important in understanding specific injury risks in high school baseball players (Saper et al. 2018).

Within the high school training room setting, there are multiple injury surveillance systems. These range from the nation-wide electronic platforms mentioned above, (Schroeder et al. 2015; Comission 2019) to traditional pen and paper systems that are used for internal use only. Pen and paper systems allow for easy mobility and ad hoc adjustments, as the specific rehab session takes place. Pen and paper also allows for athletes and rehabilitation professionals to write their own thoughts, strengths and struggles throughout the session, creating a more organic and authentic representation of the rehabilitation session. The pen and paper system does have its limitations. Pen and paper does not allow for ease of communication between different healthcare professionals, nor is pen and paper able to effectively and accurately summarize medical data. This does not allow for healthcare professionals to calculate and understand the overarching injury trends that are happening within a specific baseball team or organization (Michael Sola ATC 2019).

High school athletic trainers that were interviewed for this chapter stated that pen and paper baseball injury surveillance was easier and faster than any EMR system. Further they believed that an EMR was more burdensome and required more technical know-how than the pen and paper system. However, despite these limitations, all athletic trainers believed that an EMR was worth the extra effort to document baseball injuries and medical issues, due to the benefits that the EMR systems entail. Specifically, an EMR's ability to summarize injury data, create a more effective communication system, and embed imaging and other pertinent medical data. One athletic trainer stated, pertaining to the benefits of using an EMR, "I think at the end of the day, switching to an EMR system has been beneficial because of all the capabilities that it has. The additional time that it may require greatly outlays all the benefits that it brings. Like with all documentation, you get what you put into it" (Michael Sola ATC 2019). Each individual high school has their own budget, culture, and communication systems concerning medical monitoring. Having a system that works for each high school's specific circumstances is important in creating a baseball medical monitoring system that allows for baseball personnel to capture and understand the injury and medical trends for their own specific baseball program.

Phone Application Medical Monitoring

Currently, 80% of people worldwide own a cellphone, with 90% of all smartphone owners use their cellphone at least one time per day. Also, 70% of all adolescents own a cellphone. (Go-Gulf) Technology allows for portable, available online platforms for the user to interact with monitoring mediums, for fast, on the go data collection. Smart phone applications, better known as 'Apps,' are able to provide a personalized monitoring system, to help create an individualized monitoring and surveillance experience (van Mechelen, van Mechelen, and Verhagen 2014).

The ease and utility of monitoring applications creates a plethora of phone applications designed for sport medical monitoring. Sport monitoring phone applications are relatively cheap (average cost is $1.67), and can be downloaded for most devices (van Mechelen, van Mechelen, and Verhagen 2014). Despite these positives, there are many reported issues with sport medical monitoring applications. In a systematic review on sport injury phone applications, out of 64,873 applications, 18 were included in the review, with only four having any evidence backing up their claims. Furthermore, the majority of the reviewed phone applications had bugs, and required users to retrieve additional content from the web (van Mechelen, van Mechelen, and Verhagen 2014).

Due to the overall paucity of scientifically based sport injury monitoring applications, (van Mechelen, van Mechelen, and Verhagen 2014) a word of caution is proposed for using baseball specific medical phone applications. It is recommended to perform a full background check and talk to medical experts, prior to purchasing and using any baseball phone application. Furthermore, it is recommended to evaluate each application on its user ability. User ability can be categorized into four categories: presence of bugs, content (including scientific rigor and evidence), the need to search for content or videos from outside the application, and the merit of the claims made by the application (van Mechelen, van Mechelen, and Verhagen 2014).

Despite this caution, it is important to still overview specific baseball phone applications. The most popular and scientifically based baseball phone application is the Throw Like a Pro 2.0 phone application, developed in collaboration with Kevin Wilk PT, DPT and James Andrews, MD (Misra, Escamilla, and Trivedi 2018). The Throw Like a Pro application has four main categories: Overview, Preseason, In Season, and About. The application can track pitching and innings counts, provides age specific pitch limit and rest day recommendations, and offers specific videos and instructions on the Throwers 10 baseball injury prevention program. The information and instruction is all scientifically sound and backed by strong empirical evidence (Misra, Escamilla, and Trivedi 2018). However, despite these strengths, there are limitations. The application is expensive, costing $9.99, with multiple price points to add information. The application is also wordy at times, with some scientific jargon, decreasing the usability of the system (Misra, Escamilla, and Trivedi 2018).

Baseball Specific Patient Reported Outcome Monitoring

Patient reported outcome measures are a quick and easy tool to assess patient perspectives and gain insight into symptoms, physical function, mental health, and wellbeing (Nelson et al. 2015). These outcome measures are filled out by patient or athletes, and can be administered through pen and paper or electronically (Marshall, Haywood, and Fitzpatrick 2006; Greenhalgh and Meadows 1999). Patient reported outcome measures can help "narrow the gap" between the athlete and the clinician, and can assist in creating a better understanding of the patient's perspective of their health status (Nelson et al. 2015). Patient reported outcome measures also enable improved communication and decision making between the patient and clinician (Nelson et al. 2015; Valderas et al. 2008). Due to the ease and positive outcomes associated with administering these measures, (Valderas et al. 2008; Greenhalgh and Meadows 1999; Nelson et al. 2015) patient reported outcome measures have become a part of standardized care (Nelson et al. 2015).

One baseball specific patient reported outcome measure is The Kerlan-Jobe Orthopaedic Clinic Overhead Athlete Shoulder and Elbow Score (KJOC). The KJOC is a 10-item questionnaire that is specifically designed to evaluate throwing athlete health, practice patterns, and performance (Domb et al. 2010; Alberta et al. 2010; Franz et al. 2013; Kraeutler et al. 2013; Neri et al. 2011; Paci 2015). Questions assess warm up ability (*'how difficult is it for you to get loose or warm up prior to competition or practice?'*), pain, strength, arm instability, relationship with coaches (*'how much have arm problems affected your relationship with your coaches, management, and agents?'*), throwing velocity, throwing endurance, pitching control, and performance (*'how much do you feel your arm affects your current level of competition in your sport (i.e., is your arm holding you back from being at your full potential?'*). Each question uses a 10-cm visual analog scale (VAS), which a throwing athlete marks an 'X' on the reported scale. The 10-cm VAS is scored on a 10-point scale. For example, if an athlete marked an 'X' at 8.5 cm, the questions would be scored as an 8.5. The KJOC is scored on a 0 to 100 scale, with 0 reporting no throwing function, and 100 reporting perfect throwing function (Alberta et al. 2010). The KJOC has high reliability and validity in English, (Alberta et al. 2010) Italian, (Merolla et al. 2017) Turkish, (Turgut and Tunay 2018) Korean, (Oh et al. 2017) and can be effectively administered over the phone (B. J. Erickson et al. 2018).

The KJOC has been found to be sensitive to throwing specific pain and injuries (Domb et al. 2010; Alberta et al. 2010; Neri et al. 2011; Fronek et al. 2015). The KJOC was more responsive to throwing athlete pain and injury than the Disabilities of the Arm Shoulder and Hand (DASH) (Domb et al. 2010; Alberta et al. 2010). The KJOC was more accurate in evaluating pitchers' ability to return to play following labrum surgery compared to the American Shoulder and Elbow Surgeons score (Neri et al. 2011). Non-injured professional pitchers scored higher on the KJOC than injured professional pitchers (Fronek et al. 2015). Collegiate pitchers with scapular dyskinesis reported lower KJOC scores compared to pitchers without scapular dyskinesis (Tsuruike, Ellenbecker, and Hirose 2018).

There are specific limitations when using the KJOC. The entire questionnaire must be used, due to specific line items have not been validated (Chasse et al. 2018). This does not allow for coaches and clinicians to draw specific conclusions between warm up, pain, strength, etc. (Chasse et al. 2018). The KJOC is also not validated in Spanish. With a large population of Spanish speaking baseball players, the outcome measure cannot be used in this population (G. S. Bullock, Chapman, et al. 2018). The outcome also does not have specific cut off measures. While different outcome score thresholds have been proposed, (Kraeutler et al. 2013) there are no specific cut off scores to help identify at risk throwers.

Another baseball specific patient reported outcome measure is The Functional Arm Scale for Throwers (FAST) (Sauers et al. 2017; Huxel Bliven et al. 2017). FAST is a patient reported outcome focusing on health-related quality of life (Sauers et al. 2017). Health related quality of life is a multiple domain construct which examines the person's mental and physical perceptions, beliefs, and expectations of their health related experience (Testa and Simonson 1996). There are five domains to FAST, including: pain, throwing, activities of daily living (ADL's), psychological impact, and advancement (Sauers et al. 2017). FAST was specifically designed to capture the whole-person dynamic of high level throwers (Sauers et al. 2017; Huxel Bliven et al. 2017). Traditional patients reported outcomes do not account for the upper extremity, nor designed for high level athletes. This causes health-related quality of life outcome measures to report a ceiling effect with throwing athletes (Sauers et al. 2017; Denegar, Vela, and Evans 2008). A ceiling effect is defined when patient reported outcome measure scores are continually at the maximum score. Capturing a ceiling effect does not allow for an accurate representation of the patient, decreasing the usability of such outcome measures (Denegar, Vela, and Evans 2008). For example, a high-level thrower that is in need of ulnar collateral ligament reconstruction surgery, may still report high functioning scores with the Disabilities of the Arm, Shoulder and Hand (DASH) outcome measure. Solely using the DASH score, this high-level thrower would seem to not need medical attention. When in reality, this thrower cannot perform any throwing activities (Sauers et al. 2017).

FAST is scored on a 0 to 100 scale with a higher score demonstrating decreased health related of quality of life. FAST is a 22-item questionnaire, with an additional 9 item pitcher module. There are sport and non-sport related questions. Fast has been found to have high reliability and validity in throwing populations (Sauers et al. 2017; Huxel Bliven et al. 2017). Currently there are no additional studies that have utilized FAST since the publication of the original papers. Thus, it is not possible at this time to report on the strength and limitations of this patient reported outcome measure.

The Conway-Jobe Scale was designed to assess overhead throwing athlete's ability to return to sport following ulnar collateral ligament reconstruction (Conway et al. 1992). This scale was first introduced in 1992, and has been used routinely in a plethora of publications, mostly in baseball populations (Makhni et al. 2017). The outcome is scored on an ordinal scale of excellent, good, fair, and poor. An excellent score is achieved if a thrower returns to the same or higher competition level. A good score is achieved if a thrower competes at a lower competition level for ≥12 months or can throw batting practice without issues. A fair score is achieved if a thrower can play on a recreational level. A poor score is achieved if a thrower cannot throw without pain and cannot compete (Conway et al. 1992). Limitations of the Conway-Jobe scale include that this outcome measure has not been validated nor a minimum clinically important difference has not been determined (Smith et al. 2012).

PHYSICAL MONITORING

Success in baseball, as in all sports, depends on player health and performance (Stan Conte, Camp, and Dines 2016b; Brandon J Erickson et al. 2016). When players are not healthy, they will either miss games or have difficulty performing at their highest level. Athlete availability is the first parameter in evaluating player success; however, it is only half of the equation. The other contribution of player success comes from optimizing performance. Physical monitoring is incorporated in order to maximize player health and performance. While the basic human response to training is understood, (Halson 2014) clinicians, coaches, and sports performance professionals also recognize that individual differences exist (Bourdon et al. 2017). This makes it increasingly important to determine how athletes respond to training with regard for individual uniqueness (Bourdon et al. 2017; Halson 2014). Physical monitoring seeks to optimize training and performance by determining each athlete's physical response to loading (Halson 2014; Gabbett 2016). To assess the response to training, coaches and performance specialists need methods to monitor and track athletes to make sure they are being adequately challenged without forfeiting health (Gabbett 2016; Saw, Main, and Gastin 2016).

Baseball, at all competitive levels, demands an intensive schedule where multiple games are played in a week, often requiring multiple days in a row, or occasionally multiple games in a day. Where other sports such as football play only one game per week, baseball's competitive schedule creates a need to measure the challenging workload. While difficult to quantify, monitoring is necessary to gauge the unique stress baseball creates and ensure adequate athlete recovery (Brandon J Erickson et al. 2016; Saper et al. 2018). A professional baseball season occurs over a six-month period where athletes will play 162 games (Suchomel and Bailey 2014). Minor league players will compete in 140 games over a five-month period (Suchomel and Bailey 2014). College players will endure upward of 70 games and high school level play 20-30 games without including additional team play (Suchomel and Bailey 2014; Olsen et al. 2006). Youth and high school baseball carries the added risk of playing on multiple teams throughout the year. A majority of school-aged players do not heed the rest recommendations for pitch count and rest, taking less than two months off from baseball per year (Saper et al. 2018; Olsen et al. 2006). Further, despite the recommendations for youth pitchers, many do not take the suggested rest days or the rest period of four months (Yang et al. 2014). Without adequate rest and recovery, baseball players may exhibit signs of fatigue, possibly decreases in performance, and at worst, time loss from injury. (Suchomel and Bailey 2014; Halson 2014). Due to baseball's unique physical loading parameters, it is necessary to assess fatigue in baseball players to enhance performance, but also protect against overuse injury (Schroeder et al. 2015; Brandon J Erickson et al. 2016).

Physical monitoring techniques continue to develop as technology advances (Cardinale and Varley 2017) Tracking distance ran, weights lifted, practice time, and number of competitive games is incomplete and only represents half of what is needed to monitor training prescription. (Saw, Main, and Gastin 2016). To create a holistic representation of optimal training prescription, one must monitor an athlete's response to that training. It becomes necessary to look at external and internal parameters to create a full picture of an athlete's status (Blanch and Gabbett 2016).

External Load and Internal Load Monitoring

Teams experience more success when their best players are on the field and playing at their full potential (Arnason et al. 2004; Eirale et al. 2013). Increasing the availability of a team starts with appropriate training programs, focused on developing and optimizing the physical attributes associated with high performance and low injury (Foster, Daniels, and Yarbrough 1977; Gabbett 2016, 2010; Hulin et al. 2014). Physical traits must not only be enhanced, but overtraining, fatigue and injury must be mitigated (Gabbett 2016; Blanch and Gabbett 2016; Gabbett and Ullah 2012; Hulin et al. 2016).

A proper balance in training load and fatigue is needed to ensure adequate training for the desired physical result (Lyman et al. 2002; Racinais et al. 2014; Taha and Thomas 2003). When there is an imbalance between high stress followed by inadequate recovery, various symptoms contribute to an overtraining effect where performance decreases (Mourot et al. 2004; Kellmann 2010). Overtraining syndrome thus refers to the state of an athlete after excessive training without proper recovery, causing detrimental psychological and physiological effects. There is no on single indicator to determine overtraining syndrome, making a comprehensive approach more applicable (Gabbett 2016, 2010, 2004; Halson 2014). Manifestations of fatigue or overtraining can be measured based on performance metrics, but in research it is most often determined through objective physiologic effects (Knicker et al. 2011; Callister et al. 1990). For example a decrease in blood lactate levels, (Jeukendrup et al. 1992; Lehmann et al. 1998) decreased in glycogen levels, (Snyder et al. 1995; Costill et al. 1988) reduced maximal cortisol levels, (Snyder et al. 1995) decreased oxygen uptake, (Snyder et al. 1995) or lower heart rate variability may appear in athletes experiencing symptoms of overtraining (Halson and Jeukendrup 2004; Kreher and Schwartz 2012; Kellmann 2010).

Monitoring training load provides a data driven approach to examine athlete training load, competition load, and response to this work, and athlete training (Bourdon et al. 2017; Borresen and Lambert 2009; Gabbett 2016; Taha and Thomas 2003). Through internal and external load monitoring, players and coaching staff can examine fatigue level, determine recovery status, and alter training when necessary (Bourdon et al. 2017; Halson 2014; Borresen and Lambert 2009). External load is defined as the amount of work being performed, while internal load measures how an athlete is responding to external load (Gabbett 2016; Bourdon et al. 2017). External load is often easier to measure and refers to the amount of work an athlete completes in a given amount of time (Akubat, Barrett, and Abt 2014; Bourdon et al. 2017). Common examples of external load monitoring include global positioning systems, power output, pitch count, power generation, and mechanical forces (Bourdon et al. 2017; Gabbett 2016; Cornell, Paxson, Caplinger, Seligman, Davis, and Ebersole 2017; N.B. Murray et al. 2017). Internal load investigates the physiological and psychological stresses an athlete experiences during a given workout or competition (Bourdon et al. 2017; Gabbett 2016). Internal load monitoring examples include rate of perceived exertion, heart rate, heart rate variability, blood lactate, and oxygen consumption (Blanch and Gabbett 2016; Gabbett 2016; Callister et al. 1990; Cornell, Paxson, Caplinger, Seligman, Davis, and Ebersole 2017; Cornell, Paxson, Caplinger, Seligman, Davis, Flees, et al. 2017).

The combination of internal and external load gives a representation of how an athlete is responding to training and whether training adjustments need to be made (Gabbett 2016; Bourdon et al. 2017; Halson 2014). Where many baseball teams utilize external load monitoring such as pitch count, rest days, and even GPS monitoring, external load cannot exist in isolation (Windt and Gabbett 2017; Bourdon et al. 2017). Given an identical training session, an athlete will respond differently due to variables such as previous night sleep, prior training sessions, and emotional state, regardless of identical training intensity and duration (Halson 2014; Halson et al. 2002; Hulin et al. 2014; Hulin et al. 2016). Combining both external and internal load monitoring allows for a comprehensive quantification and understanding of an athlete's training, fatigue and readiness to compete (Hulin et al. 2016; Halson 2014; Bourdon et al. 2017).

Internal Load Monitoring

Heart Rate Variability

The autonomic nervous system (ANS) plays a major role in controlling the cardiovascular system, which in turn effects heart rate (Daanen et al. 2012; Dong 2016; O'Sullivan and Bell 2000). The ANS is made up of the parasympathetic and the sympathetic nervous systems (Borresen and

Lambert 2008; Hautala, Kiviniemi, and Tulppo 2009). These two systems regulate the cardiovascular response, and work in contrast to each other (Aubert, Seps, and Beckers 2003; Daanen et al. 2012). Specifically, the sympathetic nervous system raises heart rate in order to respond to the increased metabolic demand, while the parasympathetic nervous system decreases cardiac output when activity ceases (Daanen et al. 2012). Although both systems are active during rest, the sympathetic nervous system is more predominant during training and the parasympathetic more dominant during recovery (Dong 2016; Hautala, Kiviniemi, and Tulppo 2009).

Due to the role the ANS plays in regulating heart rate, heart-rate recovery (HRR) was an initial proposed way to determine athlete training response. (Daanen et al. 2012) It was hypothesized that measuring how heart rate responded directly after training, one could determine an athlete's ability to recovery (Daanen et al. 2012; Borresen and Lambert 2008; Kannankeril et al. 2004; Jeukendrup et al. 1992; Halson et al. 2002). The theory suggested that a more adaptable ANS would return to a resting heart rate faster than a less recovered state (Halson et al. 2002; Achten and Jeukendrup 2003). However, this hypothesis was not substantiated by research, with no observed differences in HRR between recovered and over trained athletes (Achten and Jeukendrup 2003; Snyder et al. 1995; Daanen et al. 2012). When observing resting heart rate changes, there is little variation (Pichot et al. 2000). A change of a few beats may be statistically significant, but practically misrepresented. Heart rate can be affected by many other factors besides the level of recovery, making it an inferior method for monitoring (Daanen et al. 2012; Pichot et al. 2000). Mental stress, caffeine, and environmental factors all affect heart rate (Pichot et al. 2000; Halson 2014). For this reason, the more reliable and valid (Makivić, Nikić Djordjević, and Willis 2013) method of heart rate variability (HRV) should be considered (Hautala, Kiviniemi, and Tulppo 2009).

Heart rate variability represents the time interval, or R-R interval, between each consecutive heartbeat (Billman 2011; Electrophysiology 1996). When examined in a healthy individual, these oscillations demonstrate the ability of the ANS to adjust and respond to an ever changing environment. (Electrophysiology 1996) Both sympathetic and parasympathetic innervations contribute to HRV, with parasympathetic influence causing higher HRV, and sympathetic inputs producing lower HRV (Dong 2016). As stated earlier, the sympathetic nervous system dominates during training, resulting in the "fight-or-flight" response (Aubert, Seps, and Beckers 2003; Dong 2016). Thus, a lower HRV suggests a stressed state and a higher HRV demonstrates a better ability to adapt and return to homeostasis.

Heart rate variability initially gained traction as a non-invasive way to predict mortality after a myocardial infarction (Electrophysiology 1996). The advent of the electrocardiogram (ECG) allowed the ability to connect variations in the heart rate rhythm with pathological conditions in patients (Electrophysiology 1996; Billman 2011). Since proving clinical relevance of HRV in the cardiac population, (Kleiger et al. 1987) it now provides a window into the ANS for sport and performance coaches (Aubert, Seps, and Beckers 2003; F. Shaffer and Ginsberg 2017; Makivić, Nikić Djordjević, and Willis 2013; Mourot et al. 2004; Borresen and Lambert 2008).

Optimizing performance relies on the ability to assess whether or not an athlete has recovered (Daniel J Plews et al. 2013; Seiler, Haugen, and Kuffel 2007). Heart rate variability offers the meaningful measure when monitoring athlete response to training load and competition stress (Makivić, Nikić Djordjević, and Willis 2013; Pichot et al. 2000; Aubert, Seps, and Beckers 2003). While monitoring total athlete workload is useful, HRV provides insight into how the ANS is responding to training stress (Uusitalo, Uusitalo, and Rusko 2000; Aubert, Seps, and Beckers 2003; Hautala, Kiviniemi, and Tulppo 2009; Dong 2016; Daniel J Plews et al. 2013; Seiler, Haugen, and Kuffel 2007). Heart rate variability can also evaluate whether an athlete is nearing an overtraining effect or has returned to pre-training or near pre-training state (Mourot et al. 2004; Saboul et al. 2016; Dong 2016; Aubert, Seps, and Beckers 2003; Borresen and Lambert 2009; Kaikkonen et al. 2012; Hedelin et al. 2000; Stan Conte, Camp, and Dines 2016b). Research shows that a less uniform HRV will signal an athlete is not in a trainable state due to its correlated sympathetic dominance (Polanczyk et al. 1998; Dong 2016; Aubert, Seps, and Beckers 2003).

Heart rate variability measures are most meaningful when there are multiple daily recordings, combined with weekly averages (Daniel J. Plews et al. 2014). Heart rate variability offers insight into recovery states both before and after training, making it necessary to have accessible means for measurement. The gold standard for measuring HRV is the electrocardiogram (ECG), but this is not feasible from a financial, environmental or time efficiency standpoint (Vanderlei et al. 2009). These convenience and cost issues were solved by using cardiofrequency meters in which software captures and translates the final heart rate variability metric (Vanderlei et al. 2009).

Heart rate variability is an effective tool in determining whether an athlete is ready for training (Billman 2011; Aubert, Seps, and Beckers 2003). Due to the long and demanding season, teams look to meticulously monitor internal load to optimize performance and mitigate injury (Stan Conte, Camp, and Dines 2016b; Ahmad et al. 2014). Yet, measuring the total work during practice and games remains challenging due to the different requirements of each position (Szymanski 2009). Because heart rate variability can identify an overtraining effect, monitoring at the beginning of day can help dictate that training session (Kiviniemi et al. 2010) and monitoring at the end can measure an individual's response (Aubert, Seps, and Beckers 2003; Achten and Jeukendrup 2003). Research shows that when using HRV to prescribe a training day, athletes demonstrate greater improvements with VO2peak and maximal running velocity compared to those athletes that were given a generic workout not based off HRV (Kiviniemi et al. 2010). Using HRV measurements to determine training may allow greater gains and less risk of fatigue.

Not only can heart rate variability determine an athlete's readiness, it can be used for training design (Aubert, Seps, and Beckers 2003; Cornell, Paxson, Caplinger, Seligman, Davis, and Ebersole 2017; Dong 2016). Lower trained athletes display lower heart rate variability in response to training compared to their higher trained peers. This suggests that HRV can be used to determine when to increase training, especially at the beginning of the season when players are less conditioned. Heart rate variability also shows a decrease during an interval training regimen compared to a constant intensity training session (Kaikkonen et al. 2012). Knowing the response to these trends can allow coaching to determine the type, intensity, and frequency of training depending on how athletes present (Uusitalo, Uusitalo, and Rusko 2000; Makivić, Nikić Djordjević, and Willis 2013; Kaikkonen et al. 2012).

In athletes that were intentionally over trained, there was a correlated decrease in HRV, making it possible to expose when an athlete is nearing fatigue. Signs of fatigue may be observed in baseball pitchers since HRV is seen to decrease after a start, until it rebounds by day three post-start, suggesting recovery (Cornell, Paxson, Caplinger, Seligman, Davis, and Ebersole 2017). The same gradual decline in HRV was seen with athletes undergoing intense training until a recovery week was instituted. These athletes' HRV was restored following this mandated recovery period (Seiler, Haugen, and Kuffel 2007). This suggests that built in periods of lighter exertion during the season may be able to help athletes recover (Cornell, Paxson, Caplinger, Seligman, Davis, and Ebersole 2017; Seiler, Haugen, and Kuffel 2007).

The most popular measurement tools for HRV remain watches paired with chest straps, chest strap systems, and the use of photoplethysmography (PPG) through smart phone applications (Daniel J. Plews et al. 2017). Photoplethysmography uses the flash from the smart phone to determine the amount of light that is reflected back through the skin (Daniel J. Plews et al. 2017; Bouts et al. 2018). Studies have shown that both the chest strap and smart phone application both yield acceptable comparison with the ECG (Daniel J. Plews et al. 2017; Vanderlei et al. 2009).

The Omegawave technology system and Polar S810i are reliable and valid devices when monitoring HRV using chest straps (Parrado et al. 2010). Where the Polar S810i is more affordable, the Omegawave uses leads in conjunction with a chest strap to more closely resemble an ECG setup (Parrado et al. 2010). Omegawave uses electrodes placed on the body to collect ECG and direct current potential (Parrado et al. 2010). The Omegawave device demonstrates compliance with the measurement guidelines proposed by the European Society of Cardiology for heart rate variability (Camm et al. 1996).

As stated earlier in the chapter, caution is advised when utilizing phone applications. Yet, affordability and ease of use make phone applications desirable for monitoring HRV(Bouts et al. 2018). The applications Runtastic and Instant Heart Rate show weak correlations to ECG metrics (Bouts et al. 2018). However, HRV4Training application demonstrates acceptable levels of correlation with the ECG (Daniel J. Plews et al. 2017; Altini, Van Hoof, and Amft 2017; K.H.C. Li et al. 2019). HRV4Training costs $9.99 to download the application onto a smartphone. While the cost is low, it is not without drawbacks (Bouts et al. 2018; K.H.C. Li et al. 2019). Phone applications sample at 30 Hz, which is below the recommended 200 Hz, (Polimeni et al. 2014) and may not offer the same accuracy as other monitoring methods (Gregoski et al. 2012). Finally, user errors may confound results such as skin tone, pressure on camera, and movement during reading (K.H.C. Li et al. 2019).

Biochemical Monitoring

Biochemical and physiological measures reflect internal load responses during training, making them of interest when monitoring athletes (Halson 2014; Halson and Jeukendrup 2004). While research tries to identify multiple biochemical markers, very few show significance when determining the training state or the risk of approaching overtraining (Halson 2014; Meeusen et al. 2013; Kenttä, Hassmén, and Raglin 2001; Lehmann et al. 1998).

Not only is research lacking, but testing methods prove to be challenging and at times unrealistic for regular monitoring (Lehmann et al. 1998; Kellmann 2010; Meeusen et al. 2013). The large amount of time, high costs, and level of expertise needed to interpret the findings deters many from using these measures (Taylor et al. 2012). In addition, the time of day, diet of the athlete, presence of supplements, and a non-fasting state may all confound the results (Taylor et al. 2012). The difference between individuals and the difficulty determining desired measures makes this method increasingly challenging to implement on a regular basis (Taylor et al. 2012; Coutts, Wallace, and Slattery 2007). The intricacies of the endocrine system produce further difficulties when monitoring hormonal responses to training

(Axel Urhausen, Gabriel, and Kindermann 1995; Meeusen et al. 2013). The endocrine system functions as a feedback system in which changes are interconnected rather than isolated (Meeusen et al. 2013; Axel Urhausen, Gabriel, and Kindermann 1995). Training will not affect a single hormone or a single marker and will instead cause an interactive response in which the endocrine system manipulates multiple biochemical variables (Meeusen et al. 2013; Szymanski 2009). This integration of the endocrine system would therefore require the measurement of multiple hormones due to the interplay and feedback system (Meeusen et al. 2013).

Blood lactate levels, (W Kindermann 1986; Axel Urhausen and Kindermann 2002; Bourdon et al. 2017) oxygen consumption, (Halson and Jeukendrup 2004; Bourdon et al. 2017) and urea concentrations (Axel Urhausen and Kindermann 2002) can help determine athletes nearing an overtraining state in aerobic competition. However, the physical demands during a baseball game rely on strength and power, which are anaerobically based (Jeffrey A Potteiger, Blessing, and Wilson 1992b). Pitching requires 0.145 seconds (Dillman, Fleisig, and Andrews 1993) from foot contact of the stride leg to ball release, making maximum effort less than 1 second (Jeffrey A Potteiger, Blessing, and Wilson 1992b). This is then followed by a rest of about eighteen seconds before the next pitch is thrown (Jeffrey A Potteiger, Blessing, and Wilson 1992b). These energy demands may explain why lactate and serum glucose measures showed no change when measured pre and post one inning pitched (Jeffrey A Potteiger, Blessing, and Wilson 1992b; Szymanski 2009). That is not to assume blood lactate measures did not change, but rather the amount of rest was adequate to resume homeostasis (Warren, Szymanski, and Landers 2015). Further, maximal volume of oxygen uptake during a simulated game reached only 45%, suggesting that these measures do not offer the same meaningfulness as in runners or other aerobic based sports (Szymanski 2009; Uusitalo, Uusitalo, and Rusko 2000).

While not correlated with overtraining, creatine kinase (CK) does provide useful information in athlete recovery (Jeffrey A Potteiger, Blessing, and Wilson 1992b; Szymanski 2009). Creatine kinase appearance suggests possible muscle fiber damage in response to training (J. A. Potteiger,

Blessing, and Wilson 1992a). Creatine kinase in the blood results from muscle contractions especially eccentric contractions (J. A. Potteiger, Blessing, and Wilson 1992a; Newham et al. 1983). Researchers speculate that CK measurement may allow information regarding injury reduction due to impaired muscular strength and fatigue associated with its release (J. A. Potteiger, Blessing, and Wilson 1992a; A Urhausen et al. 1998). This measure would be useful if it was able to deduce which muscles are producing increased CK levels (Wilfried Kindermann 2016). However, currently it is not possible to identify specific muscle degradation via CK measurement, making it impossible to conclude if pitching arm muscle overuse is occurring (J. A. Potteiger, Blessing, and Wilson 1992a; Jeffrey A Potteiger, Blessing, and Wilson 1992b).

Self-Reporting

While there is debate among which biological and physiological measures should be used, there is support for the use of self-reporting scales when monitoring an athlete's response to training (Meeusen et al. 2013; Bourdon et al. 2017; Slimani et al. 2017; Suchomel and Bailey 2014; Taylor et al. 2012; Saw, Main, and Gastin 2016; Drew and Finch 2016; Main and Grove 2009; W. Morgan et al. 1987). Methods show that self-reporting scores are sensitive to both dosage alterations and performance changes during training (Saw, Main, and Gastin 2016; Halson et al. 2002; Fry et al. 1994; Meeusen et al. 2013; W. Morgan et al. 1987). This relationship allows the use of self-reporting to determine when an athlete may be approaching an overtraining state (Fry et al. 1994; Meeusen et al. 2013; W. Morgan et al. 1987). Because the consequences of overtraining are psychological as well as physical, self-reporting identifies three main domains for assessment: mood disturbance, perceived stress or exertion, and a combination of both (Main and Grove 2009; Halson et al. 2002; Saw, Main, and Gastin 2016; Drew and Finch 2016).

Mood Disturbance

Decreased mood scores can identify when an individual is approaching overreaching and overtraining (Fry et al. 1994; Halson et al. 2002). Mood disturbance scores reflect when training dosage increases and then respond when a taper is introduced (Berger et al. 1999; Meeusen et al. 2013). Where the Daily Analyses of Life-Demands in Athletes (DALDA) shows little support for monitoring overtraining, (Rushall 1990) the Profile of Mood States (POMS) consistently demonstrates acceptable levels of reliability and validity when measuring response to training (Meeusen et al. 2013; LIAO and LUO 2004; Yokoyama et al. 1990; W. Morgan et al. 1987).

In situations where biochemical markers are unable to detect trending toward overtraining, the POMS results demonstrate a correlation (Slivka et al. 2010). The POMS questionnaire requires roughly five minutes to complete and can offer an efficient and inexpensive method to determine athlete response to training (LIAO and LUO 2004; Yokoyama et al. 1990.) The questionnaire contains multiple statements that respondents rank on a five point Likert Scale (Terry and Lane 2000). It contains six subscales (tension, depression, anger, vigor, fatigue, confusion, bewilderment) as well as provides a total mood disturbance score (Terry and Lane 2000).

Assessing mood does not come without difficulty (Saw, Main, and Gastin 2016). Mood may be sensitive to changes unrelated to training and it is challenging to distinguish if an athlete's mood status is influenced by emotional factors (LIAO and LUO 2004; Saw, Main, and Gastin 2016). A player's external situation may skew metrics designed to measure the athlete's load (Meeusen et al. 2013). There is a social desire to portray a false positive mood, and athletes may perceive the need to inflate responses to gain selection for play (Brener, Billy, and Grady 2003; Saw, Main, and Gastin 2015; Meeusen et al. 2013). In addition, stressors unrelated to sport such as schooling, relationships, or confidence may play a role in mood responses (Saw, Main, and Gastin 2015).

Perceived Stress or Exertion

Perceived stress or rate of perceived exertion provides athletes with the ability to report on their training status based on how they feel in regard to the level of intensity (Bourdon et al. 2017). Throughout the training session, athletes can give feedback on how hard they feel they are working. Studies suggest that an athlete's perception of stress correlates with actual training load (Saw, Main, and Gastin 2016; Halson et al. 2002; Kenttä, Hassmén, and Raglin 2001). Borg rating of perceived exertion (RPE) and session rating of perceived exertion (session-RPE) show that RPE is useful in assessing the intensity of exercise (Kenttä, Hassmén, and Raglin 2001; Borges et al. 2014). Previous research shows that athletes can in fact reproduce levels of intensity by working at a specific rate of perceived exertion (Kenttä, Hassmén, and Raglin 2001; W.P. Morgan 1994). Session-RPE has also been linked to average percentage of heart rate reserve and percentage of maximal heart rate (Meeusen et al. 2013). Validation and reliability studies substantiate the use of RPE as a method for determining an overtraining state (Borges et al. 2014). Rate of perceived exertion allows a fast and valid appreciation of intensity during said training session, but also over the course of the entire season (Borges et al. 2014; Suchomel and Bailey 2014).

While RPE does give a representation of training load, it should be noted that a low fitness level may impact response (Borges et al. 2014). Less experience may contribute to the meaningfulness of RPE as younger athletes have been shown to be more unreliable in their report (Bourdon et al. 2017; Borges et al. 2014). Both inexperience and undertraining may cause a player to rate their perceived exertion higher regardless of the load (Bourdon et al. 2017). Players may rate perceived exertion higher than the desired training level expected by coaches and training staff(Wallace, Slattery, and Coutts 2009). This disconnect further supports the need for both internal and external monitoring to give a more comprehensive quantification of load.

Comprehensive Self-Reporting

The Recovery Stress Questionnaire for Athletes (RESTQ-S) uses a combination of social, physical, and behavioral aspects of training and recovery (Coutts, Wallace, and Slattery 2007; Saw, Main, and Gastin 2016). The questionnaire correlates to different training loads suggesting that it may be used as a response to training assessment (Saw, Main, and Gastin 2016).

Subjective measures are useful when measuring the response to both acute training and chronic training loads, and may do so at early stages of overtraining (Halson et al. 2002; Coutts, Wallace, and Slattery 2007; Saw, Main, and Gastin 2016). The RESTQ-S questionnaire was able to show change in overtraining status when biochemical and physiological measures could not (Coutts, Wallace, and Slattery 2007). Research supports the questionnaires reliability and validity for use in sport(Martinent et al. 2014).

Subjective self-reporting allows for an inexpensive, efficient, and non-invasive tool way to assess athlete response to training (Saw, Main, and Gastin 2016; Main and Grove 2009). Athletic RPE is reproducible and RPE and mood disturbance measures correlate with increased training and tapering (Axel Urhausen and Kindermann 2002; Bourdon et al. 2017). This suggests that both RPE and mood patient reported outcome measures are valid instruments to evaluate an athlete's overtraining state (Axel Urhausen and Kindermann 2002; Bourdon et al. 2017). Their use, however, does not come without difficulties. Self-reporting can be manipulated by an athlete trying to change the course of training (Bourdon et al. 2017). In some cases, athletes may give a false representation of their self-report to appear more fatigued, or in a poorer mood, in order that their training intensity will be lessened (Meeusen et al. 2013). Mood monitoring poses complications due to when the athlete's baseline wellbeing is unknown making it difficult to distinguish when overtraining is approaching (Chambers et al. 2015).

External Load Monitoring

Triaxial Global Positioning Systems and Inertial Measurement Units

While global positioning system (GPS) was initially developed for military use, its prevalence in sport, recreation, and aviation continues to increase (Larsson 2003; Maddison and Mhurchu 2009). The communication between satellites and GPS receivers allows the transmission of player positioning at any given time (MacLeod et al. 2009; Hongu et al. 2013). Global positioning systems provide information that can be used to establish the external training loads involved in an athlete's training (Scott et al. 2013).

Global positioning system monitoring has been found to be valid for positioning, (MacLeod et al. 2009; Cummins et al. 2013) velocity, (MacLeod et al. 2009; Cummins et al. 2013) and distance travelled

(MacLeod et al. 2009; Maddison and Mhurchu 2009) by an athlete. However, sports that require short bursts throughout the game, such as baseball, have not been validated (Szymanski 2009). Where total distance and speed zones provide meaningful data in aerobic sports such as soccer (Akubat, Barrett, and Abt 2014; Cummins et al. 2013) and field hockey, (MacLeod et al. 2009) GPS cannot provide the necessary data for acceleration, deceleration, and quick movements required of an anaerobic sport (MacLeod et al. 2009; Cummins et al. 2013). Global positioning systems alone also have a lowered validity and reliability when assessing faster speeds over shorter distances and sudden directional changes as seen in baseball (Cummins et al. 2013; Jennings et al. 2010). The use of GPS in isolation is better suited for sports with constant movement over large distances (Cummins et al. 2013).

Global positioning systems with built in inertial measurements through accelerometers, magnetometers and gyroscopes add a meaningful level of data when monitoring sport (R.T. Li et al. 2016; Roell et al. 2018). Where using GPS gives speed and distance information, the addition of an accelerometer, magnetometer and gyroscope allows for the measurement of acceleration, body orientation, and rotational movements respectively (Roell et al. 2018; N.B. Murray et al. 2017). The addition of accelerometers, magnetometers and gyroscopes provide valid real-time measurements of acceleration and deceleration when compared to three dimentional (3D) motional analysis (Roell et al. 2018). Where reliability and validity for GPS decreases for faster speeds, its combination with inertial measurements continue to be valid even at high speeds (Weaving et al. 2017). Measuring distance, acceleration, deceleration, and speed of an athlete's movements allows quantification of external training loads (Cummins et al. 2013; Scott et al. 2013). A triaxial global positioning system, with triaxial accelerometers, can quantify multi-dimensional movements (Scott et al. 2013; Barrett, Midgley, and Lovell 2014). Incorporating a mathematical algorithm, it creates a representation known as PlayerLoad (Scott et al. 2013; Barrett, Midgley, and Lovell 2014; Garrett S Bullock et al. 2017).

The GPS monitoring systems by Catapult Sports are some of the most used systems in athletics to monitor GPS and PlayerLoad (Garrett S Bullock et al. 2017; Barrett, Midgley, and Lovell 2014). Catapult combines inertial sensors with the traditional positional metrics to give a more robust representation of external load (Gabbett 2016). This addition can permit monitoring of non-locomotor tasks like pitching and throwing (Gabbett 2016; Chambers et al. 2015). The athlete wears the device which includes a triaxial accelerometer, gyroscope, and GPS monitoring system (Weaving et al. 2017). While the device has been shown to be valid and reliable in treadmill running, it may be less reliable for multi-planar movement (Nicolella et al. 2018). The device demonstrates good intradevice reliability for PlayerLoad, although the actual total load is consistently lower than the calculated total load (Nicolella et al. 2018; Luteberget, Holme, and Spencer 2017). Further, interdevice reliability is low, making the collective team monitoring less conclusive (Nicolella et al. 2018; Scott et al. 2013).

The use of GPS monitoring in baseball is limited due to the inability to measure upper extremity load (Luteberget, Holme, and Spencer 2017). That in combination with the lowered validity and reliability at high speeds over short distances makes the use less meaningful (Weaving et al. 2017).

Force Plates

Force plates have the ability to measure the kinetic components involved in sport and performance movements (Beckham, Suchomel, and Mizuguchi 2014; Bourdon et al. 2017). Kinetics quantify both the forces and torques to determine why a specific movement occurs (G.S. Fleisig et al. 1995). Force plates can then be used to determine the forces created by athletes and analyze ground reaction force (GRF) (Beckham, Suchomel, and Mizuguchi 2014). The force plate measures the reactive force returned by the ground to complete the movement (Claudino et al. 2017).

The ability to quantity the kinetic variables of athletes allows the use of the force plate for neuromuscular fatigue monitoring. Neuromuscular fatigue has been linked to altered landing mechanics from a jump, (Kernozek, Torry, and Iwasaki 2008) decreased velocity, (Sanchez-Medina and González-Badillo 2011) and decreased spinal stabilization (Granata, Slota, and Wilson 2004). Neuromuscular fatigue refers to the decline or inability to complete physical movements (Enoka and Duchateau 2008). It is the point at which physiological responses causes a decrease in the force output (Enoka and Duchateau 2008). Force plates enable these forces to be calculated and used to monitor athlete fatigue (R.J. Gathercole et al. 2015a).

Multiple tests incorporating force plates have been used to monitor athlete fatigue, (R.J. Gathercole et al. 2015a; Beckham, Suchomel, and Mizuguchi 2014; Suchomel and Bailey 2014; Claudino et al. 2017) but the countermovement jump (CMJ) has been the most utilized in sport (Beckham, Suchomel, and Mizuguchi 2014; Claudino et al. 2017). The countermovement jump is an accepted measure to determine athlete fatigue (Claudino et al. 2017). Various countermovement jump measures can be assessed from power, peak force, and peak velocity to ascertain an objective marker of fatigue (Healy et al. 2014; Claudino et al. 2017). To perform the CMJ, the athlete starts standing and then loads into a position resembling a squat, and lastly transitions as quickly as possible into a maximal vertical jump (Laffaye, Wagner, and Tombleson 2014). The force plate measures total height, peak power, peak force, and peak velocity (Raymond et al. 2018). While peak power, force and jump height are used, (R. Gathercole, Sporer, and Stellingwerff 2015) the relation of flight time to contraction time may be closely linked to neuromuscular fatigue (Cormack, Newton, and McGuigan 2008).

The force plate created by Fitness Technology is commonly used among researchers and performance specialists (R. Gathercole, Sporer, and Stellingwerff 2015; Cormack, Newton, and McGuigan 2008; R. Gathercole et al. 2015b). The force plate utilizes Ballistic Measurement System (BMS) software to analyze CMJ (Cormack, Newton, and McGuigan 2008). These force plates have been found to be reliable and valid for CMJ (Cormack et al. 2008; Claudino et al. 2017) (Garcia-Lopez et al. 2005). The benefits include portability, affordability, and ease of everyday use (Claudino et al. 2017).

Within baseball, force plates can be used to measure neurological fatigue. One study found that CMJ remained decreased after 72-hours (Claudino et al. 2017; R.J. Gathercole et al. 2015a). These findings suggest CMJ scores can be used to monitor fatigue and also give insight into whether fatigue has affected mechanics (R.J. Gathercole et al. 2015a). Investigating measures such as eccentric components show that when fatigued, a CMJ may take longer to perform (R.J. Gathercole et al. 2015a). Force plates have also been used to assess hitting and pitching (Fortenbaugh et al. 2011). Evidence supports that the batter's weight shift adjustment is necessary for success against different pitches (Fortenbaugh et al. 2011). When swinging against change-ups and fastballs, a greater GRF was correlated with greater success hitting (Fortenbaugh et al. 2011). The use of force plates also validated the relationship between wrist velocity and leg drive, suggesting that the lower extremity plays a role in the throwing motion (MacWilliams et al. 1998). Those pitchers that were able to create the greatest forces in the direction of the pitch were able to throw faster pitches (MacWilliams et al. 1998). Most research in biomechanics looks at the upper extremity, but there is evidence that leg drive affects arm velocity and should not be overlooked (MacWilliams et al. 1998). The GRF during pitching showed that reducing stride length may decrease physiologic demand when pitching without decreasing velocity, but may come at the expense of other biomechanical factors (Crotin et al. 2014).

Biomechanics

Technology fuels man's desire to learn more about human movement. Biomechanics evaluates the underlying kinematic properties during complex skills. This information enables coaches and players to have a deeper understanding of sport movement (Mündermann, Corazza, and Andriacchi 2006). The development and continual progress of 3D motion capture paves the way for the use of biomechanical analysis in athlete monitoring (Camp et al. 2017). The baseball pitching motion is one of the fastest human movements (Dillman, Fleisig, and Andrews 1993). Over half of all baseball injuries are to the upper extremity. As a result, it is critical to understand the forces acting on the joints and muscles(Stan Conte, Camp, and Dines 2016b).

In order to discuss the biomechanics affecting injury risk, an understanding of pitching biomechanics is necessary. By looking at the biomechanics associated with pitching, researchers have been able to identify typical patterns in the kinetics and kinematics of the movement

(G.S. Fleisig et al. 1999; G.S. Fleisig et al. 1995; Fortenbaugh, Fleisig, and Andrews 2009; Dillman, Fleisig, and Andrews 1993). As defined earlier, kinetics determine why a movement occurs and kinematics observe how a movement occurs. Further, kinematics identifies angular displacement and velocity (G.S. Fleisig et al. 1995).

Motion capture technology provides the means to map these movements into a 3D representation (Stodden et al. 2005; G.S. Fleisig et al. 1999; G.S. Fleisig 2018). Reflective markers are placed on bony landmarks and are tracked by the motion capture camera (G.S. Fleisig et al. 1995). The equipment captures the markers throughout the movement and converts tracking into information and data (van der Kruk and Reijne 2018). Motion Analysis manufactures the most widely used system in baseball research and monitoring (Dillman, Fleisig, and Andrews 1993; G.S. Fleisig et al. 1995; G.S. Fleisig et al. 1999; Fortenbaugh, Fleisig, and Andrews 2009; Stodden et al. 2005). Most of these studies utilized four to eight 200-Hz charged-coupled device cameras worked in tandem with the markers and calculation software (Stodden et al. 2005). Three-dimensional motion capture performs exceptionally well at field tests for repeatability and precision (Richards 1999). The reliability and validity make 3D motion capture the gold standard for baseball biomechanics monitoring (Stodden et al. 2005; Huber et al. 2015; Theobalt et al. 2004; Hurd and Kaufman 2012; van der Kruk and Reijne 2018; Camm et al. 1996; Richards 1999).

Due to the high velocity of pitching, it is expected that there will be high kinetic measures (Fortenbaugh, Fleisig, and Andrews 2009). The problem originates when certain kinematic movements increase kinetic measures without any increase in velocity (Fortenbaugh, Fleisig, and Andrews 2009). These patterns then become determinantal rather than beneficial and may result in injury (Fortenbaugh, Fleisig, and Andrews 2009; G.S. Fleisig and Escamilla 1996). Researchers have identified and agreed upon six stages of pitching flowing from one to the next (Fortenbaugh, Fleisig, and Andrews 2009; Dillman, Fleisig, and Andrews 1993; G.S. Fleisig and Escamilla 1996). These six phases include: wind-up, stride, arm cocking, acceleration, arm deceleration, and follow-through (G.S. Fleisig et al. 1995). While all phases are important, special attention is given to arm cocking (foot contact to maximal external rotation (MER)), acceleration (MER to ball release), and arm deceleration (ball release to maximal internal rotation (MIR)) due to the maximal kinetic measures at these time points (G.S. Fleisig et al. 1995).

During the arm cocking phase, the arm experiences a period of maximal anterior shoulder force, internal rotation torque, horizontal adduction torque and elbow valgus torque (Fortenbaugh, Fleisig, and Andrews 2009). Shoulder external rotation (ER) and rotation at both the pelvis and upper torso produce a maximal shoulder internal rotation (IR) torque and a large valgus torque at the elbow (Dillman, Fleisig, and Andrews 1993). A maximum elbow varus torque is then produced in response right before MER (G.S. Fleisig et al. 1995; Dillman, Fleisig, and Andrews 1993). To prevent the distraction of the elbow joint, a maximum compressive force is created (Dillman, Fleisig, and Andrews 1993; G.S. Fleisig and Escamilla 1996). The arm cocking phase exposes periods of vulnerability to injury (G.S. Fleisig and Escamilla 1996). The measure of maximal elbow varus at MIR was found to correlate with elbow injuries (Fortenbaugh, Fleisig, and Andrews 2009). At the same time, enough elbow varus torque must be generated to prevent tension medially, impingement posteromedially, and compression laterally (G.S. Fleisig et al. 1995).

When observing the acceleration phase, the arm reaches a maximal flexion torque (Fortenbaugh, Fleisig, and Andrews 2009). This causes the elbow flexors to add stability to the joint by producing a compressive force (Fortenbaugh, Fleisig, and Andrews 2009). To accomplish this the biceps brachii responds with increased tension. The tension created coupled with the role of the biceps brachii in generating shoulder compression may contribute to labral tears (G.S. Fleisig et al. 1995).

At arm deceleration from ball release to MIR, the shoulder and the elbow undergo a maximal proximal force (G.S. Fleisig et al. 1995). The instant of maximal compressive for during this phase creates another critical period for possible injury (G.S. Fleisig et al. 1995). Too much traction at this point will put the labrum in a vulnerable position due to the position of the humeral head (Stodden et al. 2005; G.S. Fleisig et al. 1995). A translation of the humeral head either anteriorly or posteriorly can cause trapping of the labrum or subacromial impingement (Dillman, Fleisig, and Andrews 1993; G.S. Fleisig et al. 1995). Subacromial impingement also occurs possibly due to the positioning of abduction, horizontal adduction, and internal rotation of the shoulder joint (G.S. Fleisig et al. 1995). To resist this horizontal adduction and distraction during deceleration, the rotator cuff and posterior shoulder muscles provide stabilization (G.S. Fleisig et al. 1995). This becomes more challenging in a shoulder with capsular weakness or increased laxity putting the rotator cuff at risk of tensile failure (G.S. Fleisig et al. 1995). The biceps plays a role in resisting deceleration and may cause tearing at its attachment at the labrum (G.S. Fleisig et al. 1995).

Forces and torque contribute to injury risk when they are repeated in high quantities (Fortenbaugh, Fleisig, and Andrews 2009). Because pitching requires such a high load of force and torque, it becomes necessary to minimize any pitching inefficienies (Dillman, Fleisig, and Andrews 1993; Fortenbaugh, Fleisig, and Andrews 2009). Studies show that there is little variation in pitching mechanics between age groups, but kinetics increase with age (G.S. Fleisig et al. 1999). This lack of variation makes it very beneficial to teach proper mechanics from a young age (G.S. Fleisig et al. 1999). As player experience increases, many kinematic parameters become more uniform (G. Fleisig et al. 2009). The largest differences in biomechanics exist between youth and high school pitchers (G. Fleisig et al. 2009). This may be attributed to experience or may be the result of growth slowing.

Portable Biomechanical Devices

While marker-based motion capture has answered the need for insight into the biomechanics of pitching and throwing, it is costly and challenging to interpret (Boddy et al. 2019). Inertial measurement units (IMU) can be a solution when there is not access to 3D motion capture (Boddy et al. 2019). Inertial measuring units are comprised of accelerometers and gyroscopes that can offer the same information as 3D biomechanical analysis, without taking the pitcher off the field (Waltz 2015; Makhni et al. 2018). These devices have the ability to measure elbow torque, arm slot, arm speed, and shoulder rotation (Makhni et al. 2018). Elbow varus torque, alterations in arm slot, and throwing loads have all been linked to increased injury risk (Camp et al. 2017; Makhni et al. 2018). Monitoring these can have profound effects on maintaining pitchers on the active roster and preventing additions to the disabled list (Brandon J Erickson et al. 2016).

The Motus Throw or other previous products by Motus Global have been the wearable device of choice for both athletic teams and researchers. The device contains a sensor including a triaxial accelerometer and triaxial gyroscope that can be contained in the sleeve that is worn on the pitching arm (Waltz 2015). Information regarding pitching load, elbow height at release, arm slot, release point and arm speed is sent to a phone application in real-time (Waltz 2015). The validity and precision of the device are acceptable for use during the pitching motion (Makhni et al. 2018). Studies have observed that these devices can offer much of the information captured by motion analysis, but can do so on the field and with players of all levels (Makhni et al. 2018; Boddy et al. 2019). Research found that the sensor is comparable to 3D motion capture in regards to arm speed, arm rotation, arm slot, and elbow varus torque (Camp et al. 2017).

Motion capture may provide extensive insight into biomechanics, but its feasibility proves challenging for baseball (van der Kruk and Reijne 2018). Motion capture 3D biomechanics requires a laboratory setting, computer software, and both time and expertise for the interpretation of results (van der Kruk and Reijne 2018; Boddy et al. 2019). The Motus Throw allows a player to wear the sleeve without disrupting practice. A pitcher will go through their motion as usual while the sleeve collects information. The benefit to the Motus Throw is that real-time data is sent to the cell phone. This can allow coaches and players to get immediate feedback when working on pitching. The affordability and portability make theis device feasible for players of all ages. This is in stark contrast to the expensive costs and unnatural setting required for 3D motion capture.

Pitch count is one variable that correlates with injury in a multitude of literature (Slenker et al. 2014; N.B. Murray et al. 2017; Rawashdeh, Rafeldt, and Uhl 2016; Fortenbaugh, Fleisig, and Andrews 2009). While recommendations urge coaches to keep track of pitch count, this number can be an inaccurate representation of load because positional throws and warm-up pitches are often not included (Rawashdeh, Rafeldt, and Uhl 2016). When validating the use of IMUs for pitch count, findings suggest that they can keep track of total pitch count with acceptable accuracy (Rawashdeh, Rafeldt, and Uhl 2016; Boddy et al. 2019). The device has shown good sensitivity without missing a pitch thrown, but had slightly lower specificity due to counting incidental movements (Rawashdeh, Rafeldt, and Uhl 2016).

The Motus Throw is useful in rehabilitation as well as prevention. As discussed in the section on biomechanics, elbow varus torque is correlated with elbow injuries (G.S. Fleisig and Escamilla 1996). Findings show that elbow varus torque increases during an interval throwing program when transitioning from partial effort to full effort (Slenker et al. 2014). This is not surprising since kinetics increase with velocity and velocity will increase with effort, but it gives rise to the possibility that the Motus Throw can be used to monitor effort given and force during return to sport throwing programs (Slenker et al. 2014; G.S. Fleisig and Escamilla 1996).

In agreement with motion capture, the Motus Throw also found fastballs to produce more torque than change-ups (Camp et al. 2017). One study found that arm slot and the angle at ball release of the forearm in relation to the ground, could influence elbow varus torque (Camp et al. 2017). As discussed previously, elbow varus torque can influence medial elbow injuries (G.S. Fleisig and Escamilla 1996; Camp et al. 2017). Lateral flexion of the trunk, shoulder abduction, and elbow flexion produce arm slot position and can result in increased medial forces (Camp et al. 2017). Findings show that a pitch delivered over the top as opposed to at a side angle create less overall varus torque (Matsuo, Nakamoto, and Kageyama 2017). All of these findings suggest the versatility for using the Motus Throw in baseball. Players and coaches can use the device to monitor pitch count (Rawashdeh, Rafeldt, and Uhl 2016) with ease and accuracy (R.T. Li et al. 2016). The sleeve also provides players insight into their throwing mechanics. The use of the Motus Sleeve can increase the awareness and real-time feedback for players of all levels.

PRACTICAL APPLICATIONS: HEART RATE VARIABILITY MONITORING

Jason Shut PT, DPT is a physical therapist, strength and conditioning coach, and movement specialist. He is currently a sports medicine provider for the St. Louis Cardinals.

Figure 2. Jason Shutt, PT, DPT.

As discussed in the section, the ability to monitor internal and external load can help determine appropriate training approaches. This ability to monitor internal loading becomes even more important when athletes are returning from injury. The level of workload may play a role in reinjury and must be carefully considered when working through a return to sport continuum. Finding the correct balance of stress and rest is necessary to make generic protocols more unique to the athlete. Heart rate variability allows a window into the training response of an athlete by signifying if an athlete is trending more toward a sympathetic state. This approach can be applied to rehabilitation to assess the appropriateness of interventions throughout the plan of care.

Heart rate variability monitoring was implemented with a Major League Baseball player after he underwent an anterior cruciate ligament reconstruction (ACL). Heart rate variability was used to determine response to previous session and readiness for the next session. With this particular player, the goal was not simply to have him complete the rehabilitation plan of care or to have him return to pitch in a single game. The goal was to have him complete the season as a productive and effective member of the pitching rotation. For this reason, he was not going to have an extended period of taper at the end of the rehabilitation process. Heart rate variability allowed monitoring throughout the rehabilitation process with the end goal of seasonal play.

How Did You Use HRV to Determine Appropriate Rehabilitation and Training Load?

Heart rate variability was chosen because it was a way to be consistent with measurements. These measurements were taken multiple times throughout the day to gauge his readiness for each session. However, a single measurement does not hold tremendous power. The value lies in trends and changes over time. These short-term and long-term trends provided the ability to adjust the structure of each session. When determining each session, we would compare to the day prior, the week prior, and when available the month prior. A single day does not give a true representation. We would carry out our plan for rehabilitation and then heart rate variability would provide the representation of how he was responding to that plan of care.

If on a given day his numbers were trending more to a sympathetic state, we would modify our exercises to reflect a less demanding session. Additional information should not make a situation more confusing. In this case we had clear priorities, objective standards and a plan for each session. With a plan in place, the HRV information was a luxury or bonus allowing us to adjust. If it was within the normal range, we completed the session as planned. If HRV was outside the normal range, we looked back at the priorities to see what was most necessary to accomplish. In regard to loading specifically when we had a HRV outside the normal range, we looked to decrease the physiologic toll of the season. There are many options to decrease load, decrease sets to allow for longer rest, decrease exercise complexity, decrease speed, any combination of those things. We may have worked on improving mobility and improving his tissue extensibility rather than performing a more strength-based session. We would take a break from working on something like power, and transition into something physiologically different. Days where heart rate variability was consistently trending low, we could work on knee extension for example if it was stiff from the previous workout. Because a single day can drop without a pattern, we would try a steady-state warm-up and see if his HRV rebounded. The benefit to HRV is that you can check your intervention and get immediate feedback moving forward.

Did His HRV and RPE Agree or Were There Times Where They Varied?

There were instances of both circumstances throughout his rehabilitation. There were times when he had a good HRV, but self-reported fatigue, and days with a poor HRV where he self-reported feeling great. This relates back to not allowing more information to cloud your judgment, you do not want to ignore the athlete in front of you. If he self-reported fatigue, but HRV was acceptable, a lengthened warm-up could often eliminate the feeling of fatigue. When successful, we would continue with the session as planned. However, if he still felt fatigued, then we would adjust the plan in the same way as if HRV was poor.

Were There Any Patterns You Noticed with His HRV and His Sessions?

In general, there was a trend to become more sympathetic throughout the training week. This became more common as rehabilitation progressed and his external training load increased. When he trended toward more sympathetic for an extended period of time, we would give more opportunities for recovery. As the process continued, he also became more aware of his body. He started to recognize that more soreness may not result in a lower HRV.

What Are Some Challenges to HRV Monitoring?

As discussed earlier, HRV is only meaningful when you get consistent and reliable data. While monitoring methods can often prove challenging, this professional athlete demonstrated exceptional compliance and made the process of monitoring possible. When athletes are only minimally compliant, the data becomes weaker. Getting client buy-in is necessary for effectiveness with HRV monitoring. It is important to note that many other things play into the HRV measurement. Supplements, mood state, sleep quality, and emotional stress can all cause variations in HRV. We used the morning standardized protocol to get a reading before the any effects of caffeine, and then we would monitor again after the morning training. He would lie down in a quiet room for several minutes to decrease outside influences.

PERFORMANCE MONITORING

Since baseball's inception, people have been trying to quantify an individual's performance (Rader 2008). Unlike other team games such as football or basketball, it is very easy to tabulate each individual's actions during a baseball game. Due to the nuances of individual player's actions, baseball enthusiasts have been trying to ever increase precision and accuracy of an individual's true performance value (James, Albert, and Stern 1993).

The original baseball performance monitoring stemmed from baseball's heritage in cricket. Henry Chadwick, an English statistician, altered the cricket batting average to help quantify the performance ability of individual baseball batters (Rader 2008). As the game progressed, different statisticians, or in baseball what are termed sabermetricians, have been debating the efficacy of these standard performance metrics such as batting average and earned run average (ERA). In response, sabermetricians have created alternative, next generation performance metrics, such as fielding independent pitching (FIP) and wins above replacement (WAR), to better quantify baseball performance (James, Albert, and Stern 1993; James and Solutions 2018; James 2010).

Since the creation of the batting average, baseball players, coaches, scouts, and organizations have been trying to better understand the underlying factors that help separate high performing from low performing baseball players (James, Albert, and Stern 1993; James and Solutions 2018; James 2010; Lewis 2004). The first recorded attempt to understand one of these factors was the testing of Washington Senators' pitcher Walter Johnson in 1912. Walter Johnson, the greatest pitcher of his era, had great pitching success, much of what was allotted to having the best fastball in the Major Leagues. Due to the limitations of technology at the time, no one knew how to quantify pitching velocity. This caused inconsistency in a Major League team's ability to properly scout pitching prowess. As a result, Walter Johnson's fastball was first analyzed at the Abderdeen Proving Grounds, at the Remington Arm Company bullet testing facility (Thomas 1998). Since this first initial test, (Thomas 1998) other means have been developed to quantify pitching velocity, from testing Bob Feller's fastball against a motorcycle, to the stop watch (Sickels 2004). However, it was not until the development of the radar gun, and the first official in game test of Nolan Ryan, in 1974, that modern baseball performance monitoring was born (Rader 2008).

Since the advent of the first radar gun, there has been an ever increasing arms race in trying to capture the underlying variables that best can predict baseball players' performance (MayorsCitySports 2018). They have ranged from measuring sprinting speed,[1,2] to modern approaches such as quantifying pitch spin rate (Jinji and Sakurai 2006). Presently, there are multiple devices and systems on the market that are used to try to quantify these factors (Jinji and Sakurai 2006; Garrett S Bullock, Schmitt, et al. 2018; Sawicki, Hubbard, and Stronge 2003).

Pitch Velocity Monitoring

Pitch velocity is essential to pitching performance. Pitchers with higher velocity, on average, have improved performance compared to slower pitchers (Fortenbaugh, Fleisig, and Andrews 2009). One mile per hour (mph) increase at the Major League level equals 0.3 runs saved per nine innings for a starter (R. Arthur 2017). A pitched baseball at 90 mph reaches home plate in 400 ms (D.M. Green and Swets 1966). The faster a pitch, the less reaction time the hitter has to judge pitch type, location, and the quality of the pitch (Gray 2010).

As described previously, measuring pitch velocity was one of the initial attempts to quantify factors that directly contribute to baseball performance (Thomas 1998). Since the initial testing of the radar speed gun, more commonly known as the radar gun, this device has improved technologically, and is currently a portable easy to operate device that is used in ball parks throughout the world (G.S. Fleisig et al. 1999). Radar is an

---

[1] The best story of trying to quantify running speed pertains to the allegedly fastest baseball player of all time, James 'Cool Papa' Bell. James Bell would race horses to test his speed.

[2] Freedman L. African American Pioneers of Baseball: A Biographical Encyclopedia. Greenwood Press, Westport, CT. 2007.

acronym derived from World War Two, standing for Radio Detection And Ranging (Brown 1999). Radar guns use the principle of the Doppler effect to measure the speed of objects. Radio waves are sent from the 'gun' and are then bounced back after striking an object. The Doppler effect principle is used to measured how the radio waves react to a moving object. If the object is moving towards them, the radio wave frequency will be greater when the waves return. If the object is moving away, the radio waves will return at a lower frequency. The radio wave frequency difference, from initial emission, to return, can be calculated to generate a velocity of the moving object (Cadotte Jr and Koscica 2000). The velocity is calculated from the following equation:

$$v = \frac{\Delta f}{f} \frac{c}{2}$$

where Δf is change in frequency, f is original frequency, and c is the speed of light (Cadotte Jr and Koscica 2000).

When using a radar gun, in order to accurately quantify pitching velocity, the gun must be stationary. This allows for the radar gun to accurately assess the change in radio wave frequency. The second stipulation is that the radar gun must be directly behind the catcher. Trying to use the radar gun at an angle to the pitcher creates what is known as angle error. Measuring at an angle does not allow for an accurate Doppler effect to be established, creating error. The farther away from directly behind the catcher one stands, the more error there will be in measuring pitching velocity (Inc. 2018).

Currently, there are two radar gun devices that are used precipitously in baseball. These devices include the Stalker (Applied Concepts, Inc., Plano, TX) and Jugs (Jugs Sports, Tulatin OR) radar guns. Neither has been found to have greater precision in measuring pitching velocity, nor are there differences in portability or usability (Sandomir 2006).

Since measuring pitch velocity became a standard procedure in the 1980's, fastball velocity has continued to rise. The average Major League fastball velocity in 2001 was 88.5 mph, in 2015, it was just under 92 mph. Further, the number of 95+ mph pitchers has significantly increased in just the last decade. In 2008, 4.82% of pitchers threw on average 95+ mph, now the average is 9.14% (R. Arthur 2017). Due to the continued measurement of pitching velocity, velocity has become a more pertinent tool in evaluating pitchers. Since 1990, baseball scouts have given more weight to pitching velocity, causing for faster pitchers to be more highly recruited and selected in the Major League Draft (B.L.R. Arthur 2019).

Pitch Track Monitoring

Pitch velocity is only one factor that contributes to pitching performance (A. Nathan 2012a; A.M. Nathan 2012b). Other factors include movement and pitch location (A. Nathan 2012a; A.M. Nathan). To have a better understanding of these factors, an understanding of physics must first be given. Once the baseball has been propelled from the hand, there are multiple forces that affect baseball pitch trajectory (A. Nathan 2012a). These forces are gravity and aerodynamics. Gravity is a downward pull on the baseball. This is the reason for baseball trajectories to have a curvilinear arc. Aerodynamic forces can be divided into two separate factors: the drag force and magnus force. The drag force, also known as air resistance, impedes baseball velocity, but does not have an effect on ball direction. The magnus force effects ball direction, but does not affect velocity (A. Nathan 2012a). The magnus force is affected by the spin rate and spin axis of the baseball, helping to create baseball movement (A.M. Nathan 2007; A. Nathan 2012a; A.M. Nathan).

Creating movement during a pitch is a way to effect baseball performance. Movement can be created in two ways: 1. Throwing different pitches with different spin (curveball, slider, or changeup), 2. Masking pitches so that they appear they will end at one location, but by creating 'late break,' allows them to terminate at different locations (e.g., four seam fastball versus a cutter or a sinker). 'Late break' is the perception that a pitch is on one trajectory, but at the last second, moves in a different direction. An example would be Max Scherzer's slider. His slider appears to be going to one location, but at the last second, the pitch seems to break down and away from a right-handed hitter. (A. Nathan 2012a) While 'late break' is an actual impossibility, creating later movement on a pitch allows for less reaction time for a hitter, decreasing the chance of reaching base (A. Nathan 2012a; James and Solutions 2018). During the trajectory of a baseball pitch, the hitter has to begin his swing no later than when the baseball is 20 feet from home plate. If a pitch has the same trajectory as a straight four seam fastball, until the 20 feet mark, the hitter will begin to initiate his swing to this specific trajectory. However, changes in the magnus force (i.e., spin of the baseball), will allow the baseball to end in a different trajectory (A. Nathan 2012a).

From these examples, one can see that spin rate, spin axis, and ultimate pitch location have an influence on pitching performance (A.M. Nathan 2007; A. Nathan 2012a; A.M. Nathan 2012b). Further, different pitchers produce different spin rates and orientation of the spin axis, even on the same pitch type (Nagami, Higuchi, and Kanosue 2013). It has not been until recently that spin rate and spin axis could be measured (A.M. Nathan; Kagan and Nathan 2017; A.M. Nathan 2012b). In the following sections, the most popular pitch trajectory devices will be detailed.

Pitchf/x® is a video based baseball tracking system owned and operated by Sportvision. From 2007 to 2017, every Major League Baseball stadium was fitted with Pitchf/x®. Pitchf/x® consists of two 60 HZ cameras, above the field of play. These cameras measure the area between the mound and home plate. The baseball is tracked from five feet after pitch is released to 50 feet. A series of images are captured during the baseball trajectory, with a total of 20 images captured per pitch. From these data, pitch velocity, baseball movement, and pitch location can be garnered (A. Nathan 2012a)/. Pitchf/x® uses a 'real time pattern classification algorithm' to identify different pitch types. (Healey 2017) Pitchf/x® can also capture the trajectory of batted balls (Hitf/x®), and to a lesser degree capture fielder, baserunner, and umpire movements (Fieldf/x®) (A. Nathan 2012a). The limitation of Pitchf/x® is its inability to calculate absolute maximum pitch velocity due to Pitchf/x® only begins to track the baseball five feet after the pitcher releases the baseball.

Pitchf/x® was integral in changing baseball player and umpire evaluation. One of the first noticeable influences was in umpire strike zone recognition. Due to Pitchf/x®, the strike zone increased from 435 inches^2 in 2009, to 475 inches^2 in 2014. Pitchf/x® was also important in evaluating catcher pitch framing ability. Pitchf/x® was able to determine how a catcher caught a pitch would affect the probability of an umpire calling a strike. These data assisted in the rise of strike outs in the last decade (Healey 2017).

Another baseball pitch tracking device is Trackman®. Trackman® is an infrared baseball tracking system that uses the same basic Doppler principles as the radar gun. However, instead of one radar source, three emitters are placed above the field of play. An antenna transmits at 10.5 GHz, and uses the three-array system to triangulate the ball in space. This allows for the ball to be assessed directly out of the hand, permitting for absolute maximum pitching velocity to be quantified. Further, spin rate, spin axis of the ball, and release slot can be assessed. Trackman® was found to have similar reliability to Pitchf/x® in calculating pitch velocity (A.M. Nathan). Trackman® is also used in batted ball monitoring. Since 2017, Trackman® replaced Pitchf/x® in Major League Baseball stadiums for baseball tracking (A.M. Nathan). Limitations include the price point (upwards of $30,000) and poor reliability of pitches with low spin rate such as knuckleballs and splitters, and with line drive batted balls (Matsuo, Nakamoto, and Kageyama 2017).

Rapsado® is a relatively new pitch tracking device that uses a combination of radar and video. This device is designed for baseball teams that cannot afford the higher priced point baseball tracking devices, with a price point set at around $4,000. Rapsado® uses a single device that sits on a tripod six feet behind the catcher. It is designed to withstand pitches up to 100 mph, and uses Wi-Fi or USB to connect to a smart phone of computer. Rapsado® can calculate spin rate, spin axis, velocity, and pitch break. (Rapsado) Rapsado® uses a different spin rate algorithm to calculate spin, subtracting gravity and drag. Thus, its spin outputs are dissimilar from other baseball tracking devices. Limitations include that no objects can block the view of baseball trajectory, the device must be six feet behind the catcher, which is not always possible, and the inability to export data into a spreadsheet for further analyses (Prusaczyk 2017).

Batter Monitoring

While the ability to assess pitch velocity available since 1974, (Rader 2008) the capacity to evaluate hitting factors has been more tenuous. Historically, the speed and skill required to become a high performing hitter has only been able to be assessed through direct output, such as batting average, runs batted in (RBI's), and home runs (Rader 2008). With the advent of new era statistics, these metrics have evolved to included statistics such as on base percentage, slugging percentage, and batting average on balls in play BABIP (James and Solutions 2018). Evaluating hitting tools was even more arbitrary, with grading hitting contact ability, hitting power, or strike zone discernment. However, it was not until the last decade that being able to assess hitting ability could be truly quantified (R. Arthur 2016).

As with the pitching monitoring section above, before diving into hitting monitoring, one must understand the physics behind, as Ted Williams once said, "Hit(ting) a round ball with a round bat squarely" (Seidel 2003).

The baseball swing is a composite of multiple highly involved motor programs (B. Shaffer et al. 1993; Welch et al. 1995). The baseball swing must be initiated during baseball flight, (Gray 2010) before the baseball reaches 20 feet in front of home plate (A. Nathan 2012a). This requires baseball batters to predict where the ball will end up in space, and decide if and where to swing the bat in space (Gray 2010; D.M. Green and Swets 1966). Better hitters will be able to more precisely and effectively swing their bat, and create superior contact and velocity compared to poorer hitters (Gray 2010).

Within baseball, a home run produces an automatic run (Sawicki, Hubbard, and Stronge 2003). Home runs are created by hitting a pitched baseball over the outfield fence, with outfield fences being 300 to 400 feet away from home plate (Rader 2008). Due to these requirements, baseballs that are hit farther in the air will have a greater probability of becoming home runs (Sawicki, Hubbard, and Stronge 2003).

The probability of hitting a home run is effected by multiple variables including spin of the baseball, angle of contact, and velocity hit off of the bat (Sawicki, Hubbard, and Stronge 2003; Gray 2010; Rex 1985; Watts and Baroni 1989). As previously described, when the ball is pitched, spin is instituted on the baseball as it moves towards home plate (Nagami, Higuchi, and Kanosue 2013). Depending on the pitch, different spin axes are produced (Sawicki, Hubbard, and Stronge 2003). For example, a four seam fastball produces bask spin and a curveball produces top spin. When the ball and bat make contact, the friction of the bat, in conjunction with the momentum created by the swing, can alter the spin of the baseball (Rex 1985). Different baseball spins can affect baseball distance. For example, backspin can cause a baseball to fly over ten meters (32 feet) farther (Sawicki, Hubbard, and Stronge 2003). Hitters can have control of what type of spin is created on a batted baseball by where they hit the ball. Hitting the baseball 1 to 2 cm below the center of the baseball allows for backspin to be created (Sawicki, Hubbard, and Stronge 2003; Rex 1985). Being able to consistently hit the baseball below the center of the baseball allows for the baseball to travel farther, increasing the probability of hitting success (Gray 2010; Sawicki, Hubbard, and Stronge 2003).

The angle in which the bat makes contact with the baseball, known as launch angle, also affects hitting success (Sawicki, Hubbard, and Stronge 2003; Gray 2010). Launch angle measures the vertical direction of the ball as it is propelled off of the bat (R. Arthur 2016). A zero-degree launch angle would be a perfect line drive. Launch angles with positive numbers depict baseballs that are hit upward (i.e., fly balls), and launch angles with negative numbers depict baseballs that are hit downward (i.e., ground balls) (R. Arthur 2016).

As previously described, hitting home runs is an automatic successful hitting outcome, which is affected by the distance the ball is hit and the ball's trajectory in the air (Sawicki, Hubbard, and Stronge 2003). There is an optimum trajectory for a baseball to travel, to garner the greatest distance (Sawicki, Hubbard, and Stronge 2003; Gray 2010). In order to achieve optimum launch angle, the batter must swing with a slight upper cut swing, to produce a launch angle of around 25 degrees (Sawicki, Hubbard, and Stronge 2003).

Better hitters produce more consistent launch angles, compared to worse hitters who have greater changes in launch angle (Gray 2010). One of the best hitters in baseball, Mike Trout, 2019 launch angle was 20.7 degrees. This is in comparison to one of the worst hitters, Chris Davis, whose average 2019 launch angle was 17.8 degrees. Chris Davis's launch angle average was still high due to his skill as a power hitter (Savant). However, baseball players that rely on their speed to achieve success will have launch angles that are closer to zero in order to have a greater chance of reaching base (R. Arthur 2016). One example would be Lorenzo Cain, a high average hitter that relies on his speed and high contact ability to achieves hitting success. His average 2019 launch angle was 5.7 degrees (Savant).

While baseball spin and launch angle are important, (Rex 1985; Gray 2010; Sawicki, Hubbard, and Stronge 2003) without substantial exit velocity, batted balls in play will not reach great distance, decreasing hitting success probability (Sawicki, Hubbard, and Stronge 2003). Hitters that make contact at the optimal launch angle of 25 degrees, without significant exit velocity, will create short fly outs to the infield (R. Arthur 2016). Even small increments in exit velocity can have substantial changes in batted ball distance. An increase in 1 m/s (2 mph) increases ball distance by 5 meters (11 feet) (Sawicki, Hubbard, and Stronge 2003).

Increased exit velocity is mostly correlated with improved probability of hitting success. As exit velocity increases, infield fly balls turn into base hits, which eventually can lead to a home run. There is a drop in hitting success probability (known as the 'doughnut hole) due to balls hit in the 80 to 90 mph range that reach the outfielders. However, 90 mph is considered the threshold for high probability of hitting success. Batted balls with exit velocities above 90 mph have a greater percentage of extra base hits and home runs, compared to below batted balls below 90 mph (Sawicki, Hubbard, and Stronge 2003).

The initiation of baseball hitting monitoring has increased home run potential at the Major League level. Since 2015, the first year that hitting monitoring was ubiquitous at all Major League Baseball games, home runs have increased precipitously (Committe 2018). In 2015, there were a total of 4,909 home runs hit, in 2017, there were 6,105 home runs, a 24% increase (Butterworth 2018). While some of this increase has been due to changes in baseball manufacturing, (Committe 2018) much of this upsurge in overall home runs has been attributed to hitters training to hit at optimal launch angles, and focusing on increasing exit velocity (Butterworth 2018). Strike outs have also increased for eleven straight years, with strikeouts tallying 21.6% of plate appearances in 2018. This has been attributed to hitters trying to increase home run potential, specifically by focusing on launch angle and exit velocity (Greenberg 2019).

Many devices that assessed hitting have already been previously described, including Trackman® and Pitchf/x®. One device that has not been described is HitTrax®. HitTrax® is a batting simulation device that combines infrared and video monitoring systems. HitTrax® assesses spin, launch angle, exit velocity and strike zone aptitude. The system also simulates baseball flight and trajectory. Different parks and stadiums can be integrated into the simulation, so that a hitter can know where the baseball would have landed in real time. All data is automatically updated to the cloud, where web based leader boards are continuously updated. The major limitation of this device is the price, which can cost up to $30,000 (HitTrax 2019).

Baseball Game Monitoring

Since the advent of baseball, people have been trying to capture every movement of the game. This originally was through the box score (Rader 2008). However, the box score only tabulated event outcomes, leaving many other actions left unrecorded. Bill James, the creator of sabermetrics, tried to increase the quantification of player actions by introducing project score sheet in 1984 (James 2010). However, not every movement or action was truly quantified.

It was not until 2015 that every person on the baseball field has been tabulated. Every movement by each player and umpire, can now be monitored throughout each Major League Baseball game. While the technology is still nascent, the effect of this technology is already being felt within the game. The ability to better quantify defence has greatly improved. Defence has always been a skill in which was assessed more qualitatively. However, now each player's true defensive range, run saving ability, and ability to read baseballs off of the bat, can be recorded and analysed. Other improvements include ability to measure running speed in the field and on the base paths, and also a better understanding of umpire movements (Lage et al. 2016).

The system that allows for true baseball game monitoring to occur is Statcast. Statcast is an overarching baseball game monitoring system that combines radar and camera systems. It is a mixture of hardware (the actual monitoring systems) and software (programs to process and export data). Statscast originally used Pitchf/x® for baseball tracking, but since 2017 had used Trackman®. Released in 2015, it is currently in every Major League ballpark (Lage et al. 2016). Each game outputs 7 terabytes of data, much of which is noise (Healey 2017). Baseball games are stored as a series of actions, termed *gameplay*. The *gameplay* data is used to create visual and quantifiable outputs that are delivered real time to fans and also for player and game analyses (Healey 2017).

Statcast tracks every player and umpire on the field, through a Cartesian grid system at 30 Hz. Home plate is placed as $(0, 0)$, and the y axis is towards the pitchers' mound, and the x-axis is to the right (Figure 2). Three cameras track all players, and then compresses these data into a two-dimensional format. All three cameras are 15 meters apart, and are usually placed high above the third base line (Healey 2017).

The Statcast Metrics Engine uses these data and can reproduce an entire baseball game. *Gameplay* actions are split into three categories: pitch (from windup to when the ball reaches home plate), the hit (from when the ball is batted into play until it is fielded), and the field (actions following when the ball is fielded) (Lage et al. 2016).

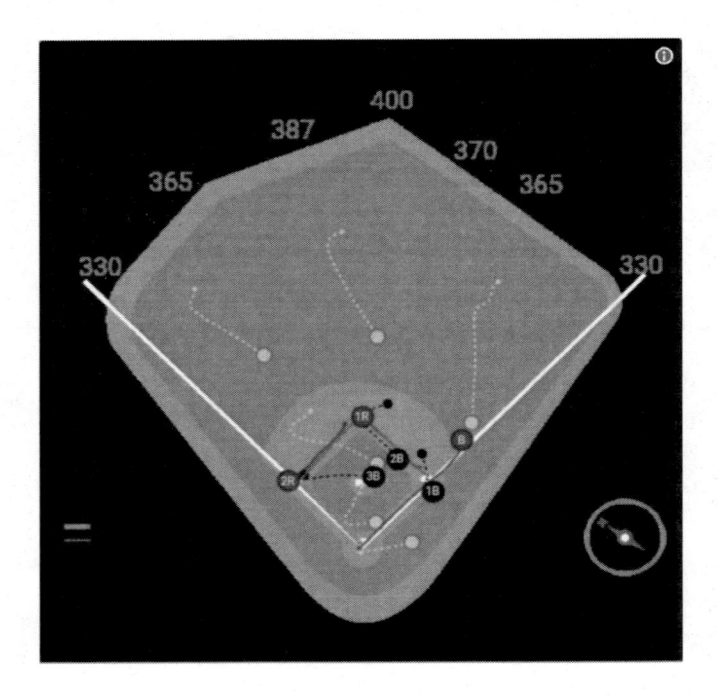

Figure 3. Statcast output of a 5-4-3 double play.

The data from Stacast is uploaded real time for audience consumption. The raw data is also available to each Major League team to use for internal analytics. There is currently a debate on how much data availability should be given to fans. This debate stems from the underlying use of Statcast. Is it a tool to increase the fan experience, or is it designed for deep analytics? While the debate continues, the use of full baseball game monitoring will continue to be explored (Anderson 2017).

INTERVIEW AND PRACTICAL APPLICATIONS OF SPIN RATE AND SPIN AXIS

Eric Niesen is a former collegiate and professional pitcher, playing 10 years professionally. Niesen is the current pitching coach for Georgetown University.

Figure 4. Eric Niesen.

How Do You Look at Spin Rate and Spin Axis for Pitchers You Are Coaching?

Spin rate is the new hot metric in baseball. However, spin rate as an overall number is only the tip of the iceberg. You need context about spin rate to truly understand what is needed when you evaluate and teach a pitcher or to recognize its value. First, spin rate is the overall spin (or rotations of the baseball) from the release of a pitcher's hand described in the terms of rotations per minute (RPM). This spin rate can tell you a lot about the movement and level of difficulty of a hitter making contact. In general, the higher the spin rate, the more movement this pitch will have, with the caveat being the spin axis (direction of the spin) and spin efficacy (spin that leads to movement) of the pitch.

From a performance standpoint, when looking at a pitcher's spin rate and spin axis, you typically start with their fastball. Now, spin rate for a pitcher's fastball isn't so much about how to fix it or change the spine rate, but how to identify whom that pitcher is as an individual and how to best utilize or compliment what he already possesses. You can use this information to help determine who to recruit, because spin rate can be unique to the individual.

Spin axis is just the direction of the spin of the baseball, which will help to determine which way the ball will move. Again, a certain axis will create a certain shape to a pitch. Changing or manipulating the spin axis in different ways can alter the movements of a pitch to compliment the pitcher's skillset.

Depending on Spin Rate, How Will That Change How You Coach a Pitcher to Use His Pitches?

Spin rate will help dictate to me, first, who that pitcher is as an individual. So, much goes into what causes an individual's fastball spin rate, we still do not know fully all the factors that affect spin rate. However, I look at the fastball as the leading indicator to help me determine the "identity" of any pitcher.

For example, if a pitcher has a high spin rate ($\geq$2300 RPM for a fastball) with high spin efficacy ($\geq$ 90%), with an axis anywhere from 10:45-1:15, we can determine that this pitch will have a lot of 'ride' or lift that makes the baseball seem to 'rise.' This has been proven to create more swing and misses when being used at the top of the strike zone. I would take this pitcher's fastball profile and teach him to pitch at the top of the zone while creating off speed pitches that will "tunnel" or track that same line, then breaking off of that line in different directions as it approaches the hitting zone.

Now someone with lower spin ($\leq$2250 RPM.) you would teach this pitcher to pitch at the bottom of the zone due to the sinking action that would be created.

After you have identified the fastball spin rate and spin axis, you can make slight changes to grips and locations to help create the best probability of success.

Depending on Spin Rate, What Type of Pitches Will You Try to Create in Their Pitching Repertoire?

Generally, spin rate combined with spin axis will help determine movement and what pitches to create. Once you have identified a pitcher's fastball spin rate and spin axis, you can begin to shape his overall repertoire. Creating deception and late movement to a fastball is what every pitcher and pitching coach is looking for. Making something look like something else is always the creative and artistic part of pitching. Fortunately, now we have the science to make it even more masterful. If a hitter cannot notice any difference in spin or release patterns, the harder it is to hit. Recognizing a pitch as early as possible is key to hitter's success, and the longer I can keep that from happening the better.

I would typically approach this is by looking at the fastball spin axis. Does the pitcher create a lot of horizontal movement due to the spin axis (9-10 or 2-3 spin axis)? If so, then maybe a slider best fits his 'tunnelling.' Let's say you have a left-handed pitcher with a fastball spin axis of 10:30-10:45. I would recommend throwing a slider or slurve, that has a spin axis of 4:30 or 4:15, that will mimic and channel his fastball path.

So, all that being said, I try to create pitches using what the data and metrics lead me to. It is more about what will channel the pitcher's fastball, which he throws 60-70% in a game. Thus, it becomes relative to the identity of the pitcher's fastball, what pitch we will try to create or expand his pitching repertoire. It is much easier to teach amateurs, in my opinion, new grips for off-speed than fastballs because they have done it less over the years and can feel the difference quickly. After we determine the fit, we will work on making the spin harder, tighter, and locating it wherever we want.

How Does Spin Axis Determine What Type of Pitches You Recommend for a Pitcher to Throw?

All of these measurements are intertwined, you first need to know how spin axis, spin rate, and spin efficiency work together. You need to understand the metric readings and the physics behind them. Spin axis is really essential when it comes to determining the context and effectiveness of a pitch. Gyroscopic spin, which makes a bullet stay true, or a football more accurate, is essentially spin that keeps the ball stable in flight and limit movement. So, if you are throwing a fastball, you want more movement and less gyroscopic spin. The more movement a pitch has, the harder it is to hit. That is what we want to achieve using spin axis, spine rate, and spin efficacy. You want to get the most use out of the spin each pitcher creates.

Spin efficiency is the measurement of that force and how much of your overall spin leads to movement. This can change for different types of pitches. Sliders are low efficiency, typically ranging from 15-30%. If you have a slider above that, say from 35% to 50%, you may actually have more of a slurve. Again, that doesn't necessarily mean it's a bad pitch, but you may be able to create both if you can teach the pitcher to manipulate the spin when he wants too. Again, high speed camera work and biomechanical feedback goes hand in hand here to speed up the process.

When Recruiting a Pitcher, How Much Do You Look at Spin Rate and Spin Axis?

When you can get the data, it is a huge metric to look at, at least for me. This tells me so much more than just seeing the velocity on a radar gun. First, it will tell me what direction his ball is moving and why hitters may or may not be swinging through it or making solid contact. Sometimes you see a fastball that is 88 miles per hour (mph), but hitters are having really high exit velocity against his pitches. Or on the other hand, another pitcher is throwing at 88 mph, and hitters are never really squaring up, or swinging through a lot of his pitches. Spin rate and the spin axis gives us a hint to why these pitching outcomes are happening. One thing I look for to compare different fastballs is something called a Bauer unit. A Bauer unit is essentially overall spin rotations per minute (rpm) divided by velocity.

In context, if you have an 88 mph fastball with a spin rate of 2000 rpm, the fastball Bauer unit will 22.7 units. Now take an 88 mph with a spin of 2500, and you get 28.4 Bauer units. That is a difference of 6 points which can lead an evaluator to believe that the pitcher with 28 Bauer units fastball will get more swing and misses with the same velocity. It is another way to separate talent at a more advanced level.

Again, for me I want to see what 'raw materials' these pitchers have. At any level, I am trying to find hidden value that I can exploit and make individuals players better. There are a lot of 88-91mph pitchers out there, but not all fastballs are the same, even if the velocity is. Data and specifically spin rate and spin axis, give me a chance to dig through numbers to find hidden value. Also, we can hopefully drastically change the career and futures of young pitchers. There is so much value being passed up out there, that the data, depending how you use it, can give you a chance to find gold. The next step, if not already being utilized, is finding and optimizing that value in huge data sets.

THE FUTURE OF BASEBALL MONITORING

Baseball monitoring has evolved over the century and a half of play. Since the original box scores and the first batting average calculation, baseball has seen changes that would have been improbable to the games' founders (Rader 2008). At the Major League level, one can now quantify every player movement, from the first step reaction of a batted ball, to a pitcher's spin rate and spin axis (Lage et al. 2016). These futuristic technologies are not relegated to the elite. You can now find hitting simulations and analytical software at most local baseball training facilities (Prusaczyk 2017).

Baseball monitoring will evolve as clinicians, coaches, and players continue to pursue a deeper understanding of the data being outputted by current baseball monitoring technologies. Hordes of statistical advisors and analysts have been hired by Major League teams in the last decade to manage and interpret the terabytes of data being produced at every Major League Baseball game (B.L.R. Arthur 2019). As more and more data is being tabulated and analysed, greater robust inferences can be made, continuing to change how the game is interpreted and played.

The future of baseball monitoring is being able to handle, interpret, and extrapolate predictions from the masses of data being collected. These monitoring abilities will be attempted through different data driven approaches: from machine learning and artificial intelligence, to traditional statistical methods. In the ever-increasing Major League Baseball arms race, the team that can correctly and succinctly shift and consolidate through these data, will gain the edge necessary to win.

As technology progresses, different baseball monitoring systems and devices will continue to become cheaper and more ubiquitous at the amateur levels. More and more of the techniques and analytical approaches currently only used at the Major League level, will become standard in the amateur ranks. One day soon you may see college scouts predominantly recruiting off of exit velocity and spin rate, taken at a local training facility, without ever seeing in person these college prospects; or, see little leaguers worried about their average launch angle, where once you heard them discussing their home run tally.

Baseball, like no other sport, is a game of history, conservatism, and unspoken rules. Changes to the National Pastime will continue to be felt, at all levels, due to the rise in baseball monitoring. These changes will continue to create a discussion between the games' purists and the modern analytical observants, causing an ever tug of war between the heralded past and the undiscovered future. The future of baseball monitoring can be best summed up by the late great Yogi Berra, "When you come to a fork in the road, take it" (Berra and Kaplan 2001).

REFERENCES

Achten, Juul, and Asker E Jeukendrup. 2003. "Heart rate monitoring." *Sports medicine* 33 (7): 517-538.

Adirim, Terry A, and Tina L Cheng. 2003. "Overview of injuries in the young athlete." *Sports medicine* 33 (1): 75-81.

Ahmad, Christopher S, Randall W Dick, Edward Snell, Nick D Kenney, Frank C Curriero, Keshia Pollack, John P Albright, and Bert R Mandelbaum. 2014. "Major and minor league baseball hamstring injuries: epidemiologic findings from the major league baseball injury surveillance system." *The American journal of sports medicine* 42 (6): 1464-1470.

Akubat, Ibrahim, Steve Barrett, and Grant Abt. 2014. "Integrating the internal and external training loads in soccer." *International journal of sports physiology and performance* 9 (3): 457-462.

Alberta, FG, NS. ElAttrache, S Bissell, K Mohr, J Browdy, L Yocum, and F Jobe. 2010. "The development and validation of a functional assessment tool for the upper extremity in the overhead athlete." *Am J Sports Med* 38 (5): 903-11. https://doi.org/10.1177/0363546509355642.

Altini, Marco, Chris Van Hoof, and Oliver Amft. 2017. "Relation between estimated cardiorespiratory fitness and running performance in free-living: an analysis of HRV4Training data." 2017 IEEE EMBS International Conference on Biomedical & Health Informatics (BHI).

Anderson, RJ. 2017. How Statcast has changed MLB and why not everybody seems all that happy about it. Accessed April 10, 2019.

Arnason, Arni, Stefan B Sigurdsson, Arni Gudmundsson, Ingar Holme, Lars Engebretsen, and Roald Bahr. 2004. "Physical fitness, injuries, and team performance in soccer." *Medicine & Science in Sports & Exercise* 36 (2): 278-285.

Arthur, Beth Lindbergh & Rob. 2019. *We Got Our Hands on 73,000 Never-Before-Seen MLB Scouting Reports. Here's What We Learned.*

Arthur, Rob. 2016. "The New Science of Hitting." *FiveThirtyEight.* Accessed April 10. https://fivethirtyeight.com/features/the-new-science-of-hitting/.

---. 2017. *Pitchers Are Slowing Down To Speed Up.* Accessed April 10, 2019.

Association, National Collegiate Athletic. 2019. *"Estimated probability of competing in college baseball."* http://www.ncaa.org/about/resources/research/baseball.

Associations, National Federation of State High School. Accessed April 2, 2019. https://www.nfhs.org/.

Aubert, André E, Bert Seps, and Frank Beckers. 2003. "Heart rate variability in athletes." *Sports medicine* 33 (12): 889-919.

Barrett, Steve, Adrian Midgley, and Ric Lovell. 2014. "PlayerLoad™: reliability, convergent validity, and influence of unit position during treadmill running." *International journal of sports physiology and performance* 9 (6): 945-952.

Beckham, George, Tim Suchomel, and Satoshi Mizuguchi. 2014. "Force plate use in performance monitoring and sport science testing." *New Studies in Athletics* 3: 25-37.

Berger, Bonnie G, Robert W Motl, Brian D Butki, David T Martin, John G Wilkinson, and David R Owen. 1999. "Mood and cycling performance in response to three weeks of high-intensity, short-duration overtraining, and a two-week taper." *The Sport Psychologist* 13 (4): 444-457.

Berra, Yogi, and Dave Kaplan. 2001. *When you come to a fork in the road, take it!: Inspiration and wisdom from one of baseball's greatest heroes.* Hachette UK.

Billman, George. 2011. "Heart Rate Variability – A Historical Perspective." *Frontiers in Physiology* 2 (86). https://doi.org/10.3389/fphys.2011. 00086. https://www.frontiersin.org/ article/10.3389/fphys.2011.00086.

Blanch, Peter, and Tim J Gabbett. 2016. "Has the athlete trained enough to return to play safely? The acute: chronic workload ratio permits clinicians to quantify a player's risk of subsequent injury." *Br J Sports Med* 50 (8): 471-475.

Boddy, Kyle J, Joseph A Marsh, Alex Caravan, Kyle E Lindley, John O Scheffey, and Michael E O'Connell. 2019. "Exploring wearable sensors as an alternative to marker-based motion capture in the pitching delivery." *Peer J* 7: e6365.

Borges, Thiago Oliveira, Nicola Bullock, Christine Duff, and Aaron J Coutts. 2014. "Methods for quantifying training in sprint kayak." *The Journal of Strength & Conditioning Research* 28 (2): 474-482.

Borresen, Jill, and Michael I Lambert. 2008. "Autonomic control of heart rate during and after exercise." *Sports medicine* 38 (8): 633-646.

Borresen, Jill, and Michael Ian Lambert. 2009. "The quantification of training load, the training response and the effect on performance." *Sports medicine* 39 (9): 779-795.

Bourdon, Pitre C, Marco Cardinale, Andrew Murray, Paul Gastin, Michael Kellmann, Matthew C Varley, Tim J Gabbett, Aaron J Coutts, Darren J Burgess, and Warren Gregson. 2017. "Monitoring athlete training loads: consensus statement." *International journal of sports physiology and performance* 12 (Suppl 2): S2-161-S2-170.

Bouts, Alexa M, Lauren Brackman, Elizabeth Martin, Adam M. Subasic, and Edward S. Potkanowicz. 2018. "The Accuracy and Validity of iOS-Based Heart Rate Apps During Moderate to High Intensity Exercise." *International journal of exercise science* 11 (7): 533-540. https://www.ncbi.nlm.nih.gov/pubmed/29541341 https://www.ncbi.nlm.nih.gov/pmc/articles/PMC5841680/.

Brener, Nancy D, John OG Billy, and William R Grady. 2003. "Assessment of factors affecting the validity of self-reported health-risk behavior among adolescents: evidence from the scientific literature." *Journal of adolescent health* 33 (6): 436-457.

Brown, Louis. 1999. *Technical and military imperatives: a radar history of World War 2*. CRC Press.

Bullock, GS, T Chapman, T Joyce, R Prengle, T Stern, and RJ Butler. 2018. "Examining Differences in Movement Competency in Professional Baseball Players Born in the United States and Dominican Republic." *J*

Sport Rehabil 27 (5): 397-402. https://doi.org/10.1123/jsr.2016-0251.

Bullock, Garrett S, Abigail C Schmitt, Patrick Chasse, Barrett A Little, Lee H Diehl, and Robert J Butler. 2017. "Heart rate response does not differ between pitch types in college baseball pitchers." *International Journal of Performance Analysis in Sport* 17 (5): 774-782.

Bullock, Garrett S, Abigail C Schmitt, Patrick M Chasse, Barrett A Little, Lee H Diehl, and Robert J Butler. 2018. "The Relationship Between Trunk Rotation, Upper Quarter Dynamic Stability, and Pitch Velocity." *The Journal of Strength & Conditioning Research* 32 (1): 261-266.

Butterworth, Trevor. 2018. "Why did home runs surge in baseball? Statistics provides twist on hot topic." *Phys Org* Accessed April 10. https://phys.org/news/2018-07-home-surge-baseball-statistics-hot.html.

Buzas, D, NA Jacobson, and LG Morawa. 2014. "Concussions from 9 Youth Organized Sports: Results from NEISS Hospitals Over an 11-Year Time Frame, 2002-2012." *Orthop J Sports Med* 2 (4): 2325967114528460. https://doi.org/10.1177/2325967114528460.

Cadotte Jr, Roland, and Thomas E Koscica. 2000. Doppler radar speed measuring unit. Google Patents.

Callister, Robin, Robert J Callister, Steven J Fleck, and GARY A Dudley. 1990. "Physiological and performance responses to overtraining in elite judo athletes." *Med Sci Sports Exerc* 22 (6): 816-824.

Camm, A John, Marek Malik, J Thomas Bigger, Günter Breithardt, Sergio Cerutti, Richard J Cohen, Philippe Coumel, Ernest L Fallen, Harold L Kennedy, and RE Kleiger. 1996. *"Heart rate variability: standards of measurement, physiological interpretation and clinical use. Task Force of the European Society of Cardiology and the North American Society of Pacing and Electrophysiology."*

Camp, Christopher L, Travis G Tubbs, Glenn S Fleisig, Joshua S Dines, David M Dines, David W Altchek, and Brittany Dowling. 2017. "The relationship of throwing arm mechanics and elbow varus torque: within-subject variation for professional baseball pitchers across 82,000 throws." *The American journal of sports medicine* 45 (13): 3030-3035.

Cardinale, Marco, and Matthew C Varley. 2017. "Wearable training-monitoring technology: applications, challenges, and opportunities." *International journal of sports physiology and performance* 12 (Suppl 2): S2-55-S2-62.

Carniol, Eric T, Kevin Shaigany, Peter F Svider, Adam J Folbe, Giancarlo F Zuliani, Soly Baredes, and Jean Anderson Eloy. 2015. ""Beaned" A 5-Year Analysis of Baseball-Related Injuries of the Face." *Otolaryngology–Head and Neck Surgery* 153 (6): 957-961.

Chambers, Ryan, Tim J Gabbett, Michael H Cole, and Adam Beard. 2015. "The use of wearable microsensors to quantify sport-specific movements." *Sports medicine* 45 (7): 1065-1081.

Chasse, P, GS Bullock, AC Schmitt, BA Little, LH Diehl, and RJ Butler. 2018. "The Relationship Between Trunk Rotation, Upper Quarter Dynamic Stability, and the Kerlan-Jobe Orthopaedic Clinic Overhead Athlete Shoulder and Elbow Score in Division I Collegiate Pitchers." *Int J Sports Phys Ther* 13 (5): 819-827.

Clarsen, B, G Myklebust, and R Bahr. 2013. "Development and validation of a new method for the registration of overuse injuries in sports injury epidemiology: the Oslo Sports Trauma Research Centre (OSTRC) overuse injury questionnaire." *Br J Sports Med* 47 (8): 495-502. https://doi.org/10.1136/bjsports-2012-091524.

Claudino, João Gustavo, John Cronin, Bruno Mezêncio, Daniel Travis McMaster, Michael McGuigan, Valmor Tricoli, Alberto Carlos Amadio, and Julio Cerca Serrão. 2017. "The countermovement jump to monitor neuromuscular status: A meta-analysis." *Journal of science and medicine in sport* 20 (4): 397-402.

Collins, CL, and RD Comstock. 2008. "Epidemiological features of high school baseball injuries in the United States, 2005-2007." *Pediatrics* 121 (6): 1181-7. https://doi.org/10.1542/peds.2007-2572.

Commission, United States Consumer Product Safety. 2019. *"Injury Surveillance System (NEISS)."* Accessed April 3. https://www.cpsc.gov/Research--Statistics/NEISS-Injury-Data.

Committee, Major League Baseball. 2018. "MLB receives report on increased home run rate." *Major League Baseball*. Accessed April 10.

https://www.mlb.com/press-release/major-league-baseball-receives-report-on-increased-home-run-rate-278136100.

Conte, S, CL Camp, and JS Dines. 2016a. "Injury Trends in Major League Baseball Over 18 Seasons: 1998-2015." *Am J Orthop (Belle Mead NJ)* 45 (3): 116-23.

Conte, S, RK Requa, and JG Garrick. 2001. "Disability days in major league baseball." *Am J Sports Med* 29 (4): 431-6. https://doi.org/10.1177/03635465010290040801.

Conte, Stan, Christopher L Camp, and Joshua S Dines. 2016b. "Injury trends in Major League Baseball over 18 seasons: 1998-2015." *Am J Orthop* 45 (3): 116-123.

Control, Centers for Disease, and Prevention. 2006. "Sports-related injuries among high school athletes--United States, 2005-06 school year." *MMWR: Morbidity and mortality weekly report* 55 (38): 1037-1040.

Conway, JE, Frank W Jobe, RE Glousman, and M Pink. 1992. "Medial instability of the elbow in throwing athletes. Treatment by repair or reconstruction of the ulnar collateral ligament." *The Journal of bone and joint surgery. American volume* 74 (1): 67-83.

Cormack, Stuart J, Robert U Newton, and Michael R McGuigan. 2008. "Neuromuscular and endocrine responses of elite players to an Australian rules football match." *International journal of sports physiology and performance* 3 (3): 359-374.

Cormack, Stuart J, Robert U Newton, Michael R McGuigan, and Tim LA Doyle. 2008. "Reliability of measures obtained during single and repeated countermovement jumps." *International journal of sports physiology and performance* 3 (2): 131-144.

Cornell, David J, Jeffrey L Paxson, Roger A Caplinger, Joshua R Seligman, Nicholas A Davis, and Kyle T Ebersole. 2017. "Resting heart rate variability among professional baseball starting pitchers." *Journal of strength and conditioning research* 31 (3): 575-581.

Cornell, David J, Jeffrey L Paxson, Roger A Caplinger, Joshua R Seligman, Nicholas A Davis, Robert J Flees, and Kyle T Ebersole. 2017. "In-game heart rate responses among professional baseball starting pitchers." *The Journal of Strength & Conditioning Research* 31 (1): 24-29.

Coronado, Victor G, Tadesse Haileyesus, Tabitha A Cheng, Jeneita M Bell, Juliet Haarbauer-Krupa, Michael R Lionbarger, Javier Flores-Herrera, Lisa C McGuire, and Julie Gilchrist. 2015. "Trends in sports-and recreation-related traumatic brain injuries treated in US emergency departments: the National Electronic Injury Surveillance System-All Injury Program (NEISS-AIP) 2001-2012." *The Journal of head trauma rehabilitation* 30 (3): 185.

Costill, David L, Michael G Flynn, John P Kirwan, Joseph A Houmard, Joel B Mitchell, Robert Thomas, and Sung Han Park. 1988. "Effects of repeated days of intensified training on muscle glycogen and swimming performance." *Med Sci Sports Exerc* 20 (3): 249-254.

Coutts, Aaron J, LK Wallace, and KM Slattery. 2007. "Monitoring changes in performance, physiology, biochemistry, and psychology during overreaching and recovery in triathletes." *International journal of sports medicine* 28 (02): 125-134.

Crotin, Ryan L, Karl Kozlowski, Peter Horvath, and Dan K Ramsey. 2014. "Altered stride length in response to increasing exertion among baseball pitchers." *Medicine & Science in Sports & Exercise* 46 (3): 565-571.

Cummins, Cloe, Rhonda Orr, Helen O'Connor, and Cameron West. 2013. "Global positioning systems (GPS) and microtechnology sensors in team sports: a systematic review." *Sports medicine* 43 (10): 1025-1042.

Daanen, Hein AM, Robert P Lamberts, Victor L Kallen, Anmin Jin, and Nico LU Van Meeteren. 2012. "A systematic review on heart-rate recovery to monitor changes in training status in athletes." *International journal of sports physiology and performance* 7 (3): 251-260.

Dahm, DL, FC Curriero, CL Camp, RH Brophy, T Leo, K Meister, GA Paletta, JA Steubs, BR Mandelbaum, and KM Pollack. 2016. "Epidemiology and Impact of Knee Injuries in Major and Minor League Baseball Players." *Am J Orthop (Belle Mead NJ)* 45 (3): E54-62.

Day, Meghan L, Michael R McGuigan, Glenn Brice, and Carl Foster. 2004. "Monitoring exercise intensity during resistance training using the session RPE scale." *The Journal of Strength & Conditioning Research* 18 (2): 353-358.

Denegar, Craig R, Luzita I Vela, and Todd A Evans. 2008. "Evidence-based sports medicine: outcomes instruments for active populations." *Clinics in sports medicine* 27 (3): 339-351.

Department, *St. Louis Cardinals Performance*. 2019.

Dick, R, J Agel, and SW Marshall. 2007. "National Collegiate Athletic Association Injury Surveillance System commentaries: introduction and methods." *J Athl Train* 42 (2): 173-82.

Dillman, Charles J, Glenn S Fleisig, and James R Andrews. 1993. "Biomechanics of pitching with emphasis upon shoulder kinematics." *Journal of Orthopaedic & Sports Physical Therapy* 18 (2): 402-408.

Domb, BG, JT Davis, FG Alberta, KJ Mohr, AG Brooks, NS Elattrache, L M Yocum, and FW Jobe. 2010. "Clinical follow-up of professional baseball players undergoing ulnar collateral ligament reconstruction using the new Kerlan-Jobe Orthopaedic Clinic overhead athlete shoulder and elbow score (KJOC Score)." *Am J Sports Med* 38 (8): 1558-63. https://doi.org/10.1177/0363546509359060.

Dong, Jin-Guo. 2016. "The role of heart rate variability in sports physiology." *Experimental and therapeutic medicine* 11 (5): 1531-1536.

Drew, Michael K, and Caroline F Finch. 2016. "The relationship between training load and injury, illness and soreness: a systematic and literature review." *Sports medicine* 46 (6): 861-883.

Eirale, Cristiano, JL Tol, Abdulaziz Farooq, Faten Smiley, and Hakim Chalabi. 2013. "Low injury rate strongly correlates with team success in Qatari professional football." *Br J Sports Med* 47 (12): 807-808.

Electrophysiology, Task Force of the European Society of Cardiology the North American Society of Pacing. 1996. "Heart rate variability: standards of measurement, physiological interpretation, and clinical use." *Circulation* 93 (5): 1043-1065.

Enoka, Roger M, and Jacques Duchateau. 2008. "Muscle fatigue: what, why and how it influences muscle function." *The Journal of physiology* 586 (1): 11-23.

Erickson, BJ, J Ahn, PN Chalmers, CS Ahmad, BR Bach, Jr., NN Verma, and AA Romeo. 2017. "Reasons for Retirement Following Ulnar Collateral Ligament Reconstruction Among Major League Baseball

Pitchers." *Orthop J Sports Med* 5 (12): 2325967117745021. https://doi.org/10.1177/2325967117745021.

Erickson, BJ, PN Chalmers, J Newgren, M Malaret, M O'Brien, GP Nicholson, and AA Romeo. 2018. "Can the Kerlan-Jobe Orthopaedic Clinic Shoulder and Elbow Score Be Reliably Administered Over the Phone?: A Randomized Study." *Orthop J Sports Med* 6 (8): 2325967118791510. https://doi.org/10.1177/2325967118791510.

Erickson, Brandon J, Peter N Chalmers, Charles A Bush-Joseph, and Anthony A Romeo. 2016. "Predicting and preventing injury in Major League Baseball." *Am J Orthop (Belle Mead NJ)* 45 (3): 152-156.

Finch, C. 2006. "A new framework for research leading to sports injury prevention." *J Sci Med Sport* 9 (1-2): 3-9; discussion 10. https://doi.org/10.1016/j.jsams.2006.02.009.

Fleisig, Glenn, Yungchien Chu, Adam Weber, and James Andrews. 2009. "Variability in baseball pitching biomechanics among various levels of competition." *Sports Biomechanics* 8 (1): 10-21.

Fleisig, Glenn S. 2018. Editorial commentary: Changing times in sports biomechanics: baseball pitching injuries and emerging wearable technology. Elsevier.

Fleisig, Glenn S, James R Andrews, Charles J Dillman, and Rafael F Escamilla. 1995. "Kinetics of baseball pitching with implications about injury mechanisms." *The American journal of sports medicine* 23 (2): 233-239.

Fleisig, Glenn S, Steve W Barrentine, Nigel Zheng, Rafael F Escamilla, and James R Andrews. 1999. "Kinematic and kinetic comparison of baseball pitching among various levels of development." *Journal of biomechanics* 32 (12): 1371-1375.

Fleisig, Glenn S, and Rafael F Escamilla. 1996. "Biomechanics of the elbow in the throwing athlete." *Operative Techniques in Sports Medicine* 4 (2): 62-68.

Fortenbaugh, Dave, Glenn Fleisig, Arzu Onar-Thomas, and Shihab Asfour. 2011. "The effect of pitch type on ground reaction forces in the baseball swing." *Sports biomechanics* 10 (4): 270-279.

Fortenbaugh, Dave, Glenn S Fleisig, and James R Andrews. 2009. "Baseball pitching biomechanics in relation to injury risk and performance." *Sports health* 1 (4): 314-320.

Foster, CARL, JACK T Daniels, and RICHARD A Yarbrough. 1977. "Physiological and training correlates of marathon running performance." *Aust J Sports Med* 9: 58-61.

Franz, JO, PC McCulloch, CJ Kneip, PC Noble, and DM Lintner. 2013. "The utility of the KJOC score in professional baseball in the United States." *Am J Sports Med* 41 (9): 2167-73. https://doi.org/10. 1177/0363546513495177.

Fronek, J, JG Yang, DC Osbahr, KM Pollack, NS ElAttrache, TJ Noonan, SA Conte, BR Mandelbaum, and LA Yocum. 2015. "Shoulder functional performance status of Minor League professional baseball pitchers." *J Shoulder Elbow Surg* 24 (1): 17-23. https://doi.org/10.1016/j.jse.2014.04.019.

Fry, RW, JR Grove, AR Morton, PM Zeroni, S Gaudieri, and David Keast. 1994. "Psychological and immunological correlates of acute overtraining." *British Journal of Sports Medicine* 28 (4): 241-246.

Gabbett, Tim J. 2004. "Influence of training and match intensity on injuries in rugby league." *Journal of sports sciences* 22 (5): 409-417.

---. 2010. "The development and application of an injury prediction model for noncontact, soft-tissue injuries in elite collision sport athletes." *The Journal of Strength & Conditioning Research* 24 (10): 2593-2603.

---. 2016. "The training—injury prevention paradox: should athletes be training smarter and harder?" *Br J Sports Med* 50 (5): 273-280.

Gabbett, Tim J, and Shahid Ullah. 2012. "Relationship between running loads and soft-tissue injury in elite team sport athletes." *The Journal of Strength & Conditioning Research* 26 (4): 953-960.

Garcia-Lopez, J, J Peleteiro, JA Rodriguez-Marroyo, JC Morante, JA Herrero, and JG Villa. 2005. "The validation of a new method that measures contact and flight times during vertical jump." *International journal of sports medicine* 26 (04): 294-302.

Garrison, JC, C Johnston, and JE Conway. 2015. "Baseball Players with Ulnar Collateral Ligament Tears Demonstrate Decreased Rotator Cuff

Strength Compared to Healthy Controls." *Int J Sports Phys Ther* 10 (4): 476-81.

Gathercole, Rob J, Ben C Sporer, Trent Stellingwerff, and Gord G Sleivert. 2015a. "Comparison of the capacity of different jump and sprint field tests to detect neuromuscular fatigue." *The Journal of Strength & Conditioning Research* 29 (9): 2522-2531.

Gathercole, Rob, Ben Sporer, Trent Stellingwerff, and Gord Sleivert. 2015b. "Alternative countermovement-jump analysis to quantify acute neuromuscular fatigue." *International journal of sports physiology and performance* 10 (1): 84-92.

Gathercole, Rob, Benjamin Sporer, and Trent Stellingwerff. 2015. *Countermovement Jump Performance with Increased Training Loads in Elite Female Rugby Athletes*. Vol. 36.

Go-Gulf. "Smartphone Users around the World – Statistics And Facts." Accessed April 2. http://www.go-gulf.com/blog/smartphone.

Granata, Kevin P, Greg P Slota, and Sara E Wilson. 2004. "Influence of fatigue in neuromuscular control of spinal stability." *Human factors* 46 (1): 81-91.

Gray, Rob. 2010. "Expert baseball batters have greater sensitivity in making swing decisions." *Research quarterly for exercise and sport* 81 (3): 373-378.

Green, David Marvin, and John A Swets. 1966. *Signal detection theory and psychophysics*. Vol. 1. Wiley New York.

Green, GA, KM Pollack, J D'Angelo, MS Schickendantz, R Caplinger, K Weber, A Valadka, TW McAllister, RW Dick, B Mandelbaum, and FC Curriero. 2015. "Mild traumatic brain injury in major and Minor League Baseball players." *Am J Sports Med* 43 (5): 1118-26. https://doi.org/10.1177/0363546514568089.

Greenberg, Neil. 2019. MLB batters are recording more strikeouts than hits. That's a big problem that's unlikely to soon change. Accessed April 10, 2019.

Greenhalgh, J, and K Meadows. 1999. "The effectiveness of the use of patient-based measures of health in routine practice in improving the process and outcomes of patient care: a literature review." *J Eval Clin Pract* 5 (4): 401-16.

Gregoski, Mathew J, Martina Mueller, Alexey Vertegel, Aleksey Shaporev, Brenda B Jackson, Ronja M Frenzel, Sara M Sprehn, and Frank A Treiber. 2012. "Development and validation of a smartphone heart rate acquisition application for health promotion and wellness telehealth applications." *International journal of telemedicine and applications* 2012: 1.

Halson, Shona L, 2014. "Monitoring training load to understand fatigue in athletes." *Sports medicine* 44 (2): 139-147.

Halson, Shona L, Matthew W Bridge, Romain Meeusen, Bart Busschaert, Michael Gleeson, David A Jones, and Asker E Jeukendrup. 2002. "Time course of performance changes and fatigue markers during intensified training in trained cyclists." *Journal of applied physiology* 93 (3): 947-956.

Halson, Shona L, and Asker E Jeukendrup. 2004. "Does overtraining exist?" *Sports medicine* 34 (14): 967-981.

Hautala, Arto J, Antti M Kiviniemi, and Mikko P Tulppo. 2009. "Individual responses to aerobic exercise: the role of the autonomic nervous system." *Neuroscience & Biobehavioral Reviews* 33 (2): 107-115.

Healey, Glenn. 2017. "The New Moneyball: How Ballpark Sensors are Changing Baseball." *Proceedings of the IEEE* 105 (11): 1999-2002.

Healy, Marie-Louise, James Gibney, Claire Pentecost, Mike J Wheeler, and PH Sonksen. 2014. "Endocrine profiles in 693 elite athletes in the postcompetition setting." *Clinical endocrinology* 81 (2): 294-305.

Hedelin, Rikard, Göran Kenttä, Urban Wiklund, Per Bjerle, and Karin Henriksson-Larsén. 2000. "Short-term overtraining: effects on performance, circulatory responses, and heart rate variability." *Medicine and science in sports and exercise* 32 (8): 1480-1484.

HitTrax. 2019. Accessed April 10. www.hittrax.com.

Hodgins, JL, DP Trofa, S Donohue, M Littlefield, M Schuk, and CS Ahmad. 2018. "Forearm Flexor Injuries Among Major League Baseball Players: Epidemiology, Performance, and Associated Injuries." *Am J Sports Med* 46 (9): 2154-2160. https://doi.org/10.1177/0363546518778252.

Hodgins, Justin L, Mark Vitale, Raymond R Arons, and Christopher S Ahmad. 2016. "Epidemiology of Medial Ulnar Collateral Ligament Reconstruction." *American Journal of Sports Medicine* 44 (3): 729-734. http://search.ebscohost.com/login.aspx?direct=true&db=sph&AN =113451311&site=ehost-live&authtype=ip,uid.

Hongu, Nobuko, Barron J Orr, Denise J Roe, Rebecca G Reed, and Scott B Going. 2013. "Global positioning system watches for estimating energy expenditure." *The Journal of Strength & Conditioning Research* 27 (11): 3216-3220.

Hootman, JM, R Dick, and J Agel. 2007. "Epidemiology of collegiate injuries for 15 sports: summary and recommendations for injury prevention initiatives." *J Athl Train* 42 (2): 311-9.

Huber, ME, Amee L Seitz, M Leeser, and D Sternad. 2015. "Validity and reliability of Kinect skeleton for measuring shoulder joint angles: a feasibility study." *Physiotherapy* 101 (4): 389-393.

Hulin, Billy T, Tim J Gabbett, Peter Blanch, Paul Chapman, David Bailey, and John W Orchard. 2014. "Spikes in acute workload are associated with increased injury risk in elite cricket fast bowlers." *Br J Sports Med* 48 (8): 708-712.

Hulin, Billy T, Tim J Gabbett, Daniel W Lawson, Peter Caputi, and John A Sampson. 2016. "The acute: chronic workload ratio predicts injury: high chronic workload may decrease injury risk in elite rugby league players." *Br J Sports Med* 50 (4): 231-236.

Hurd, Wendy J, and Kenton R Kaufman. 2012. "Glenohumeral rotational motion and strength and baseball pitching biomechanics." *Journal of athletic training* 47 (3): 247-256.

Huxel Bliven, KC, AR Snyder Valier, RC Bay, and EL Sauers. 2017. "The Functional Arm Scale for Throwers (FAST)-Part II: Reliability and Validity of an Upper Extremity Region-Specific and Population-Specific Patient-Reported Outcome Scale for Throwing Athletes." *Orthop J Sports Med* 5 (4): 2325967117700019. https://doi.org/10. 1177/2325967117700019.

Inc., Applied Concept. 2018. *Stalker Sport 2 Owner's Manual.*

James, Bill. 2010. *The new Bill James historical baseball abstract.* Simon and Schuster.

James, Bill, Jim Albert, and Hal S Stern. 1993. "Answering questions about baseball using statistics." *Chance* 6 (2): 17-30.

James, Bill, and Baseball Info Solutions. 2018. *The Bill James Handbook 2019.* ACTA Publications.

Jennings, Denise, Stuart Cormack, Aaron J Coutts, Luke Boyd, and Robert J Aughey. 2010. "The validity and reliability of GPS units for measuring distance in team sport specific running patterns." *International journal of sports physiology and performance* 5 (3): 328-341.

Jeukendrup, AE, MKC Hesselink, AC Snyder, H Kuipers, and HA Keizer. 1992. "Physiological changes in male competitive cyclists after two weeks of intensified training." *International journal of sports medicine* 13 (07): 534-541.

Jinji, Tsutomu, and Shinji Sakurai. 2006. "Baseball: Direction of spin axis and spin rate of the pitched baseball." *Sports Biomechanics* 5 (2): 197-214.

Kagan, David, and Alan M Nathan. 2017. "Statcast and the baseball trajectory calculator." *The Physics Teacher* 55 (3): 134-136.

Kaikkonen, Piia, Esa Hynynen, Theresa Mann, Heikki Rusko, and Ari Nummela. 2012. "Heart rate variability is related to training load variables in interval running exercises." *European journal of applied physiology* 112 (3): 829-838.

Kania, ML, BB Meyer, and KT Ebersole. 2009. "Personal and environmental characteristics predicting burnout among certified athletic trainers at National Collegiate Athletic Association institutions." *J Athl Train* 44 (1): 58-66. https://doi.org/10.4085/1062-6050-44.1.58.

Kannankeril, Prince J, Francis K Le, Alan H Kadish, and Jeffrey J Goldberger. 2004. "Parasympathetic effects on heart rate recovery after exercise." *Journal of investigative medicine* 52 (6): 394-401.

Kellmann, M. 2010. "Preventing overtraining in athletes in high-intensity sports and stress/recovery monitoring." *Scandinavian journal of medicine & science in sports* 20: 95-102.

Kenttä, Göran, Peter Hassmén, and JS Raglin. 2001. "Training practices and overtraining syndrome in Swedish age-group athletes." *International journal of sports medicine* 22 (06): 460-465.

Kernozek, Thomas W, Michael R Torry, and Mark Iwasaki. 2008. "Gender differences in lower extremity landing mechanics caused by neuromuscular fatigue." *The American journal of sports medicine* 36 (3): 554-565.

Kerr, ZY, TP Dompier, EM Snook, SW Marshall, D Klossner, B Hainline, and J Corlette. 2014. "National collegiate athletic association injury surveillance system: review of methods for 2004-2005 through 2013-2014 data collection." *J Athl Train* 49 (4): 552-60. https://doi.org/10.4085/1062-6050-49.3.58.

Kerr, ZY, RC Lynall, KG Roos, SL Dalton, A Djoko, and TP Dompier. 2017. "Descriptive Epidemiology of Non-Time-Loss Injuries in Collegiate and High School Student-Athletes." *J Athl Train* 52 (5): 446-456. https://doi.org/10.4085/1062-6050-52.2.15.

Kerr, ZY, SW Marshall, TP Dompier, J Corlette, DA Klossner, and J Gilchrist. 2015. "College Sports-Related Injuries - United States, 2009-10 Through 2013-14 Academic Years." *MMWR Morb Mortal Wkly Rep* 64 (48): 1330-6. https://doi.org/10.15585/mmwr.mm6448a2.

Kindermann, W. 1986. "Overtraining: expression of a disturbed autonomic regulation." *Dtsch Z Sportmed* 37 (4): 238-245.

Kindermann, Wilfried. 2016. "Creatine Kinase Levels After Exercise." *Deutsches Arzteblatt international* 113 (19): 344-344. https://doi.org/10.3238/arztebl.2016.0344a. https://www.ncbi.nlm.nih.gov/pubmed/27232364. https://www.ncbi.nlm.nih.gov/pmc/articles/PMC4904530/.

Kiviniemi, Antti M, Arto J Hautala, Hannu Kinnunen, Juuso Nissilä, Paula Virtanen, Jaana Karjalainen, and Mikko P Tulppo. 2010. "Daily exercise prescription on the basis of HR variability among men and women." *Medicine and science in sports and exercise* 42 (7): 1355-1363. https://doi.org/10.1249/mss.0b013e3181cd5f39. http://europepmc.org/abstract/MED/20575165. http://content.wkhealth.com/linkback/openurl?issn=0195-

9131&volume=42&issue=7&spage=1355. https://doi.org/10.1249/MSS.0b013e3181cd5f39.

Kleiger, Robert E, J Philip Miller, J Thomas Bigger, and Arthur J Moss. 1987. "Decreased heart rate variability and its association with increased mortality after acute myocardial infarction." *The American Journal of Cardiology* 59 (4): 256-262. https://doi.org/https://doi.org/10.1016/0002-9149(87)90795-8. http://www.sciencedirect.com/science/article/pii/0002914987907958.

Knicker, Axel J, Ian Renshaw, Anthony RH Oldham, and Simeon P Cairns. 2011. "Interactive processes link the multiple symptoms of fatigue in sport competition." *Sports medicine* 41 (4): 307-328.

Knowles, SB, SW Marshall, T Miller, R Spicer, JM Bowling, D Loomis, RW Millikan, J Yang, and FO Mueller. 2007a. "Cost of injuries from a prospective cohort study of North Carolina high school athletes." *Inj Prev* 13 (6): 416-21. https://doi.org/10.1136/ip.2006.014720.

Knowles, Sarah B, Stephen W Marshall, Tyler Miller, R Spicer, J Michael Bowling, D Loomis, RW Millikan, Jingzhen Yang, and FO Mueller. 2007b. "Cost of injuries from a prospective cohort study of North Carolina high school athletes." *Injury Prevention* 13 (6): 416-421.

Kraeutler, MJ, MG Ciccotti, CC Dodson, RW Frederick, B Cammarota, and SB Cohen. 2013. "Kerlan-Jobe Orthopaedic Clinic overhead athlete scores in asymptomatic professional baseball pitchers." *J Shoulder Elbow Surg* 22 (3): 329-32. https://doi.org/10.1016/j.jse.2012.02.010.

Kreher, Jeffrey B, and Jennifer B Schwartz. 2012. "Overtraining syndrome: a practical guide." *Sports health* 4 (2): 128-138.

Laffaye, Guillaume, Phillip P Wagner, and Tom IL Tombleson. 2014. "Countermovement jump height: Gender and sport-specific differences in the force-time variables." *The Journal of Strength & Conditioning Research* 28 (4): 1096-1105.

Lage, Marcos, Jorge Piazentin Ono, Daniel Cervone, Justin Chiang, Carlos Dietrich, and Claudio T Silva. 2016. "StatCast Dashboard: Exploration of spatiotemporal baseball data." *IEEE computer graphics and applications* 36 (5): 28-37.

Lapinski, Michael, Eric Berkson, Thomas Gill, Mike Reinold, and Joseph A Paradiso. 2009. "A distributed wearable, wireless sensor system for evaluating professional baseball pitchers and batters." 2009 International Symposium on Wearable Computers.

Larsson, Peter. 2003. "Global positioning system and sport-specific testing." *Sports medicine* 33 (15): 1093-1101.

Lehmann, Manfred, Carl Foster, Hans-Hermann Dickhuth, and U Gastmann. 1998. "Autonomic imbalance hypothesis and overtraining syndrome." *Medicine and science in sports and exercise* 30 (7): 1140-1145.

Lewis, Michael. 2004. *Moneyball: The art of winning an unfair game.* WW Norton & Company.

Li, Ka Hou Christien, Francesca Anne White, Timothy Tipoe, Tong Liu, Martin CS Wong, Aaron Jesuthasan, Adrian Baranchuk, Gary Tse, and Bryan P Yan. 2019. "The Current State of Mobile Phone Apps for Monitoring Heart Rate, Heart Rate Variability, and Atrial Fibrillation: Narrative Review." *JMIR mHealth and uHealth* 7 (2): e11606.

Li, Ryan T, Scott R Kling, Michael J Salata, Sean A Cupp, Joseph Sheehan, and James E Voos. 2016. "Wearable performance devices in sports medicine." *Sports health* 8 (1): 74-78.

LIAO, Ba-gen, and Xin-hua LUO. 2004. "Evaluation of POMS-R for Monitoring Overtraining [J]." *Journal of Beijing University of Physical Education* 8.

Luteberget, Live S, Benjamin R Holme, and Matt Spencer. 2017. "Reliability of wearable inertial measurement units to measure physical activity in team handball." *International journal of sports physiology and performance* 13 (4): 467-473.

Lyman, Stephen, Glenn S Fleisig, James R Andrews, and E David Osinski. 2002. "Effect of pitch type, pitch count, and pitching mechanics on risk of elbow and shoulder pain in youth baseball pitchers." *The American journal of sports medicine* 30 (4): 463-468.

MacLeod, Hannah, John Morris, Alan Nevill, and Caroline Sunderland. 2009. "The validity of a non-differential global positioning system for assessing player movement patterns in field hockey." *Journal of sports sciences* 27 (2): 121-128.

MacWilliams, Bruce A, Tony Choi, Mark K Perezous, Edmund YS Chao, and Edward G McFarland. 1998. "Characteristic ground-reaction forces in baseball pitching." *The American journal of sports medicine* 26 (1): 66-71.

Maddison, Ralph, and Cliona Ni Mhurchu. 2009. "Global positioning system: a new opportunity in physical activity measurement." *International journal of behavioral nutrition and physical activity* 6 (1): 73.

Mahure, SA, B Mollon, SD Shamah, YW Kwon, and AS Rokito. 2016. "Disproportionate trends in ulnar collateral ligament reconstruction: projections through 2025 and a literature review." *J Shoulder Elbow Surg* 25 (6): 1005-12. https://doi.org/10.1016/j.jse.2016.02.036.

Main, Luana, and J Robert Grove. 2009. "A multi-component assessment model for monitoring training distress among athletes." *European Journal of Sport Science* 9 (4): 195-202.

Makhni, Eric C, Vincent A Lizzio, Fabien Meta, Jeffrey P Stephens, Kelechi R Okoroha, and Vasilios Moutzouros. 2018. "Assessment of elbow torque and other parameters during the pitching motion: comparison of fastball, curveball, and change-up." *Arthroscopy: The Journal of Arthroscopic & Related Surgery* 34 (3): 816-822.

Makhni, Eric C, Bryan M Saltzman, Maximilian A Meyer, Vasilios Moutzouros, Brian J Cole, Anthony A Romeo, and Nikhil N Verma. 2017. "Outcomes after shoulder and elbow injury in baseball players: are we reporting what matters?" *The American journal of sports medicine* 45 (2): 495-500.

Makivić, Bojan, Marina Nikić Djordjević, and Monte S Willis. 2013. "Heart Rate Variability (HRV) as a tool for diagnostic and monitoring performance in sport and physical activities." *Journal of Exercise Physiology Online* 16 (3).

Marar, M, NM McIlvain, SK Fields, and RD Comstock. 2012. "Epidemiology of concussions among United States high school athletes in 20 sports." *Am J Sports Med* 40 (4): 747-55. https://doi.org/10.1177/0363546511435626.

Marshall, S, K Haywood, and R Fitzpatrick. 2006. "Impact of patient-reported outcome measures on routine practice: a structured review." *J Eval Clin Pract* 12 (5): 559-68. https://doi.org/10.1111/j.1365-2753.2006.00650.x.

Martinent, Guillaume, Jean-Claude Decret, Edith Filaire, Sandrine Isoard-Gautheur, and Claude Ferrand. 2014. "Evaluations of the psychometric properties of the Recovery-Stress Questionnaire for Athletes among a sample of young French table tennis players." *Psychological reports* 114 (2): 326-340.

Matsuo, Tomoyuki, Hiroki Nakamoto, and Masahiro Kageyama. 2017. "Comparison of Properties of a Pitched-Ball Rotation Measured by Three Different Methods." *ISBS Proceedings Archive* 35 (1): 115.

MayorsCitySports. 2018. "The Metrics System: How MLB's Statast is Creating Baseball's New Arms race." Accessed April 8. http://mayorcitysports.org/2018/03/the-metrics-system-how-mlbs-statcast-is-creating-baseballs-new-arms-race/.

McDonald, Clement J. 1997. "The barriers to electronic medical record systems and how to overcome them." *Journal of the American Medical Informatics Association* 4 (3): 213-221.

Mclaine, Alice J. 2005. "An overview of burnout in athletic trainers." *Athletic Therapy Today* 10 (6): 11-13.

Meeusen, Romain, Martine Duclos, Carl Foster, Andrew Fry, Michael Gleeson, David Nieman, John Raglin, Gerard Rietjens, Jürgen Steinacker, and Axel Urhausen. 2013. "Prevention, diagnosis and treatment of the overtraining syndrome: Joint consensus statement of the European College of Sport Science (ECSS) and the American College of Sports Medicine (ACSM)." *European Journal of Sport Science* 13 (1): 1-24.

Merolla, G, K Corona, G Zanoli, S Cerciello, S Giannotti, and G Porcellini. 2017. "Cross-cultural adaptation and validation of the Italian version of the Kerlan-Jobe Orthopaedic Clinic Shoulder and Elbow score." *J*

Orthop Traumatol 18 (4): 415-421. https://doi.org/10. 1007/s10195-017-0467-6.

Michael Sola ATC, PT, DPT. 2019. In *San Francisco 49ers Football Club*, edited by Garrett Bullock.

Mills, Brian M. 2017. "Technological innovations in monitoring and evaluation: Evidence of performance impacts among Major League Baseball umpires." *Labour Economics* 46: 189-199.

Misra, Anuruddh Kumar, Rafael Escamilla, and Narendra Nath Trivedi. 2018. "Throw Like a Pro V. 2.0 mobile app review." *Br J Sports Med*: bjsports-2017-098359.

Morgan, William P. 1994. "Psychological components of effort sense." *Medicine & Science in Sports & Exercise.*

Morgan, WP, DR Brown, JS Raglin, PJ O'connor, and KA Ellickson. 1987. "Psychological monitoring of overtraining and staleness." *British journal of sports medicine* 21 (3): 107-114.

Mourot, Laurent, Malika Bouhaddi, Stéphane Perrey, Sylvie Cappelle, Marie-Thérèse Henriet, Jean-Pierre Wolf, Jean-Denis Rouillon, and Jacques Regnard. 2004. "Decrease in heart rate variability with overtraining: assessment by the Poincare plot analysis." *Clinical physiology and functional imaging* 24 (1): 10-18.

Mündermann, Lars, Stefano Corazza, and Thomas P Andriacchi. 2006. "The evolution of methods for the capture of human movement leading to markerless motion capture for biomechanical applications." *Journal of neuroengineering and rehabilitation* 3 (1): 6.

Murray, James AH, Henry Bradley, William A Craigie, and Charles T Onions. 1933. *The Oxford english dictionary*. Vol. 1. Clarendon Press Oxford.

Murray, Nick B, Georgia M Black, Rod J Whiteley, Peter Gahan, Michael H Cole, Andy Utting, and Tim J Gabbett. 2017. "Automatic detection of pitching and throwing events in baseball with inertial measurement sensors." *International journal of sports physiology and performance* 12 (4): 533-537.

Nagami, Tomoyuki, Takatoshi Higuchi, and Kazuyuki Kanosue. 2013. "How baseball spin influences the performance of a pitcher." *The Journal of Physical Fitness and Sports Medicine* 2 (1): 63-68.

Nathan, A. 2012a. "Determining pitch movement from PITCHf/x data." *Available: baseball. physics. illinois. edu/Movement. pdf.*

Nathan, Alan M. "Determining the 3D Spin Axis from TrackMan Data (updated, March 31, 2015)."

---. 2007. "Analysis of pitchf/x pitched baseball trajectories." *The Physics of Baseball.*

---. 2012b. "What New Technologies Are Teaching Us About the Game of Baseball."

Neft, David S, Richard M Cohen, and Michael L Neft. 2004. *The Sports Encyclopedia: Baseball 2004.* Macmillan.

Nelson, EC, E Eftimovska, C Lind, A Hager, JH Wasson, and S Lindblad. 2015. "Patient reported outcome measures in practice." *Bmj* 350: g7818. https://doi.org/10.1136/bmj.g7818.

Neri, BR, NS ElAttrache, KC Owsley, K Mohr, and LA Yocum. 2011. "Outcome of type II superior labral anterior posterior repairs in elite overhead athletes: Effect of concomitant partial-thickness rotator cuff tears." *Am J Sports Med* 39 (1): 114-20. https://doi.org/10.1177/0363546510379971.

Newham, DJ, G McPhail, KR Mills, and RHT Edwards. 1983. "Ultrastructural changes after concentric and eccentric contractions of human muscle." *Journal of the neurological sciences* 61 (1): 109-122.

Nicolella, Daniel P, Lorena Torres-Ronda, Kase J Saylor, and Xavi Schelling. 2018. "Validity and reliability of an accelerometer-based player tracking device." *PloS one* 13 (2): e0191823.

O'Sullivan, Saoirse E, and Christopher Bell. 2000. "The effects of exercise and training on human cardiovascular reflex control." *Journal of the autonomic nervous system* 81 (1-3): 16-24.

Oh, JH, JY Kim, O Limpisvasti, TQ Lee, SH Song, and KB Kwon. 2017. "Cross-cultural adaptation, validity and reliability of the Korean version of the Kerlan-Jobe Orthopedic Clinic shoulder and elbow score." *JSES Open Access* 1 (1): 39-44. https://doi.org/10.1016/j.jses.2017.03.001.

Olsen, Samuel J, Glenn S Fleisig, Shouchen Dun, Jeremy Loftice, and James R Andrews. 2006. "Risk factors for shoulder and elbow injuries in adolescent baseball pitchers." *The American journal of sports medicine* 34 (6): 905-912.

Paci, JM, Jones, CM, Yang, J, Zhu, J, Komatsu, D, Flores, A, & Van Dyke, D. 2015. "Predictive Value Of Preseason Screening In Collegiate Baseball Pitchers." *Orthopaedic Journal of Sports Medicine* 3 (7 supplemental 2).

Parrado, E, MÁ García, J Ramos, JC Cervantes, G Rodas, and L Capdevila. 2010. "Comparison of Omega Wave System and Polar S810i to Detect R-R Intervals at Rest." *Int J Sports Med* 31 (05): 336-341. https://doi.org/10.1055/s-0030-1248319.

Petty, DH, JR Andrews, GS Fleisig, and EL Cain. 2004. "Ulnar collateral ligament reconstruction in high school baseball players: clinical results and injury risk factors." *Am J Sports Med* 32 (5): 1158-64. https://doi.org/10.1177/0363546503262166.

Pichot, Vincent, Frederic Roche, Jean-Michel Gaspoz, Franck Enjolras, Anestis Antoniadis, Pascal Minini, Frederic Costes, Thierry Busso, Jean-Rene Lacour, and Jean Claude Barthelemy. 2000. "Relation between heart rate variability and training load in middle-distance runners." *Medicine and science in sports and exercise* 32 (10): 1729-1736.

Pitney, WA 2006. "Organizational influences and quality-of-life issues during the professional socialization of certified athletic trainers working in the National Collegiate Athletic Association Division I setting." *J Athl Train* 41 (2): 189-95.

Plews, Daniel J, Paul B Laursen, Jamie Stanley, Andrew E Kilding, and Martin Buchheit. 2013. "Training adaptation and heart rate variability in elite endurance athletes: opening the door to effective monitoring." *Sports medicine* 43 (9): 773-781.

Plews, Daniel J, Paul B Laursen, Yann Le Meur, Christophe Hausswirth, Andrew E Kilding, and Martin Buchheit. 2014. "Monitoring Training with Heart-Rate Variability: How Much Compliance Is Needed for Valid Assessment?" *International Journal of Sports Physiology and*

Performance 9 (5): 783-790. https://doi.org/10.1123/ijspp.2013-0455. https://journals.humankinetics.com/doi/abs/10.1123/ijspp.2013-0455.

Plews, Daniel J, Ben Scott, Marco Altini, Matt Wood, Andrew E Kilding, and Paul B Laursen. 2017. "Comparison of Heart-Rate-Variability Recording With Smartphone Photoplethysmography, Polar H7 Chest Strap, and Electrocardiography." *International Journal of Sports Physiology and Performance* 12 (10): 1324-1328. https://doi.org/10.1123/ijspp.2016-0668. https://doi.org/10.1123/ijspp.2016-0668.

Polanczyk, Carisi A, Luis EP Rohde, Ruy S Moraes, Elton L Ferlin, Cristina Leite, and Jorge P Ribeiro. 1998. "Sympathetic nervous system representation in time and frequency domain indices of heart rate variability." *European journal of applied physiology and occupational physiology* 79 (1): 69-73.

Polimeni, Giuseppe, Alfonso Scarpino, Kurt Barbé, Francesco Lamonaca, and Domenico Grimaldi. 2014. "Evaluation of the number of PPG harmonics to assess Smartphone effectiveness." 2014 IEEE International Symposium on Medical Measurements and Applications (MeMeA).

Pollack, KM, J D'Angelo, G Green, S Conte, S Fealy, C Marinak, E McFarland, and FC Curriero. 2016. "Developing and Implementing Major League Baseball's Health and Injury Tracking System." *Am J Epidemiol* 183 (5): 490-6. https://doi.org/10.1093/aje/kwv348.

Posner, M, KL Cameron, JM Wolf, PJ Belmont, Jr., and BD Owens. 2011. "Epidemiology of Major League Baseball injuries." *Am J Sports Med* 39 (8): 1676-80. https://doi.org/10.1177/0363546511411700.

Potteiger, JA, DL Blessing, and GD Wilson. 1992a. "Effects of varying recovery periods on muscle enzymes, soreness, and performance in baseball pitchers." *Journal of athletic training* 27 (1): 27-31. https://www.ncbi.nlm.nih.gov/pubmed/16558126 https://www.ncbi.nlm.nih.gov/pmc/articles/PMC1317125/.

Potteiger, Jeffrey A, Daniel L Blessing, and G Dennis Wilson. 1992b. "The physiological responses to a single game of baseball pitching." *The Journal of Strength & Conditioning Research* 6 (1): 11-18.

Prusaczyk, Max Goder-Reiser & Julia. 2017. "Comparing the Rapsodo Baseball Device to Other Pitch Trackers." Accessed April 9. https://tht.fangraphs.com/comparing-the-rapsodo-baseball-device-to-other-pitch-trackers/.

Pytiak, AV, MJ Kraeutler, DW Currie, EC McCarty, and RD Comstock. 2018. "An Epidemiological Comparison of Elbow Injuries Among United States High School Baseball and Softball Players, 2005-2006 Through 2014-2015." *Sports Health* 10 (2): 119-124. https://doi.org/10.1177/1941738117736493.

Racinais, Sebastien, Martin Buchheit, Johann Bilsborough, Pitre C Bourdon, Justin Cordy, and Aaron J Coutts. 2014. "Physiological and performance responses to a training camp in the heat in professional Australian football players." *International journal of sports physiology and performance* 9 (4): 598-603.

Rader, Benjamin G. 2008. *Baseball: A history of America's game*. Vol. 14. University of Illinois Press.

Rapsado. Accessed April 9. https://rapsodo.com/.

Rawashdeh, Samir, Derek Rafeldt, and Timothy Uhl. 2016. "Wearable IMU for shoulder injury prevention in overhead sports." *Sensors* 16 (11): 1847.

Raymond, François, Benoit Lussier, François Dugas, Mathieu Charbonneau, Félix Croteau, Cory Kennedy, and Nicolas Berryman. 2018. "Using Portable Force Plates to Assess Vertical Jump Performance: A Metrological Appraisal." *Sports* 6 (4): 149.

Rechel, JA, CL Collins, and RD Comstock. 2011. "Epidemiology of injuries requiring surgery among high school athletes in the United States, 2005 to 2010." *J Trauma* 71 (4): 982-9. https://doi.org/10.1097/TA.0b013e318230e716.

Rex, AF. 1985. "The effect of spin on the flight of batted baseballs." *American Journal of Physics* 53 (11): 1073-1075.

Richards, James G. 1999. "The measurement of human motion: A comparison of commercially available systems." *Human movement science* 18 (5): 589-602.

Roell, Mareike, Kai Roecker, Dominic Gehring, Hubert Mahler, and Albert Gollhofer. 2018. "Player monitoring in indoor team sports: concurrent validity of inertial measurement units to quantify average and peak acceleration values." *Frontiers in physiology* 9: 141.

Rowen, Ben. 2018. "Chasing the 'Holy Grail' of Baseball Performance." The Atlantic. Accessed April 9. https://www.theatlantic.com/magazine/archive/2018/07/finding-the-formula-for-team-chemistry/561722/.

Rushall, Brent S. 1990. "A tool for measuring stress tolerance in elite athletes." *Journal of Applied Sport Psychology* 2 (1): 51-66.

Saboul, Damien, Pascal Balducci, Grégoire Millet, Vincent Pialoux, and Christophe Hautier. 2016. "A pilot study on quantification of training load: The use of HRV in training practice." *European Journal of Sport Science* 16 (2): 172-181. https://doi.org/10.1080/17461391.2015.1004373. https://doi.org/10.1080/17461391.2015.1004373.

Sanchez-Medina, Luis, and Juan José González-Badillo. 2011. "Velocity loss as an indicator of neuromuscular fatigue during resistance training." *Medicine and science in sports and exercise* 43 (9): 1725-1734.

Sandomir, Richard. 2006. "Clocking Pitches, Give or Take 3 MPH." New York Times Accessed Aprill 8. https://www.nytimes.com/2006/10/13/sports/baseball/13sandomir.html.

Saper, MG, LA Pierpoint, W Liu, RD Comstock, JD Polousky, and JR Andrews. 2018. "Epidemiology of Shoulder and Elbow Injuries Among United States High School Baseball Players: School Years 2005-2006 Through 2014-2015." *Am J Sports Med* 46 (1): 37-43. https://doi.org/10.1177/0363546517734172.

Sauers, EL, RC Bay, AR Snyder Valier, T Ellery, and KC Huxel Bliven. 2017. "The Functional Arm Scale for Throwers (FAST)-Part I: The Design and Development of an Upper Extremity Region-Specific and Population-Specific Patient-Reported Outcome Scale for Throwing Athletes." *Orthop J Sports Med* 5 (3): 2325967117698455. https://doi.org/10.1177/2325967117698455.

Savant, Baseball. "Statcast-Batting." Major League Baseball Accessed April 10. https://baseballsvant.mlb.com/savant-player/.

Saw, Anna E, Luana C Main, and Paul B Gastin. 2015. "Monitoring athletes through self-report: factors influencing implementation." *Journal of sports science & medicine* 14 (1): 137.

---. 2016. "Monitoring the athlete training response: subjective self-reported measures trump commonly used objective measures: a systematic review." *Br J Sports Med* 50 (5): 281-291.

Sawicki, Gregory S, Mont Hubbard, and William J Stronge. 2003. "How to hit home runs: Optimum baseball bat swing parameters for maximum range trajectories." *American Journal of Physics* 71 (11): 1152-1162.

Schroeder, AN, RD Comstock, CL Collins, J Everhart, D Flanigan, and TM Best. 2015. "Epidemiology of overuse injuries among high-school athletes in the United States." *J Pediatr* 166 (3): 600-6. https://doi.org/10.1016/j.jpeds.2014.09.037.

Scott, Brendan R, Robert G Lockie, Timothy J Knight, Andrew C Clark, and Xanne AK Janse de Jonge. 2013. "A comparison of methods to quantify the in-season training load of professional soccer players." *International journal of sports physiology and performance* 8 (2): 195-202.

Seidel, Michael. 2003. *Ted Williams: a baseball life*. U of Nebraska Press.

Seiler, Stephen, Olav Haugen, and Erin Kuffel. 2007. "Autonomic recovery after exercise in trained athletes: intensity and duration effects." *Medicine & Science in Sports & Exercise* 39 (8): 1366-1373.

Shaffer, Benjamin, FRANK W Jobe, Marilyn Pink, and Jacquelin Perry. 1993. "Baseball batting. An electromyographic study." *Clinical orthopaedics and related research* (292): 285-293.

Shaffer, Fred, and JP Ginsberg. 2017. "An overview of heart rate variability metrics and norms." *Frontiers in public health* 5: 258.

Shanley, E, MJ Rauh, LA Michener, TS Ellenbecker, JC Garrison, and CA Thigpen. 2011. "Shoulder range of motion measures as risk factors for shoulder and elbow injuries in high school softball and baseball players." *Am J Sports Med* 39 (9): 1997-2006. https://doi.org/10.1177/0363546511408876.

Sickels, John. 2004. *Bob Feller: Ace of the Greatest Generation*. Brassey's Inc.

Slenker, Nicholas R, Orr Limpisvasti, Karen Mohr, Arnel Aguinaldo, and Neal S ElAttrache. 2014. "Biomechanical comparison of the interval throwing program and baseball pitching: upper extremity loads in training and rehabilitation." *The American journal of sports medicine* 42 (5): 1226-1232.

Slimani, Maamer, Philip Davis, Emerson Franchini, and Wassim Moalla. 2017. "Rating of perceived exertion for quantification of training and combat loads during combat sport-specific activities: a short review." *The Journal of Strength & Conditioning Research* 31 (10): 2889-2902.

Slivka, Dustin R, Walther S Hailes, John S Cuddy, and Brent C Ruby. 2010. "Effects of 21 days of intensified training on markers of overtraining." *The Journal of Strength & Conditioning Research* 24 (10): 2604-2612.

Smith, Matthew V, Ryan P Calfee, Keith M Baumgarten, Robert H Brophy, and Rick W Wright. 2012. "Upper extremity-specific measures of disability and outcomes in orthopaedic surgery." *The Journal of Bone and Joint Surgery. American volume.* 94 (3): 277.

Snyder, AC, HARM Kuipers, B Cheng, RODRIQUE Servais, and ERIK Fransen. 1995. "Overtraining following intensified training with normal muscle glycogen." *Medicine and science in sports and exercise* 27 (7): 1063-1070.

Stodden, David F, Glenn S Fleisig, Scott P McLean, and James R Andrews. 2005. "Relationship of biomechanical factors to baseball pitching velocity: within pitcher variation." *Journal of applied biomechanics* 21 (1): 44-56.

Suchomel, Timothy J, and Christopher A Bailey. 2014. "Monitoring and managing fatigue in baseball players." *Strength & Conditioning Journal* 36 (6): 39-45.

Swenson, DM, EE Yard, CL Collins, SK Fields, and RD Comstock. 2010. "Epidemiology of US high school sports-related fractures, 2005-2009." *Clin J Sport Med* 20 (4): 293-9. https://doi.org/10.1097/JSM.0b013e3181e8fae8.

Szymanski, David J. 2009. "Physiology of baseball pitching dictates specific exercise intensity for conditioning." *Strength & Conditioning Journal* 31 (2): 41-47.

Taha, Tim, and Scott G Thomas. 2003. "Systems modelling of the relationship between training and performance." *Sports Medicine* 33 (14): 1061-1073.

Taylor, K, D Chapman, J Cronin, Michael J Newton, and Nicholas Gill. 2012. "Fatigue monitoring in high performance sport: a survey of current trends." *J Aust Strength Cond* 20 (1): 12-23.

Terry, Peter C, and Andrew M Lane. 2000. "Normative values for the Profile of Mood States for use with athletic samples." *Journal of applied sport psychology* 12 (1): 93-109.

Testa, Marcia A, and Donald C Simonson. 1996. "Assessment of quality-of-life outcomes." *New England journal of medicine* 334 (13): 835-840.

Thacker, SB, and RL Berkelman. 1988. "Public health surveillance in the United States." *Epidemiol Rev* 10: 164-90.

Thacker, SB, JR Qualters, and LM Lee. 2012. "Public health surveillance in the United States: evolution and challenges." *MMWR Suppl* 61 (3): 3-9.

Theobalt, Christian, Irene Albrecht, Jörg Haber, Marcus Magnor, and Hans-Peter Seidel. 2004. "Pitching a baseball: tracking high-speed motion with multi-exposure images." ACM Transactions on Graphics (TOG).

Thomas, Henry W. 1998. *Walter Johnson: Baseball's Big Train*. U of Nebraska Press.

Tsuruike, M, TS Ellenbecker, and N Hirose. 2018. "Kerlan-Jobe Orthopaedic Clinic (KJOC) score and scapular dyskinesis test in collegiate baseball players." *J Shoulder Elbow Surg* 27 (10): 1830-1836. https://doi.org/10.1016/j.jse.2018.06.033.

Turgut, E, and VB Tunay. 2018. "Cross-cultural adaptation of Kerlan-Jobe Orthopaedic Clinic shoulder and elbow score: Reliability and validity in Turkish-speaking overhead athletes." *Acta Orthop Traumatol Turc* 52 (3): 206-210. https://doi.org/10.1016/j.aott.2018.02.007.

Urhausen, A, HHW Gabriel, B Weiler, and W Kindermann. 1998. "Ergometric and psychological findings during overtraining: a long-term follow-up study in endurance athletes." *International journal of sports medicine* 19 (02): 114-120.

Urhausen, Axel, Holger Gabriel, and Wilfried Kindermann. 1995. "Blood hormones as markers of training stress and overtraining." *Sports medicine* 20 (4): 251-276.

Urhausen, Axel, and Wilfried Kindermann. 2002. "Diagnosis of overtraining." *Sports medicine* 32 (2): 95-102.

Uusitalo, ALT, AJ Uusitalo, and HK Rusko. 2000. "Heart Rate and Blood Pressure Variability During Heavy Training and Overtraining in the Female Athlete." *Int J Sports Med* 21 (01): 45-53. https://doi.org/10.1055/s-2000-8853.

Valderas, JM, A Kotzeva, M Espallargues, G Guyatt, CE Ferrans, MY Halyard, DA Revicki, T. Symonds, A Parada, and J Alonso. 2008. "The impact of measuring patient-reported outcomes in clinical practice: a systematic review of the literature." *Qual Life Res* 17 (2): 179-93. https://doi.org/10.1007/s11136-007-9295-0.

van der Kruk, Eline, and Marco M Reijne. 2018. "Accuracy of human motion capture systems for sport applications; state-of-the-art review." *European journal of sport science* 18 (6): 806-819.

van Mechelen, DM, W van Mechelen, and EA Verhagen. 2014. "Sports injury prevention in your pocket?! Prevention apps assessed against the available scientific evidence: a review." *Br J Sports Med* 48 (11): 878-82. https://doi.org/10.1136/bjsports-2012-092136.

Vanderlei, Luiz Carlos Marques, Carlos Marcelo Pastre, Rosângela Akemi Hoshi, Tatiana Dias de Carvalho, and Moacir Fernandes de Godoy. 2009. "Basic notions of heart rate variability and its clinical applicability." *Brazilian Journal of Cardiovascular Surgery* 24 (2): 205-217.

Velentgas, Priscilla, Nancy A Dreyer, Parivash Nourjah, Scott R Smith, and Marion M Torchia. 2013. *Developing a protocol for observational comparative effectiveness research: a user's guide*. Government Printing Office.

Wallace, Lee K, Katie M Slattery, and Aaron J Coutts. 2009. "The ecological validity and application of the session-RPE method for quantifying training loads in swimming." *The Journal of Strength & Conditioning Research* 23 (1): 33-38.

Waltz, Emily. 2015. "A wearable turns baseball pitching into a science [News]." *IEEE Spectrum* 52 (9): 16-17.

Warren, Courtney D, David J Szymanski, and Merrill R Landers. 2015. "Effects of three recovery protocols on range of motion, heart rate, rating of perceived exertion, and blood lactate in baseball pitchers during a simulated game." *The Journal of Strength & Conditioning Research* 29 (11): 3016-3025.

Watts, Robert G, and Steven Baroni. 1989. "Baseball–bat collisions and the resulting trajectories of spinning balls." *American Journal of Physics* 57 (1): 40-45.

Weaving, Dan, Sarah Whitehead, Kevin Till, and Ben Jones. 2017. "Validity of Real-Time Data Generated by a Wearable Microtechnology Device." *The Journal of Strength & Conditioning Research* 31 (10): 2876-2879. https://doi.org/10.1519/jsc. 0000000000002127. https://journals.lww.com/nsca-jscr/Fulltext/2017/10000/Validity_of_Real_Time_Data_Generated_by_a_Wearable.27.aspx.

Welch, Christian M, Scott A Banks, Frank F Cook, and Pete Draovitch. 1995. "Hitting a baseball: A biomechanical description." *Journal of orthopaedic & sports physical therapy* 22 (5): 193-201.

Wilk, KE, LC Macrina, GS Fleisig, KT Aune, RA Porterfield, P Harker, TJ Evans, and JR Andrews. 2014. "Deficits in glenohumeral passive range of motion increase risk of elbow injury in professional baseball pitchers: a prospective study." *Am J Sports Med* 42 (9): 2075-81. https://doi.org/10.1177/0363546514538391.

Wilk, KE, LC Macrina, GS Fleisig, R Porterfield, CD Simpson, 2nd, P Harker, N Paparesta, and JR Andrews. 2011. "Correlation of glenohumeral internal rotation deficit and total rotational motion to shoulder injuries in professional baseball pitchers." *Am J Sports Med* 39 (2): 329-35. https://doi.org/10.1177/0363546510384223.

Windt, Johann, and Tim J Gabbett. 2017. "How do training and competition workloads relate to injury? The workload—injury aetiology model." *Br J Sports Med* 51 (5): 428-435.

Yang, Jingzhen, Barton J Mann, Joseph H Guettler, Jeffrey R Dugas, James J Irrgang, Glenn S Fleisig, and John P Albright. 2014. "Risk-prone pitching activities and injuries in youth baseball: findings from a national sample." *The American journal of sports medicine* 42 (6): 1456-1463.

Yokoyama, K, S Araki, N Kawakami, and T Tkakeshita. 1990. "Production of the Japanese edition of profile of mood states (POMS): assessment of reliability and validity." [*Nihon koshu eisei zasshi*] *Japanese journal of public health* 37 (11): 913-918.

Young, Kevin. 1993. "Violence, risk, and liability in male sports culture." *Sociology of sport journal* 10 (4): 373-396.

BIOGRAPHICAL SKETCH

Garrett Scott Bullock

Affiliation:
1. Centre for Sport, Exercise and Osteoarthritis Research *Versus Arthritis,* University of Oxford, United Kingdom
2. Nuffield Department of Orthopaedics, Rheumatology, and Musculoskeletal Sciences, University of Oxford, Oxford, United Kingdom

Education:
Wake Forest University, Bachelor of Arts, Field of Study: History
Duke University, Doctor of Physical Therapy, Field of Study: Physical Study
University of Oxford, Doctor of Philosophy Candidate, Field of Study: Musculoskeletal Science: Biomedical Data Science

Business Address:

Nuffield Department of Orthopaedics, Rheumatology, and Musculoskeletal Sciences

University of Oxford

B4495

Oxford, United Kingdom

OX3 7LD

Research and Professional Experience:

2013: Research Technician, Human Performance Lab, North Carolina Research Campus, Appalachian State University

2013-2014: Research Assistant, Exercise and Sport Science Laboratory, Queens University of Charlotte

2014-2017: Research Assistant, Michael W. Krzyzewski Human Performance Lab, Department of Orthopaedic Surgery, Duke University

2016-Present: Research Assistant, Functional Movement Systems

2018-Present: Member, Arden Group: Epidemiology of Musculoskeletal Diseases, University of Oxford

2018-Present: Member, Centre for Sport, Exercise and Osteoarthritis Research *versus Arthritis,* University of Oxford

Professional Appointments:

2009-2014: Professional Baseball Player, Houston Astros Organization

2014-2017: Graduate Student, Duke University, Physical Therapy Program

2016-Present: Data Analyst, Functional Movement Systems

2017-2018: Team Leader, Mountain River Physical Therapy

2018-Present: Graduate Student, University of Oxford

Honors:

2009: Captain, Wake Forest Baseball

2010: Greeneville Houston Astros Minor League Affiliate Pitcher of the Year

2014-2017: Class President, Duke University, Physical Therapy Program

2017: Degree Marshall, Duke University

2018-2021: Clarendon Scholar, Oxford University Press, University of Oxford

Publications from the Last 3 Years:

Butler RJ, Bullock GS, Arnold TW, Plisky PJ, Queen R. Competition level differences on the Lower Quarter Y Balance Test in Baseball Players. *J Athl Train.* 2016; 51(12):997-1002.

Bullock GS, Arnold TW, Plisky PJ, Butler RJ. Basketball players' dynamic performance across competition level. *J Strength Cond Res.* 2018;32(12):3528-3533.

Bullock GS, Brookreson N, Knab AM, Butler RJ. Examining fundamental movement competency and closed chain upper extremity dynamic balance in swimmers. *J Strength Cond Res.* 2017, 31(6):1544-1551.

Bullock GS, Schmitt AC, Shutt JM, Cook G, Butler RJ. Kinematics and kinetic variables differ between kettlebell swing styles. *Int J Sport Phys Ther.* 2017, 12(3):324-332.

Bullock GS, Kraft LM, Amsden K, Gore W, Prengle R, Wimsatt J, Leidbetter L, Covington JK, Goode A. The prevalence and effect of burnout on graduate healthcare students. *Canadian Medical Education Journal.* 2017;8(3).

Bullock GS, Chapman T, Joyce T, Prengle R, Stern T, Butler RJ. Examining differences in movement competency in professional baseball players born in the United State and Dominican Republic. *J Sport Rehabil.* 2017;12;1-22.

Bullock GS, Schmitt AC, Chasse P, Little BA. Diehl LH, Butler RJ. Heart rate response between different pitch types in collegiate baseball pitchers. *Int J Perform Anal Sport.* 2017;11;1-9.

Harnish C, Bullock GS. Physical, performance, and functional movement characteristics of NCAA Division III women's soccer and volleyball players. *J Research Sports Med.* 2017; 2(1);27-33.

Bullock GS, Arnold TW, Plisky PJ, Butler RJ. Basketball players' dynamic performance across competition level. *J Strength Cond Res.* 2018;32(12):3528-3533.

Bullock GS, Schmitt AC, Chasse P, Little BA. Diehl LH, Butler RJ. The relationship between trunk rotation, upper quarter dynamic stability, and pitch velocity. *J Strength Cond Res.* 2018;32(1):261-266.

Peters S, Bullock GS, Goode A, Garrigues GE, Ruch DS, Reiman MR. The Success of Return to Sport after Ulnar Collateral Ligament Injury in Baseball: A Systematic Review and Meta-Analysis. *J Shoulder Elbow Surg.* 2018;27;561-571.

Bullock GS, Faherty MS, Ledbetter L, Thigpen CA, Sell TC. Is shoulder range of motion associated with baseball arm injuries: A systematic review and meta-analysis. *J Athl Train.* 2018;53(12):1190-1199.

Chasse P, Bullock GS, Schmitt AC, Little BA. Diehl LH, Butler RJ. The relationship between trunk rotation, upper quarter dynamic stability, and the Kerlan-Jobe Orthopaedic Clinic Overhead Athlete Shoulder and Elbow Score in Division I collegiate pitchers. *Int J Sports Phys Ther.* 2018;13(5):819-827.

Helmkamp JK, Bullock GS, Amilo NR, Ledbetter LS, Guerrero EM, Sell TC, Garrigues GE. The clinical impact of center of rotation lateralization in reverse shoulder arthroplasty: A systematic review. *J Shoulder Elbow Surg.* 2018:27(11):2099-2107.

Coughlin RP, Bullock GS, Shanmugaraj A, Sell TC, Garrigues GE, Ledbetter L, Taylor DC. Outcomes After Arthroscopic Rotator Interval Closure for Shoulder Instability: A Systematic Review. *Arthroscopy.* 2018;2;34(11):3098-3108.

Gourlay J, Bullock GS, Weaver A, Kiesel K, Plisky PJ. The relationship between the half kneeling closed chain ankle dorsiflexion test and a novel ordinal scale modified weight bearing lunge test. *Athl Train Sports Health Care.* 2019.

Krysak S, Harnish C, Plisky PJ, Knab AM, Bullock GS. Fundamental movement and dynamic balance disparities between varying competition levels in golfers. *Int J Sports Phys Ther.* 2019.

Bullock GS, Garrigues GE, Ledbetter L, Kennedy J. Rehabilitation for Anatomic and Reverse Total Shoulder Arthroplasty: A Systematic Review. *J Orthop Sports Phys Ther.* 2019; 49(5):337-346.

Losciale J, Bullock GS, Cromwell C, Pietrosimone LS, Ledbetter L, Sell TC. Hop testing lack strong association with key variables following primary anterior cruciate ligament reconstruction: A literature review and meta-analysis. *Am J Sports Med.* 2019;(5):1-12.

Bullock GS, Schmitt AC, Chasse P, Little BA. Diehl LH, Butler RJ. The relationship between Player Load and pitch type in Division I collegiate baseball: are all pitch types equal? *J Sports Biomechanics.* 2019.

In: Essential Topics in Baseball
Editor: Erik Welch

ISBN: 978-1-53616-533-3
© 2019 Nova Science Publishers, Inc.

Chapter 2

THROWING KINEMATICS TO ACHIEVE HIGH PERFORMANCE AND PREVENT INJURY

Toshiaki Takahashi, MD, PhD*

Professor of Department of Sports and Health Science,
Faculty of Collaborative Regional Innovation,
Ehime University, Ehime, Japan

ABSTRACT

The throwing motion consists of a sequence of movements from the lower limbs to the upper limbs through the trunk. Failures in the sequence of movements place excess load on the upper arm and causes various disorders. The main causes of disability are a high number of throws and inadequate throwing form. Too many throws will cause medial collateral ligament injury of the elbow and rotator cuff tear and periarthritis of the shoulder.

In the wind-up phase of the throwing motion, it is necessary to save throwing energy by turning the body so that the buttocks face home plate. In the early cocking phase, the little finger side of the throwing hand should be raised upward.

* Corresponding Author's E-mail: takahast@m.ehime-u.ac.jp.

Throwing energy decreases if the pelvis and trunk turn too early when the foot of the non-throwing side is in contact with the ground. To compensate for the loss of energy, pitchers use the upper extremities; however, this places a burden on the elbow and shoulder of the throwing arm. In the acceleration phase, the area between the waist and hip joint on the non-throwing side becomes the axis of rotation, and the straight line connecting both shoulders and upper limbs rotate quickly around this axis. In the follow-through phase, the mound tilt is used to shift the weight of the entire body forward and transmit the force to the throwing arm. If the trunk and legs do not move properly, less energy is transferred to the ball.

Therefore, a form that relies too much on the strength of the upper limbs will inevitably lead to injuries of the shoulder and elbow, and subsequent inability to throw a ball with speed. Checking and improving the throwing form is very important, so we will explain the correct pitching form that achieves high pitching performance and reduces the risk of injury.

INTRODUCTION

Baseball is one of the most popular participatory sports in Japan, where approximately seven million male and female individuals play at professional, amateur, and recreational levels.

Japan has the world's second largest baseball player population next to the United States. The wide popularity of baseball among Japanese students and adults is largely attributable to the use of rubber baseballs dating back to 1919. Presently, approximately fifty thousand teams in rubber-ball baseball in Japan. Regular baseball is played on a more competitive level than rubber-ball baseball, by high-school, collegiate, and professional league players. The population of Japanese baseball players has gradually been shrinking in recent years because of Japan's declining birth rate and the increasing popularity of soccer, basketball, and other sports.

Shoulder and elbow injuries in immature youth and adolescent players are a major concern for parents, coaches, and sports medicine professionals, and their effective prevention is a frequent subject of discussion. Pitching injuries are attributable to excessive pitch counts, poor pitching mechanics, and the susceptibility of the developing skeleton in children and young adults (Thompson 2018). In a previous unpublished study, we found that shoulder and elbow injuries occurred in both pitchers and position players, suggesting that repeated improper mechanical motions are a more fundamental etiology than overuse. In particular, skeletally immature young players are at high risk of injury to the dominant medial elbow and shoulder. Thus good throwing mechanics taught at a young age are key to minimizing the risk of pitching injuries (Fleisig 2018; Fehr 2016). This article will describe biomechanically correct throwing motions for pitchers, catchers, and fielders to help protect their elbows and shoulders.

Gripping

The correct gripping technique is to place the ulnar side of the thumb directly underneath the ball (Figure 1a). This grip allows for a maximum degree of forearm pronation when the hand moves back (Figure 2a). By contrast, when the ball is supported by the palmar side of the thumb (Figure 1b), there is insufficient forearm pronation and the pitch is less powerful (Figure 2b).

Figure 1. How to grip a ball. The correct way to grip a ball is to place the ball on the ulnar side of the thumb (a). Holding the ball using the palmar side of the thumb fails to impart maximum momentum to the ball (b).

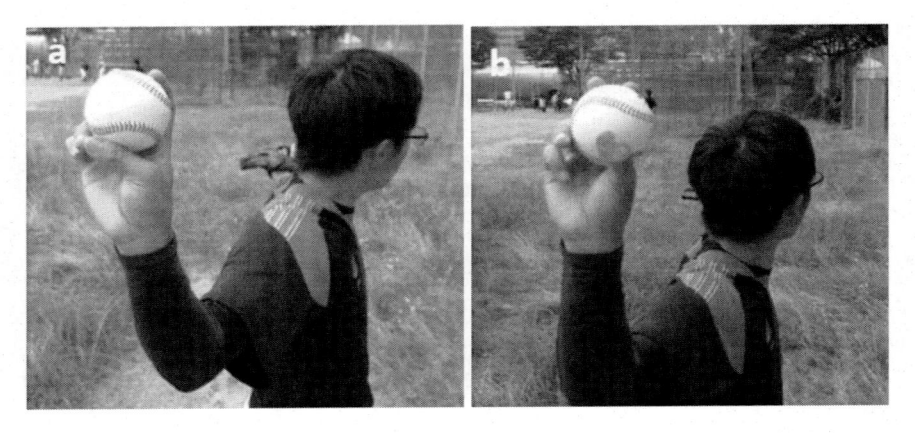

Figure 2. Ball at the highest position. The correct grip (a) helps the forearm to achieve a greater angle of pronation than the incorrect grip (b).

Players are encouraged to acquire the proper grip form through daily practice.

Basics of Throwing Motions

An accurate and high-speed throw requires an efficient kinematic chain of movements that involves the coordination of the legs, hip joints, body trunk, shoulder joint, elbow, wrist, and fingers. Directing the pitcher's mass towards the target by striding with the front leg (on the glove side) is critical for precise and powerful pitching.

A pitcher over 180cm tall with well-developed upper extremity muscles can throw fastballs relying on his muscle power and taking advantage of the long lever arm. However, pitchers throwing in this manner will suffer from shoulder or elbow injuries due to excessive stress.

Pitchers who wish to throw fastballs for most of their career should learn to coordinate their lower extremities and other body segments to dissipate the biomechanical stress on the upper extremities. Young athletes with developing skeletons should be instructed about proper mechanics to avoid heavily relying on upper extremity force (Fleisig and Andrews 2012).

Pitching Motion

Windup Phase: Starting Stance to Maximum Knee Height

It is important to direct the front hip towards home plate to maximize power production. During the leg lift, the pitcher lifts with the knee, which should be angled back away from home plate (Figure 3a). When the pitcher lifts the knee of his lead leg to its maximum height, he should have a stable center of gravity. This is necessary to avoid any weight shift and power loss outside the line between home plate and second base. If the pitcher lifts his front leg using only hip joint flexion (Figure 3b), his center of mass is shifted in a non-throwing direction, which will require him to make adjustments to the throwing direction using his upper body during the acceleration phase. Minimizing the need for upper body adjustments is critical for accurate pitching.

Early Cocking Phase: Maximum Knee Height to Landing

Figure 4 presents a top-down illustration of a pitcher in a throwing motion. The knee of the lead leg should move straight towards the catcher. This enables a correct weight shift towards the target and thereby allows maximum force to be applied to the ball. If the pitcher moves his front leg around in an arc (marked with a dotted line in Figure 4), it will cause two major problems. First, it will interfere with efficient energy transfer because it compromises the maximum weight shift along the line between home plate and second base. Second, because this motion deviates the weight shift direction from the proper line, the pitcher will need to adjust the ball release direction after his front foot lands.

The pitcher moves his front hip towards the catcher, with the trunk positioned upright. This movement is followed by shoulder abduction and internal rotation, elbow flexion, and forearm pronation. Specifically, as the throwing arm moves back and brings the ball to the highest point (shoulder abduction), the shoulder joint rotates internal and the forearm pronates (Davis 2009).

By turning the ulnar side of the hand up and the radial side down, the elbow can be positioned above the shoulder without difficulty.

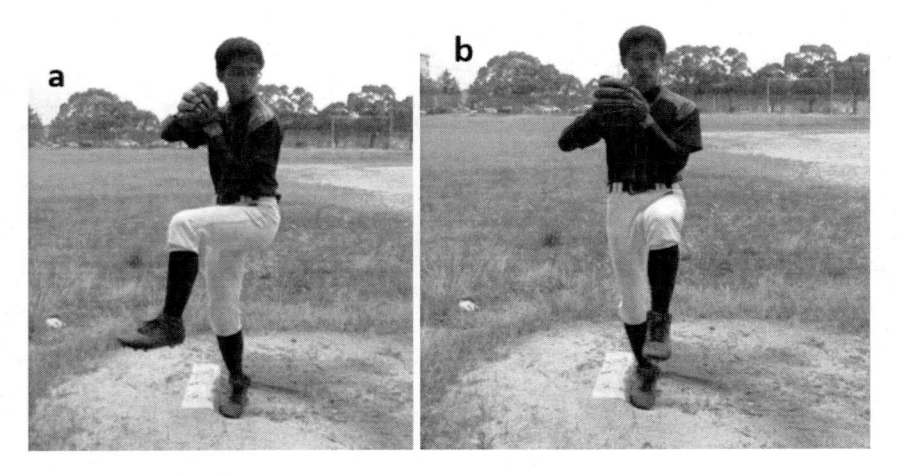

Figure 3. Knee at the highest point. In the proper form, the knee of the stride leg is elevated high and angled away from home plate by hip joint adduction (a). It is improper to lift the knee only by hip joint flexion (b).

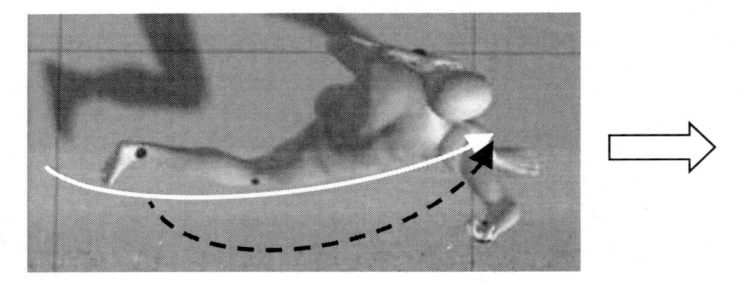

Figure 4. A top-down illustration of a pitcher in a throwing motion. The correct movement of the knee of the stride leg is indicated by a solid line, and the incorrect movement is indicated by a dotted line. Large white arrow: direction of home plate.

The pitcher can attain this optimal form more easily by paying attention to the ulnar side of the hand rather than to the elbow position (Figure 5).

During shoulder abduction, the pitcher should also pay attention to the degree of wrist cocking (dorsal flexion). The maximum cocking should be achieved when the throwing hand reaches the highest point (top form). The pitcher should preferably extend his pitching arm as he moves it in a backward circle.

Figure 5. Early cocking phase. The pitcher can bring the dominant hand above the shoulder line more easily by turning the ulnar side of the hand upward rather than raising the elbow position. As with the throwing arm, the glove arm is abducted with the forearm pronated. It is important to close the front shoulder. The thumb of the glove hand points to the ground.

However, if this is not possible because of restrictions in the range of motion of the scapula or shoulder, or difficulty coordinating this movement with forearm pronation, the radius of the circular movement may be suboptimal. Importantly, the pitcher should be more concerned about turning the ulnar side of the hand up and the radial side down at the top form than about achieving the maximum circle radius.

As with the throwing arm, the glove arm is abducted in the early cocking phase, with the forearm pronated. The pitcher extends the elbow while pointing the thumb downward (Barfield 2018). It is important to keep the front shoulder closed. When the pitcher lands his stride foot it should be directed towards home plate, and his shoulder should be at the greatest angle of abduction (Figure 5). At this time point, the front shoulder should point towards the target. Early rotation of the pelvis and trunk will compromise the pitcher's power production. In an attempt to compensate the power loss, the pitcher may want to rely on upper extremity mechanics. However, this can adversely impact the elbow and shoulder. The pitcher should rotate the upper body after the front foot lands and stabilizes the body.

Late Cocking Phase: Landing to Maximum External Shoulder Rotation

In this part of the pitching motion, the pitcher starts to rotate his hip and trunk as he moves his weight towards home plate, and the upper body becomes dorsally extended. As the trunk rotates towards home plate, the shoulder undergoes horizontal extension while the elbow remains above the shoulder until it reaches the maximum angle of external rotation (Figure 6). At this position, the elbow joint is flexed over 90 degrees and the forearm is pronated (Figure 6-a, b). Since the torque of the trunk rotation is critically related to the pitching performance, the pitcher should improve both the strength and flexibility of the trunk to maximize the ball velocity and prevent injury (Aguinaldo 2009; Oyama 2014).

Acceleration Phase: Maximum External Shoulder Rotation to Ball Release

The pitcher moves his weight further forward, supported by the front leg. The pitcher's upper body starts to flex while rotating around the hip joint of the front leg. Later maximum pelvis rotation velocity is associated with greater ball speed (Aguinaldo 2019).

Figure 6. Late cocking phase. After aligning the upper limbs with the shoulder line (a, b), the pitcher swings his arm forcefully and releases the ball by shoulder internal rotation and flexion, elbow extension, and forearm pronation (c, d).

After aligning the upper limbs with the shoulder line, the pitcher swings his arm forcefully and releases the ball by shoulder internal rotation and flexion, elbow extension, and forearm pronation (Figure 6-c, d).

From stride foot landing to ball release, the front hip joint is flexed and adducted while both knees are flexed (Figure 7). By increasing the amount of time spent imparting momentum to the ball, the pitcher can throw "rising" fastballs that are not readily slowed by drag. Since larger internal and external rotation angles of the hip joint lead to greater shoulder horizontal external torque and hence faster ball speed, pitchers should perform exercises to increase their hip joint flexibility (Laudner 2015; Robbs 2010).

The acceleration phase allows the pitcher to make subtle adjustments to the pitching direction by modifying the movements of the throwing arm and hand. Contralateral trunk lean (away from the pitching arm side) increases the ball velocity (Solomito 2015). However, it should be noted that excessive contralateral trunk tilt may increase joint loading (Oyama 2013). Moreover, sagittal plane trunk tilt at ball release is positively associated with ball velocity (Solomito 2018).

Figure 7. Acceleration phase. From the landing of the front foot to ball release, the hip joint is flexed and adducted while both knees are flexed.

Taking advantage of the mound slope, the pitcher should quickly move his center of gravity forward and transfer maximum energy to the ball.

Follow-Through Phase: Ball Release to the End of the Pitching Motion

After the ball release, the hip keeps rotating and the trunk bends further, with shoulder internal rotation, horizontal flexion, and adduction. The throwing arm finishes outside of the stride foot.

Position Players

The basics of the pitching motion explained above are also applicable to non-pitchers.

Catching Base-Stealing Runners

As soon as the catcher receives and grips the ball, he abducts both shoulders while pronating the throwing forearm. Through footwork, the catcher directs the front foot towards the target. The catcher aims at a point slightly above the base, paying attention to the direction of the throw rather than ball speed.

Fielding Grounders

Immediately after catching a grounder, the fielder moves his throwing foot towards the target and then the other foot in the same direction. This footwork helps the fielder reduce the distance to the target, while also achieving efficient body mass transfer. The fielder should make quick motions to get ready for throwing. He can throw the ball powerfully by taking a step towards the target with the front foot while closing the front side of the body. In the arm-cocking phase, the shoulder line is directed towards the target. Since the fielder's upper body is lowered and thus closer to the ground when he catches a grounder, a three-quarter throw may be preferable to an overhead throw.

Quick Examination of Throwing Motions in Outpatient Clinics

In outpatient clinics for baseball players, the clients' pitching motions should be examined and taken into consideration when diagnosing the causes of their injuries.

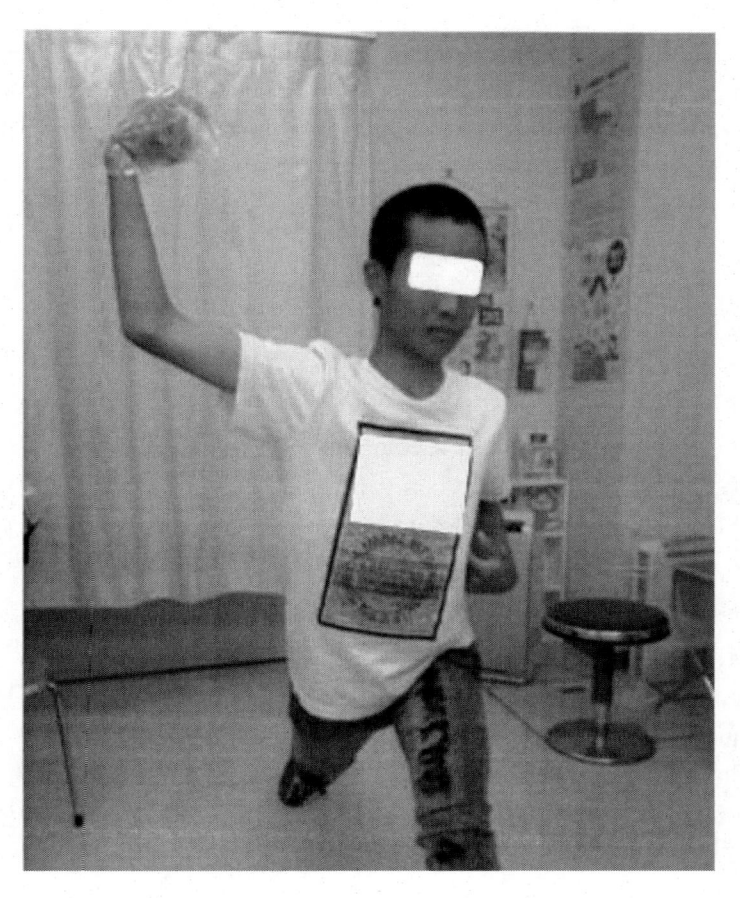

Figure 8. Pitching form simulation in a clinical setting. The client's ball-gripping hand is wrapped tightly using a transparent polyvinyl chloride bag. The client is then asked to perform his usual pitching motion for evaluation.

Ideally, patients with throwing injuries should be given the opportunity to attempt a throw on a field or in a special facility. However, this is sometimes difficult because of restrictions of time and resources. To overcome these challenges, we employ a simple, conventional way to simulate the pitching motion. Specifically, the client is asked to grip the ball, and the ball-gripping hand is wrapped tightly in a transparent polyvinyl chloride bag (Figure 8).

It is not always easy to identify biomechanical issues when we observe the client perform their usual pitching motion. However, we can identify the causes of their injury by breaking down the entire pitching motion into major phases as discussed in this article, and checking if any undesirable movements are present in each phase. During each session, we point out a maximum of two to three problems for correction. If the client is asked to make many corrections at the same time, he may develop detrimental pitching mechanics and lose confidence regarding how to pitch smoothly. Clinicians and other professionals should remember to comment on the positive aspects of their client's pitching performance if they hope to improve his condition.

Finally, suitable throwing forms differ from one player to another. Attempts to change or modify the pitching form that the client has developed should be made only if the client complains of elbow or shoulder injury or is unsatisfied with ball speed or control.

REFERENCES

Aguinaldo, A. and Escamilla, R. (2019). Segmental Power Analysis of Sequential Body Motion and Elbow Valgus Loading During Baseball Pitching: Comparison Between Professional and High School Baseball Players. *Orthop. J. Sports Med.,* 25; 7(2):2325967119827924. doi: 10.1177/2325967119827924. eCollection 2019 Feb.

Aguinaldo, A. L. and Chambers, H. (2009). Correlation of throwing mechanics with elbow valgus load in adult baseball pitchers. *Am. J. Sports Med.,* 37(10):2043 - 8. doi: 10.1177/0363546509336721.

Barfield, J. W., Anz, A. W., Andrews, J. R., Oliver, G. D. (2018). Relationship of Glove Arm Kinematics with Established Pitching Kinematic and Kinetic Variables among Youth Baseball Pitchers. *Orthop. J. Sports Med.,* 12; 6(7):2325967118784937. doi: 10.1177/ 2325967118784937. eCollection 2018 Jul.

Davis, J. T., Limpisvasti, O., Fluhme, D., Mohr, K. J., Yocum, L. A., Elattrache, N. S., Jobe, F. W. et al. (2009). The effect of pitching biomechanics on the upper extremity in youth and adolescent baseball pitchers. *Am. J. Sports Med.,* 37: 1484 - 1491. doi: 10.1177/ 0363546509340226.

Fehr, S., Damrow, D., Kilian, C., Lyon, R., Liu, X. C. (2016) Elbow Biomechanics of Pitching: Does Age or Experience Make a Difference? Sports Health, 8(5):444 - 50. doi: 10.1177/ 1941738116654863.

Fleisig, G. S., Diffendaffer, A. Z., Ivey, B., Aune, K. T., Laughlin, T., Fortenbaugh, D., Bolt, B., Lucas, W., Moore, K. D., Dugas, J. R. (2018). Changes in Youth Baseball Pitching Biomechanics: A 7-Year Longitudinal Study. *Am. J. Sports Med.,* 46(1):44 - 51. doi: 10.1177/ 0363546517732034.

Fleisig, G. S. and Andrews, J. R. (2012). Prevention of elbow injuries in youth baseball pitchers. *Sports Health*, 4(5):419 - 24.

Laudner, K., Wong, R., Onuki, T., Lynall, R., Meister, K. (2015). The relationship between clinically measured hip rotational motion and shoulder biomechanics during the pitching motion. *J. Sci. Med. Sport,* 18(5):581 - 4. doi: 10.1016/j.jsams.2014.07.011.

Oyama, S., Yu, B., Blackburn, J. T., Padua, D. A., Li, L., Myers, J. B. (2014). Improper trunk rotation sequence is associated with increased maximal shoulder external rotation angle and shoulder joint force in high school baseball pitchers. *Am. J. Sports Med.,* 42(9):2089 - 94. doi: 10.1177/0363546514536871.

Oyama, S., Yu, B., Blackburn, J. T., Padua, D. A., Li, L., Myers, J. B. (2013). Effect of excessive contralateral trunk tilt on pitching biomechanics and performance in high school baseball pitchers. *Am. J. Sports Med.,* 41(10):2430 - 8. doi: 10.1177/0363546513496547.

Robb, A. J., Fleisig, G., Wilk, K., Macrina, L., Bolt, B., Pajaczkowski, J. (2010). Passive ranges of motion of the hips and their relationship with pitching biomechanics and ball velocity in professional baseball pitchers. *Am. J. Sports Med.,* 38(12):2487 - 93. doi: 10.1177/0363546510375535.

Solomito, M. J., Garibay, E. J., Nissen, C. W. (2018). Sagittal Plane Trunk Tilt Is Associated With Upper Extremity Joint Moments and Ball Velocity in Collegiate Baseball Pitchers. *Orthop. J. Sports Med.,* 6(10):2325967118800240. doi: 10.1177/2325967118800240. eCollection 2018 Oct.

Solomito, M. J., Garibay, E. J., Woods, J. R., Õunpuu, S., Nissen, C. W. (2015). Lateral trunk lean in pitchers affects both ball velocity and upper extremity joint moments. *Am. J. Sports Med.,* 43(5):1235 - 40. doi: 10.1177/0363546515574060.

Thompson, S. F., Guess, T. M., Plackis, A. C., Sherman, S. L., Gray, A. D. (2018). Youth Baseball Pitching Mechanics: A Systematic Review. *Sports Health,* 10(2):133 - 140. doi: 10.1177/1941738117738189.

In: Essential Topics in Baseball
Editor: Erik Welch

ISBN: 978-1-53616-533-3
© 2019 Nova Science Publishers, Inc.

Chapter 3

THE ROLE OF UPPER EXTREMITY STRENGTH AND THROWING PROGRAMS ON INJURY PREVENTION IN BASEBALL PLAYERS: A LITERATURE REVIEW

Jacob W. Nigolian[1,*], Keelan R. Enseki[2,≠],
David Spaeder[3] and Adam Popchak[4]

[1]University of Pittsburgh Medical Center, Lemieux Sports Complex,
Centers for Rehab Services, Pittsburgh, PA, US
[2]Clinical Practice Innovation, Physical Therapy Residency Programs,
Orthopaedic Physical Therapy Residency Program,
University of Pittsburgh Medical Center - Rooney Sports Complex,
Centers for Rehab Services, Pittsburgh, PA, US
[3]University of Pittsburgh Medical Center,
Centers for Rehab Services, Pittsburgh, PA, US
[4]Department of Physical Therapy, University of Pittsburgh,
Pittsburgh, PA, US

---

* Corresponding Author's E-mail: Jnigolian@gmail.com.
≠ Director, Clinical Practice Innovation Administrative Director, Physical Therapy Residency Programs Director, Orthopaedic Physical Therapy Residency Program.

ABSTRACT

Overhead throwing athletes, such as baseball players, have a high incidence of upper extremity pathology. The incidence of elbow pain in high school, college, and professional baseball players is reported to be over 50% (Gregory & Nyland 2013). Approximately 20% of baseball players report shoulder pain (Myers, Oyama, & Hibberd 2013). Injuries associated with throwing are most common in the elbow and shoulder due to the extreme forces that the inherently violent motion places on each of these joints (Seroyer et al. 2010). To counteract these forces, these athletes must be able to effectively control their upper extremity throughout the throwing motion. The high injury rates call for effective and proven prevention programs. There are few evidence based programs for upper extremity injury prevention; most of the current literature relies on expert opinion.

Upper extremity strengthening is often a component of injuries prevention programs. There is some mixed evidence that upper extremity strength, particularly of the rotator cuff, may be a predictor of injury. Most recently, strength ratios of the upper extremity have been the focus of prevention programs. This literature review aims to determine whether upper extremity strength is predictive of injury, how upper extremity strength can be reliably and practically tested in the clinic, and whether or not strengthening programs will have an effect on upper extremity strength ratios as well as compare and contrast current throwing programs found in the literature.

INTRODUCTION

Overhead throwing athletes, in particular baseball players, have a high incidence of upper extremity pathology. Throwing is an inherently violent motion which requires both significant strength and range of motion. Wilk et al. (2016) describe this as the "thrower's paradox"; the shoulder must have extreme range of motion in order to throw but also have the stability to prevent injury. The incidence of elbow pain in high school, college, and professional baseball players is reported to be over 50% (Gregory and Nyland 2013), while approximately 20-35% of baseball players report shoulder pain (Myers, Oyama, and Hibberd 2013; Stephen Lyman et al. 2002; S. Lyman et al. 2001). Baseball pitchers are particularly at risk for injury; as 75% of high school baseball injuries that required surgery were in pitchers (Krajnik et al. 2010). Shoulder injuries in high school baseball players are often severe, as 10% result in surgery.

High injury rates have lead to the development of pitch limits for youth baseball pitchers from multiple organizations including: USA Baseball Medical and Safety Advisory Committee, Little League Baseball, Baseball Canada, ASMI, the American Orthopaedic Society for Sports Medicine, the American Academy of Pediatrics, and State Scholastic Athletic Boards across the country (Axe, Hurd, and Snyder-Mackler 2009). Many of these guidelines focus on limiting pitch volume. Other factors that have been identified as risk for injuries include limiting number of months pitched per year, pitching mechanics, cross-training, limiting pitching outings, avoiding showcases and playing on multiple teams. There are few studies that look prospectively into causality of injuries in baseball players which injury prevention guidelines can be drawn from (Agresta, Krieg, and Freehill 2019).

There is currently no strong consensus in the literature for the ideal method to return to throwing following injury or to start a season (Kovacic and Bergfeld 2005). Evidence based return to throwing programs in peer-reviewed sources are rare when the prevalence of injury is considered. The purpose of this literature review is to determine whether upper extremity strength is predictive of injury, how upper extremity strength can be reliably and practically tested in the clinic, the effect of strengthening protocols on upper extremity strength, and examine current return to throwing guidelines.

RESULTS

Injuries

Baseball players are at risk for a variety of elbow and shoulder injuries. As baseball players have become bigger and stronger over the years, there has been an increase in average throwing velocity (Conte, Camp, and Dines 2016). This increase in average velocity has been shown to rise linearly with injury rates in major league baseball. Shoulder injuries in baseball players include, but are not limited to: anterior glenohumeral instability, posterior impingement, superior labrum anterior to posterior (SLAP) lesion, subacromial impingement, epiphyseal plate injuries (Zaremski and Krabak 2012), scapular stress fracture, bursitis and various muscle strains such as biceps, rotator cuff, teres major, pectoralis major and latissimus dorsi (Byram et al. 2010; Oyama 2012). In an epidemiological study of high school baseball players, 38.7% of shoulder injuries were diagnosed as muscle strains (Saper et al. 2018).

Rotator cuff injuries are often a result of internal impingement related to the late cocking phase of throwing when the humerus in abducted and maximally externally rotated (Weiss et al. 2013). This position is believed to impinge the supraspinatus tendon, causing tissue damage. Adolescent baseball players are less likely to have a rotator cuff tear than older baseball players. They are more likely to experience an avulsion fracture of the greater or lesser tuberosity of the humerus than adult baseball players. Rotator cuff tendinopathy is common in adolescent baseball players and is characterized by pain at the point of ball release and through deceleration (Zaremski and Krabak 2012). Rotator cuff tendinopathy often occurs at the beginning of a competitive season; particularly if the athlete has not completed an interval throwing program to build a tolerance to throwing (Wilk, Meister, and Andrews 2002). Subscapularis injuries in adolescent athletes may be attributed to uncontrolled maximal external rotation range of motion in the late cocking phase (Weiss et al. 2013).

Adolescent baseball players are susceptible to shoulder injuries due to open epiphyseal plates and histological differences in connective tissue when compared to adults (Zaremski and Krabak 2012). Epiphyseal plates are considered the weakest part of the kinetic chain because they are weaker than their supporting ligaments and tendons. These epiphyseal plates remain open until 17-18 years old for the proximal humerus and 16-18 years old for the glenoid (Sabick et al. 2005). Proximal humeral epiphysiolysis, is also known as Little League Shoulder, due to its high prevalence in this population. This condition is characterized by progressively worsening arm pain during throwing and is diagnosed with radiographs. This condition is thought to be caused by torsional overload on the epiphysis during maximal external rotation in the late cocking phase of throwing.

Adolescents have higher amounts of type III collagen in their ligaments and tendons which results in greater laxity than adults (Zaremski and Krabak 2012). This laxity makes it less likely for tendons or ligaments to rupture; however, this laxity creates a higher risk of microinstability in the shoulder. Acquired microinstability may lead to impingement or other injury. Shoulder impingement is common in both adolescent and adult baseball players. Primary impingement occurs due to mechanical narrowing of the subacromial space. Primary impingement is common in adults, but rare in adolescent baseball players. Secondary impingement, results from the humeral head's inability to stay centered in the glenoid fossa. This may be due to rotator cuff weakness and soft tissue laxity. Secondary impingement is more common in adolescent than adult baseball players. This may lead to compression of the rotator cuff and ultimately, rotator cuff pathology (Provencher et al. 2014). Impingement is characterised by pain with overhead activity. Baseball players are most likely to report pain in the cocking and acceleration phase of throwing.

SLAP tears are common in adult throwers, however are less common in adolescent throwers (Han et al. 2009). The mechanism is often attributed to the pull of the biceps tendon on the labrum in the cocking phase (Zaremski and Krabak 2012). This has been referred to as the "peel back mechanism." Another potential mechanism is following ball release (deceleration phase), as the biceps tendon contracts strongly to counteract the large traction force in the glenohumeral joint. Symptoms include pain, clicking, and popping in the joint. Baseball players will often report pain during the cocking phase and decreased velocity. It should be noted that although there are validated special tests for SLAP tears, most of these studies have been validated in adults and few in adolescents specifically.

Common elbow injuries in baseball players include, but are not limited to: ulnar collateral (UCL) injury (Oyama 2012; Fleisig et al. 2009), medial epicondylitis (Sakata et al. 2018), impingement, osteophytes, loose bodies, chondromalacia, ulnar neuritis, stress fracture, bursitis, osteochondral defects, and avascular necrosis (Byram et al. 2010). Youth baseball pitchers are especially at risk for medial elbow injury and osteochondritis dissecans of the humeral capitellum (Sakata et al. 2018). In a study of 294 baseball players, aged 9-12, 114 (38.7%) had reported episodes of elbow pain. Fifty-eight (19.7%) were found to have medial epicondylar fragmentation and 2 (.08%) were found to have osteochondritis dissecans of the capitellum on diagnostic ultrasound (Harada et al. 2010). The lateral side of the elbow must also withstand high compression forces during the throwing motion (Fleisig and Andrews 2012). These compressive forces may lead to many of the bony pathologies mentioned previously In an epidemiological study of high school baseball players, 42.7% of elbow injuries were diagnosed as ligament sprains (Saper et al. 2018).

The overhead throwing motion requires controlled movement throughout the entire kinetic chain; from hallux to the interphalangeal joints of the upper extremity (Zaremski and Krabak 2012). The complexity, and the speed at which the action occurs, make real time throwing mechanics analysis unreliable at best. Throwing analysis studies have found peak humeral internal rotation velocities of 7,700 degrees per second (Seroyer et al. 2010). Therefore, video analysis is often needed to identify most faulty mechanics.

The dynamic and static stabilizers must both work in unison to prevent injuries when forces of this magnitude are considered (Tyler et al. 2014; Byram et al. 2010). The static stabilizers of the glenohumeral joint include the negative pressure of the joint, the labrum, ligaments, joint capsule, and bony congruity (Krajnik et al. 2010; Berckmans et al. 2017; Byram et al. 2010; Zaremski and Krabak 2012). The dynamic stabilizers of the glenohumeral joint include, but are not limited to, rotator cuff muscles, pectoralis major, latissimus dorsi, and biceps brachii. The periscapular muscles, such as the trapezius, pectoralis minor, rhomboids, levator scapulae and serratus anterior must also work to stabilize and maintain correct scapular position and rhythm throughout the throwing motion. A fault anywhere in the system may lead to microinstability which can lead to tissue damage and/or internal impingement (Agresta, Krieg, and Freehill 2019; Berckmans et al. 2017). Though generally agreed upon as a risk factor, it should be noted that there has yet to be sufficient evidence demonstrating that faulty scapular mechanics, or scapular dyskinesis, is predictive of upper extremity injury in baseball players (Myers, Oyama, and Hibberd 2013).

The shoulder must remain stable in the face of large force vectors such as the internal rotation (IR) and external rotation (ER) forces. The internal rotation force is predominantly created by the subscapularis, latissimus dorsi, and pectoralis major. The external rotation force, is largely created by the weight of the forearm and ball (Wasylynko 2015). Strength of the external and internal rotators have been extensively reported as being integral in maintaining centration of the humeral head in the glenohumeral joint (Berckmans et al. 2017; Wilk et al. 2016; Tyler et al. 2014). It has been shown that adolescent baseball pitchers who report pain are more likely to have posterior shoulder weakness in the dominant arm compared to the non-dominant arm (Trakis et al. 2008). It has also been reported that preseason external rotation and supraspinatus weakness are correlated with injury and the need for surgery in professional baseball pitchers (Byram et al. 2010). Leong et al. (2016) found that overhead athletes with rotator cuff tendinopathy have decreased subacromial space, as well as weakness of the trapezius muscles and serratus anterior. This decreased subacromial space may be indicative of secondary impingement. The dynamic stabilizers also play a key role in stabilizing the glenohumeral joint at ball release, where the traction force placed on the joint may be as high as 50% of the throwers body-weight (Sabick et al. 2005). The rotator cuff and biceps must contract forcefully to help dissipate the traction force to avoid overloading the passive stabilizers.These studies support the hypothesis that weak external rotators may lead to injury in throwing athletes.

The elbow must also endure high forces during the throwing motion (Garrison, Johnston, and Conway 2015; Bruce and Andrews 2014). The elbow experiences greatest force in the late cocking and acceleration phases of the throwing motion; these phases are when an elbow injury is most likely to occur. The throwing motion places valgus and extension forces on the elbow (Fleisig et al. 2009). The flexor/pronator mass helps to dissipate valgus force at the elbow (Bruce and Andrews 2014; Gregory and Nyland 2013; Laudner, Wilson, and Meister 2012). Without the contribution of these dynamic stabilizers, the valgus force on the elbow would almost certainly be enough to damage the ulnar collateral ligament, according to cadaveric studies (Laudner, Wilson, and Meister 2012). UCL tears have become alarmingly more frequent in adolescent baseball players. One orthopaedic surgery center reports that in 1996, 3% of UCL reconstructions were completed in youth and high school players compared to 41% in 2010 (Fleisig and Andrews 2012). Total number of UCL reconstructions have been raising as well, from 31 in 1996 to 131 in 2010. Range of motion (Sakata et al. 2018) and strength of the shoulder has been shown to be predictive of elbow injury in baseball players (Hurd and Kaufman 2012). Garrison et al. (2015) retrospectively found baseball players with UCL tears had significant rotator cuff strength loss when compared to healthy controls in both the dominant and non-dominant arms.

Fatigue

Although it is commonly reported that muscular fatigue increases risk for injury, it has been reported that after a simulated game, pitchers demonstrate only moderate losses in strength and only small deviations in pitching form (Calabrese 2013). However, general fatigue has been reported to impair pitchers' ability to reach maximal external rotation in the late cocking phase which may lead to subacromial impingement. Muscle fatigue has been shown to decrease joint proprioception and neuromuscular control. Decreased neuromuscular control and proprioception may lead to microinstability of the humeral head, leading to injury. This theory is supported by multiple studies that find muscle fatigue leads to superior humeral head migration (Chen et al. 1999; Chopp et al. 2010)).

It has been theorized the internal rotators of throwing athletes develop higher fatigue resistance than external rotators, which may predispose athletes to injury (Ellenbecker and Roetert 1999). Moore et al. (2013) used the posterior shoulder endurance test to examine if a strengthening program could improve the endurance of the posterior shoulder muscles. The authors also examined what effects this strengthening program had on the internal/external rotation strength ratio. The posterior shoulder endurance test is a rep to failure test of prone horizontal abduction with 2% body weight as resistance. Subjects underwent a 20 week program addressing upper extremity strength, core strength, and lower extremity strength. The authors report robust increases in posterior shoulder endurance; from an average of 30±14 to 88±36. There was no change in IR/ER strength ratios.

Fatigue of the scapular muscles has been shown to lead to altered scapular mechanics (Wilk, Meister, and Andrews 2002; Kibler and Ben Kibler 1998; Provencher et al. 2014). This alteration in scapular mechanics has been theorized to lead to secondary impingement. As previously stated, there is not a strong correlation between scapular dyskinesis and injury rates in baseball players. Similar to the rotator cuff, fatigue of the flexor/pronator muscles of the wrist have been considered to be a risk factor for injury (Bruce and Andrews 2014). However, this too has yet to be proven in a prospective study.

Adolescents

Adolescents have different muscular physiology than adult athletes. Children have lower size-normalized strength, power, endurance, and recovery as compared to adults (Popchak et al. 2015). Adolescent baseball players have less endurance and recovery compared to adults may make them more at risk for injury. This becomes especially true during or immediately after a growth spurt (Fleisig and Andrews 2012). Under developed musculature puts a young throwing athlete at risk for injury because their body will not be able to dissipate and control the high torques placed on it by the throwing motion (Wasylynko 2015).

Strength

Berckmans et al. (2017) published a systematic review with the goal of providing an overview of evidence considering external and internal rotation isokinetic muscle strength ratios and assess the effects of exercise programs on these measures in healthy overhead athletes. The authors found 14 relevant studies (9 cross sectional, 4 randomized control trials, 1 prospective cohort). It should be noted that only 2 articles specifically looked at baseball players alone. However, the same injury mechanisms are thought to exist in other overhead sports, such as: tennis, badminton, handball, swimming, volleyball, etc. The systematic review was searching for evidence to support the idea that the eccentric ER to concentric IR ratio can predict injury. This ratio is known as the functional deceleration ratio (FDR). Some feel that the FDR may be a predictor of injury because it can predict the effectiveness of the external rotators to safely decelerate the rapidly accelerating humerus following ball release. Twelve of 14 studies measured both concentric and eccentric ER and IR. The remaining 2 studies measured only the FDR. The authors found an FDR range of .66 to 1.54 in the healthy overhead athletes' dominant arm. Other studies have found that healthy male college students have an FDR of 1.08 in the dominant arm (Scoville et al. 1997). A cut off value of 66% for the FDR has been reported to identify shoulders at risk for injury (Cools et al. 2016; Lin et al. 2015). Noffal (2003) found that although throwers have a significantly lower FDR in the dominant arm, non-throwers had no significant difference.

One study retrospectively found that volleyball players with no history of shoulder injury had an FDR of 1.14 as opposed to .92 for those with a previous injury (Stickley et al. 2008). This same study also found the ratio between concentric ER strength and eccentric IR strength. This strength ratio is known as the "cocking ratio." This cocking ratio represents the athletes ability to safely decelerate their arm as they bring it back in the cokcing phase. The authors found that those without a history of shoulder injury had an average cocking ratio of 2.16 as opposed to 1.77 for those with a history of injury. Significantly less research has been completed on the correlation between cocking ratios than FDRs.

Isokinetic testing of the shoulder musculature has been validated and is considered to be the gold standard for measuring shoulder strength. Isokinetic dynamometers have the ability to measure eccentric, concentric, and isometric strength. It should be noted that some studies have shown the test-retest reliability of isometric, and concentric strength are higher than eccentric strength (Malerba et al. 1993; Stratford and Balsor 1994) There is no standard testing protocol to measure shoulder muscle strength. For example, the starting position, degree of movement, and speed of testing will lead to different results (Lin et al. 2015). As the speed of the isokinetic test increases, the concentric internal rotation strength decreases and eccentric external rotation strength increases; this will lead to a higher FDR (Noffal 2003). Most isokinetic dynamometers can test velocities as high as 300 deg/sec. However, this is nowhere near the upwards of 7,700 deg/sec that some pitchers are able to generate(Seroyer et al. 2010). For this reason, testing protocols for studies using isokinetic dynamometry must be examined before their results can be compared.

Most studies found moderate evidence that the dominant side has higher FDRs. The mean difference in IR strength in the dominant arm to nondominant was 15.25% and 14.77% for concentric and eccentric assessments, respectively. Much smaller strength increases were noted in ER strength; 5.63% and 2.89% for concentric and eccentric assessments, respectively. Lin et al. (2015) found similar results; baseball players have significantly higher IR strength, and no significant ER strength change when compared to healthy controls. These results show that the internal rotators on the dominant side are becoming disproportionately stronger than the external rotators. Trakis et al. (2008) found that pitchers with a history of shoulder pain tend to have stronger IR in their dominant arm compared to their non-dominant arm, with no side to side difference in ER strength. Harding et al. (2018), when looking for relationships between various measures in youth pitchers, found that the number of months played in the last year had a moderate correlation with decreased ER strength (r = -.39, P = .04). Hurd et al. (2011) found that throwing arms in pitchers have stronger IR and weaker ER when tested with hand held dynamometry at 90 degrees of shoulder abduction. Relative ER weakness may diminish the external rotators ability to eccentrically decelerate the humerus, placing greater stress on the soft tissues of the posterior shoulder.

Hand held dynamometers are often used to measure shoulder strength in the literature. Numerous studies have validated the use and show good to excellent validity and reliability to measure isometric strength (Andrews et al. 1996; Byram et al. 2010; Trakis et al. 2008), with interclass coeficient (ICC) values ranging from .934-.977 (Hurd and Kaufman 2012; Moore, Uhl, and Kibler 2013; Garrison, Johnston, and Conway 2015; Merolla et al. 2010). Harding et al. (2018) reported slightly lower ICC values; ranging from .72-.81 in tests of shoulder strength. Hand held dynamometers are more practical for many clinics that do not have access to much larger, and more costly isokinetic dynamometers. Although isometric strength measures are valid and reliable, they fail to show strength throughout an arc of motion like is needed while throwing (Papotto et al. 2016). Like isokinetic dynamometry, hand held dynamometry does not have a standardized testing protocol (Merolla et al. 2010; Sakata et al. 2017; Hurd and Kaufman 2012; Amin et al. 2015; Tyler et al. 2014; Byram et al. 2010; Moore, Uhl, and Kibler 2013). Studies differ in method of stabilization, upper extremity positioning, positioning of the dynamometer, and type of test (make vs break test). The difference in testing protocol may yield different results; therefore, studies using hand held dynamometry must be examined carefully before a comparison can be made. There have been multiple studies that report normative data for isometric strength using hand held dynamometers (Westrick et al. 2013; Van Harlinger, Blalock, and Merritt 2015). One study created regression equations for hand held dynamometer strength that take into account hand dominance, body weight, age, and sex (Andrews et al. 1996). Normative data and regression equations may have utility in setting goals for isometric strength using hand hand dynamometers in some athletes where the opposite limb is unable to be used for comparison.

Isometric strength has been correlated with concentric strength, however, there is less of a correlation with eccentric strength. Results from isokinetic studies on strength characteristics in overhead athletes show that often, concentric and eccentric strength see similar rates of improvements (Berckmans et al. 2017). It may be extrapolated with caution that an increase in isometric strength is therefore likely associated with an eccentric strength increase, though more research is needed to confirm this hypothesis.

Isometric ER to IR ratios of less than 75-100% have been reported to identify shoulders at risk for injury (Cools et al. 2016). It is advised that the dominant side should only have an increased strength of approximately 10%

compared to the non-dominant side in both ER and IR (Cools et al. 2016). Baseball pitchers are typically reported as having external to internal strength ratios between 60-80% (Byram et al. 2010). The larger latissimus dorsi, pectoralis major, and strengthening from the throwing motion have been attributed to higher internal rotation strength.

Tyler et al. (2014) used hand held dynamometry to prospectively identify if preseason strength can be predictive of injury in high school baseball pitchers. One-hundred and sixty-six pitcher-seasons from 101 different pitchers were tracked over a course of 4 years. The authors measured bilateral internal and external rotation, supraspinatus, and scapular retraction strength. There were 28 injuries reported during the course of the study (19 shoulder, 9 elbow) which amounted to 0.58 injuries per 1000 pitches. The results showed that supraspinatus weakness associated with injury (Relative Risk ratio of 4.58). The authors were unable to correlate other weakness with risk of injury.

Byram et al. (2010) also used hand held dynamometry to identify pitchers at risk of injury. This study found that preseason prone and seated ER weakness as well as supraspinatus weakness were all significantly associated with shoulder injury. Furthermore, the authors established that prone ER to IR ratio was associated with incidence of shoulder injury. The median prone ER to IR strength ratio was reported at 1.05 (.91-1.19 represent the 25th and 75th percentile, respectively). Supraspinatus strength was found to correlate with this ratio. This is an important finding as prior studies have demonstrated that supraspinatus weakness in associated with higher injury rates (Tyler et al. 2014).

Hada et al. (2010) reported that ER strength over 80N and/or IR strength over 100N are predictive of elbow injuries in baseball players between the ages of 9 and 12. Although not statistically significant, those with stronger grip strengths were more likely to sustain an elbow injury as well. These results may indicate that the stronger the thrower, the more force will be transferred through the elbow and therefore, will be more at risk for injury.

It should be noted that although the majority of the literature focuses on ER and IR strength and their relation to injury, other strength measures have also been examined. Scapular retraction to protraction as well as elevation to depression strength ratios and their relationship to injury have also been examined in overhead athletes. Studies have found that overhead athletes are likely to have weak scapular retractors, protractors, and depressors (Wilk et al. 2016; Wilk, Meister, and Andrews 2002). Strength ratios of the upper to lower trapezius, upper to middle trapezius, and upper trapezius to serratus anterior have also been examined with the goal of balancing each ratio at 1. These strength ratios have been reported mostly in healthy overhead athletes but there is little evidence proving the effect on risk of injury. In addition to periscapular weakness in healthy baseball players, many injuries common in baseball players may cause inhibition of the scapular muscles (Kibler and Ben Kibler 1998). This is particularly true for the serratus anterior and the lower trapezius.

Laudner et al. (2012) found that in 30 healthy college baseball players, the throwing arm was more likely to have wrist flexion and supination weakness than the non-throwing arm. The throwing arm was more likely to be stronger in wrist pronation and extension compared to the non-throwing arm. These results are analogous to the findings of ER weakness in the dominant arm of baseball pitchers. This study was intended to identify strength differences in the dominant versus non-dominant arm in baseball players, not to identify risk of injury.

Exercise Programs

Wilk et al. (2016) developed the Thrower's Ten program specifically for overhead athletes to be used for injury prevention and in preparation for returning to throwing. This program specifically targeted muscles of the rotator cuff, glenohumeral joint, scapula, elbow and forearm. The Advanced Thrower's Ten program was designed to more aggressively strengthen the thrower's upper extremity, develop power, endurance, and better incorporate core and lower extremity strength in preparation for a throwing program.

Sakata et al. (2018) recently published a prospective cohort study which examined elbow injury rates between baseball players, age 8-11, who performed a specific injury prevention program against those who performed their usual program. The Yokohama Baseball-9 (YKB-9) program includes 9 exercises focused on range of motion and 9 strengthening exercises which are designed to improve parameters of physical function that have been correlated with injury risk in baseball players. These interventions are targeted at the shoulder, elbow, hips, and spine. The group that performed the YKB-9 was found to improve in numerous areas that have been correlated with injury risk in baseball players. The authors reported that those in the intervention group had 49.2% decreased risk of medial elbow injury compared to the usual care group (0.8/1000 vs 1.7/1000 injuries per athlete/exposure). It should be noted that from a strengthening perspective; this program was only found to increase lower trapezius strength on the dominant side. No rotator cuff strength increases were noted. This lack of objective strength gain in the rotator cuff may be due to the program having inadequate loading.

The systematic review mentioned previously by Berckmans et al. (2017) found four studies that looked at exercise effect on rotator cuff strength in overhead athletes. The studies used various strengthening protocols including plyometric training, general shoulder strengthening, and isokinetic strengthening. All studies showed increased concentric and eccentric ER strength and eccentric IR strength. Three of four showed increased concentric IR strength. Based off of these findings, it can be safely said that a strengthening protocol can positively affect the FDR. There is currently no consensus regarding the most effective exercise program to affect the FDR.

Athletes returning to throwing after an injury should start with submaximal isometrics, progressing to concentrics, and then eccentrics. It is imperative to address the muscles of the scapula (Kibler and Ben Kibler 1998). Achieving scapular stability is needed to allow for effective rotator cuff function. Merolla et al. (2010) found that an exercise program designed to address scapular muscle strength, particularly the trapezius and serratus anterior, was effective at strengthening the supraspinatus via the empty can test and infraspinatus when measured with hand held dynamometry over 3 and 6 months. Shitara et al. (2017) found that using ER strengthening exercises as part of an injury prevention program in high school baseball players reduces the risk for injury when compared to just stretching and true controls. This validates the call for external rotation strengthening in most injury prevention programs.

Athletes returning to throwing should train throughout the force-velocity curve (Sgroi and Zajac 2018). This calls for training at 90-100% of one repetition maximum at slow speeds, as well as <30% of one repetition maximum at high speeds. Using higher velocities at lower intensities is thought to be more specific to the throwing motion. This provides a natural progression into upper extremity plyometrics. Plyometrics are an important part of returning to throwing because they mimic the stretch-shortening cycle that is required during throwing. Plyometrics should progress from more stable positions, with low loads, and slower speeds to overhead positions (mimicking the throwing motion), with higher loads and faster movement.

Because the throwing motion is complex and explosive, according to the SAIDS (specific adaptations to imposed demands) principle, some argue the most specific and beneficial way to strengthen a throwing athletes arm is by actually throwing. This is the justification behind interval progressive throwing programs. Some interval throwing programs include long toss (throwing a greater distance than a throwing athlete typically would) with the belief that it is an effective way to improve strength and endurance in a throwing athlete's arm (Axe, Hurd, and Snyder-Mackler 2009). Biomechanical studies have shown long-toss produces greater elbow and shoulder torques in the throwing arm (Fleisig et al. 2011). For this reason it is widely recommended that long-toss should be avoided until the athlete can throw from shorter distances without becoming symptomatic. Whether returning from injury, or starting to throw in preparation for an upcoming season, higher volume at shorter distances should be encouraged before progressing to long-toss.

Weighted, or de-weighted ball throwing is another activity used by some to strengthen the arm and improve arm velocity (Okoroha et al. 2019). Some have theorized that using heavier balls may lead to injury due to greater force through the shoulder and elbow. A biomechanical analysis of weighted ball throwing has shown that as ball mass increased, shoulder and elbow joint forces decreased (Fleisig et al. 2017). This is due to the throwing arm having a decreased acceleration and velocity during the throwing motion. It should be noted that heavy balls did lead to greater elbow extension forces. Based on this data, it may be appropriate to utilize heavy ball throws as an exercise to bridge the gap between resistance training and throwing. However, it should be noted that a recent study of 19 youth baseball players found that as ball weight increased, so did medial elbow torque (Okoroha et al. 2019). In another study examining the effect of a 6-week weighted baseball throwing program, the authors reported a 3.3% increase in pitch velocity in the intervention group (Reinold et al. 2018). The intervention group also experienced a 4.3 degree increase in external rotation range of motion. The authors reported a 24% injury rate in the intervention group (4 subjects). Injuries included 2 olecranon stress fractures, 1 partial UCL injury, and 1 UCL injury that surgery was recommended for. The control group had no injuries. Despite the small sample size (n = 38), this study brings to light the risk of injury that is associated with weighted ball throwing. Based on this conflicting data, further studies are needed in order to make a strong recommendation about the utility and safety of weighted ball throwing, especially in vulnerable youth baseball players.

Sgroi and Zajac (2018) recommend monitoring acute to chronic workload ratios in athletes returning to throwing. The authors point out that increases in acute to chronic workload have been linked to increased risk for injury. When acute to chronic workload is increased 5-10%, there is less than a 10% risk of injury. However, when the acute to chronic workload has increased more than 15%, there is a 21-49% risk of injury. (Gabbett 2018). Based on this data, it is recommended to monitor the amount of throws an athlete completes and increasing between 5-10% weekly.

Throwing Programs

There have been numerous interval throwing programs designed to slowly reintroduce baseball players to the forces created by the throwing motion. Reintroduction to the throwing motion is crucial for injury prevention as studies have shown that the majority of baseball related injuries occur in the first month of the season (Shanley et al. 2011). Return to throwing programs are designed to be completed as pre-season preparation for return to throwing or as a functional progression for return from injury. This slow, gradual progression is thought to reduce the chance of reinjuring healing tissues (Reinold et al. 2002). These throwing programs are to be initiated once the baseball player has completed a strengthening program and demonstrated adequate upper and lower extremity strength, endurance, range of motion, stability, as well as medical clearance and a satisfactory clinical exam by a rehabilitation professional (Cisco et al. 2019; Reinold et al. 2002). The progression through an interval throwing program should come with guidelines on when to progress, or regress, based on symptoms. Understanding and reporting symptoms while progressing through an interval throwing program is imperative. Like any plyometric exercise, throwing is likely to result in muscle soreness; this must be differentiated from pain due to tissue damage. Reinold et al. (2002) define soreness as a dull, diffuse, aching sensation in the muscles and tendons. The authors state that if sharp pain is felt, the athlete should stop until pain subsides. If pain does not subside; the athlete should undergo a physical assessment.

One popular interval throwing program was developed by Axe, Hurd and Synder-Mackler (2009). This program takes an evidence based, staged, progressive, functional, and customizable approach to returning to throwing. Where most interval based throwing programs are designed for adults, Axe et al. (1996) developed a distance-based interval throwing program for youths and adolescent athletes. The authors state that a throwing program should be reflective of the demands of a live game, be modified to meet individual needs, safe, and easy to implement and complete. This program is unique because the researchers used game data from 400 innings of little league games, field dimensions, as well as average throw speeds, to design the volume, timing, and distance of throws. This program uses age and throw velocity to determine the target distance for the long toss component of the throwing program. This allows the program to be individualized to each player. This program may be used as a rehabilitation protocol following injury or a training program for healthy athletes starting the season. The downside of this program is it is time consuming, taking about 45 minutes to complete, if followed exactly as described. It also relies on throwers pitching at 50% and 75% speed which has proven to be inaccurate (Wilk, Meister, and Andrews 2002; Slenker et al. 2014).

Reinold et al. (2002) developed a popular interval throwing program which is designed to be performed three times a week, with a day of rest in between. It is recommended that the athlete complete one set of whichever strengthening program they are using (in this case, the Thrower's Ten Program) before throwing, and the remaining two sets following throwing. This allows for the athlete to adequately warm up the shoulder muscles without causing excessive fatigue. This particular program calls for gentle arcing throws starting at 45 feet and incrementally progressing to 180 feet. Initially, flat ground throwing is used, progressing to a "crow hop" throw. All players complete this program. Pitchers do have a slightly different progression through the program. This program can also be modified to rehabilitate a thrower from injury during the season. This is designed to allow for return to competition within 21 days. The authors also developed a little league throwing program which calls for shorter distances than the adult program. These programs also rely on throwers determining how hard they are throwing, calling for throws at 50% and 75%.

Cisco et al. (2019) developed a throwing program for baseball players from little league to high school with the intent of matching the program as closely to real game demands as possible. The authors point out that although throwing programs routinely call for throws over 127 feet, throws of that distance are fairly rare in live baseball games. For that reason, this protocol calls for only a few throws over the distance required to throw diagonally across a baseball diamond. The authors also call for secondary throwing programs to be completed by pitchers and catchers before they can compete at their positions to ensure that they are ready for the increased demands that these positions place on the throwing shoulder. The amount of throws are capped at 75 per day based on research that states an athlete will rarely have to throw more than that. The program also calls for one day of rest between throwing. The authors also make recommendations for players to play certain field positions based on the ability to reach the designated distances. For example, if players cannot consistently reach on the longer throws in the program, they should play positions with fewer throwing demands, such as first or second base. It is recommended to throw with an arc on the ball as to avoid maximal effort. It also calls for the "crow hop" method of throwing in order to ensure that the athlete is utilizing their lower extremity to generate power and avoid overthrowing with their upper extremity. The program is to be completed at different speeds based on what it is being used for. An athlete who has non-specific pain, or is preparing for the season, can progress one step through the program each time they throw, taking 13 days if no setbacks. An athlete returning from a ligamentous or growth plate injury should complete each step twice before advancing, taking at minimum 27 days to complete. An athlete returning from surgery should complete each step three times before advancing, taking at minimum 41 days to complete. Similar to other interval throwing programs, soreness is permitted. If pain is produced, the athlete should terminate throwing that day and take a rest day the following day. They should then return to the prior level that was successfully completed.

Slenker et al. (2014) completed a biomechanical comparison, using a motion analysis system, of 29 healthy college baseball pitchers completing a standard interval throwing program. The purpose was to examine how different conditions called for in common throwing programs (like distance, perceived speed, distance, throwing surface, and approach) affect the loads placed on the upper extremity. The authors found that pitching at partial effort did in fact reduce the loads on the shoulder and elbow. Throwing from flat ground as compared to pitching from the mound resulted in similar forces; however, flat ground throwing resulted in significantly lower ball velocity. The authors used this as evidence to state that pitching from a mound increases the efficiency of throwing. They concluded that using a"crow hop" throw, particularly for longer throws, was an effective way to mitigate the higher forces throughout the kinetic chain.

CONCLUSION

Due to the prevalence of injuries in baseball players, especially adolescents; multiple organizations are taking steps to help reduce risk of injury. Most of these come in the form of guidelines to limit pitching volume. Studies have shown that baseball players, coaches, and parents have poor adherence to pitching guidelines put in place to protect young arms (Gregory and Nyland 2013). Many are unaware of the correct guidelines, and some that are aware, fail to comply (Fazarale et al. 2012). A study by Ahmed et al. (2012) found 31% of coaches, 28% of players, and 25% of parents did not believe that pitch volume is a risk factor for injury. This study shows how important education of proven risk factors for injury are to coaches, players, and parents. One cannot help but to consider the possibility of poor adherence even if strong, evidence backed, guidelines for injury prevention in baseball players were in place. In order to address this problem; once a strengthening or throwing program is validated, implementation studies must be completed to determine barriers to bringing these programs into practice (Lane-Fall, Curran, and Beidas 2019). Hybrid studies looking at both the effectiveness and barriers of strengthening and/or interval throwing programs should be done to further validate and achieve the goals of implementation studies mentioned previously.

Cools et al. (2015) state that in order to create a scientific based prevention program of shoulder injuries in overhead athletes, four steps must be taken. These include identifying risk factors for injury, establish that these risk factors may be used as return to play criteria with an identified cut off value based on normative data, identifying valid and reliable procedures to measure these risk factors, and creation of a program to successfully address these risk factors. In the context of shoulder strength as a risk factor for injury; it has been clearly shown that external rotation weakness is correlated with injury risk of both the shoulder and elbow. The literature lacks sufficient prospective evidence to declare a causative relationship. There is no consensus on quantifying cut-off values for risk of injury. Various authors have made recommendations based on their findings. First, a standardized testing procedure for shoulder strength should be determined.

This will be important to allow for comparison across multiple studies. Several studies have shown that through various types of strengthening programs shoulder strength can be improved. Although there is construct validity and general consensus in the sports medicine community that eccentric rotator cuff strengthening will reduce injuries in throwing athletes, that conclusion is not yet supported in the literature. There is no consensus on the ideal strengthening program. Likewise, there is still debate on the utility of long-toss and the use of weighted, or de-weighted baseballs to improve shoulder strength.

Most current standards of care agree that return to play should depend on how the athlete presents clinically, not based on imaging (Hatem, Recht, and Profitt 2006). It is widely accepted that maintaining, if not improving, muscle performance, range of motion, flexibility, and aerobic conditioning are all important components of returning a throwing athlete to play and avoiding injury. The amount that each of these factors contribute has still yet to be definitively proven.

There are various recommendations for how long an athlete should refrain from throwing. The amount of rest time should depend on the clinical diagnosis, medical procedures, and clinical presentation of the athlete. Rehabilitation professionals should be developing strength, power, stability, and endurance throughout the entire upper extremity of the throwing athlete prior to initiating a return to throwing program. This is true for those initiating throwing following injury, or healthy athletes starting the season. Rehabilitation professionals should utilize a slow return to throwing based on an established guidelines; preferably an interval throwing program or by monitoring acute to chronic workload ratios. Unfortunately, there is little evidence to support the most effective return to throwing rehabilitation program and return to throwing progression. However, generally adhering to the principles presented in this review should assist the clinician in developing a comprehensive rehabilitation / injury prevention program that is based on the best available evidence.

REFERENCES

Agresta, Cristine E., Kevin Krieg, and Michael T. Freehill. 2019. "Risk Factors for Baseball-Related Arm Injuries: A Systematic Review." *Orthopaedic Journal of Sports Medicine* 7 (2): 2325967119825557.

Ahmad, Christopher S., W. Jeffrey Grantham, and R. Michael Greiwe. 2012. "Public Perceptions of Tommy John Surgery." *The Physician and Sportsmedicine*. https://doi.org/10.3810/psm.2012.05.1966.

Amin, Nirav H., John Ryan, Stephen D. Fening, Lonnie Soloff, Mark S. Schickendantz, and Morgan Jones. 2015. "The Relationship between Glenohumeral Internal Rotational Deficits, Total Range of Motion, and Shoulder Strength in Professional Baseball Pitchers." *The Journal of the American Academy of Orthopaedic Surgeons* 23 (12): 789–96.

Andrews, A. Williams, A. Williams Andrews, Michael W. Thomas, and Richard W. Bohannon. 1996. "Normative Values for Isometric Muscle Force Measurements Obtained With Hand-Held Dynamometers." *Physical Therapy*. https://doi.org/10.1093/ptj/76.3.248.

Axe, Michael, Wendy Hurd, and Lynn Snyder-Mackler. 2009. "Data-Based Interval Throwing Programs for Baseball Players." *Sports Health: A Multidisciplinary Approach*. https://doi.org/10.1177/1941738108331198.

Axe, M. J., L. Snyder-Mackler, J. G. Konin, and M. J. Strube. 1996. "Development of a Distance-Based Interval Throwing Program for Little League-Aged Athletes." *The American Journal of Sports Medicine* 24 (5): 594–602.

Berckmans, Kelly, Annelies G. Maenhout, Lien Matthijs, Louise Pieters, Birgit Castelein, and Ann M. Cools. 2017. "The Isokinetic Rotator Cuff Strength Ratios in Overhead Athletes: Assessment and Exercise Effect." *Physical Therapy in Sport: Official Journal of the Association of Chartered Physiotherapists in Sports Medicine* 27 (September): 65–75.

Bruce, Jeremy R., and James R. Andrews. 2014. "Ulnar Collateral Ligament Injuries in the Throwing Athlete." *Journal of the American Academy of Orthopaedic Surgeons*. https://doi.org/10.5435/jaaos-22-05-315.

Byram, Ian R., Brandon D. Bushnell, Keith Dugger, Kevin Charron, Frank E. Harrell Jr, and Thomas J. Noonan. 2010. "Preseason Shoulder Strength Measurements in Professional Baseball Pitchers: Identifying Players at Risk for Injury." *The American Journal of Sports Medicine* 38 (7): 1375–82.

Calabrese, Gary J. 2013. "Pitching Mechanics, Revisited." *International Journal of Sports Physical Therapy* 8 (5): 652–60.

Chen, S. K., P. T. Simonian, T. L. Wickiewicz, J. C. Otis, and R. F. Warren. 1999. "Radiographic Evaluation of Glenohumeral Kinematics: A Muscle Fatigue Model." *Journal of Shoulder and Elbow Surgery/American Shoulder and Elbow Surgeons ... [et al.]* 8 (1): 49–52.

Chopp, Jaclyn N., John M. O'Neill, Kevin Hurley, and Clark R. Dickerson. 2010. "Superior Humeral Head Migration Occurs after a Protocol Designed to Fatigue the Rotator Cuff: A Radiographic Analysis." *Journal of Shoulder and Elbow Surgery/American Shoulder and Elbow Surgeons ... [et al.]* 19 (8): 1137–44.

Cisco, Steven, Megan Miller Semon, Paul Moraski, Joseph Smith, and Cheryl Thorndike. 2019. "Distance-Based Throwing Programs for Baseball Players from Little League to High School." *Pediatric Physical Therapy: The Official Publication of the Section on Pediatrics of the American Physical Therapy Association* 31 (3): 297–300.

Conte, Stan, Christopher L. Camp, and Joshua S. Dines. 2016. "Injury Trends in Major League Baseball Over 18 Seasons: 1998-2015." *American Journal of Orthopedics* 45 (3): 116–23.

Cools, Ann M., Dorien Borms, Birgit Castelein, Fran Vanderstukken, and Fredrik R. Johansson. 2016. "Evidence-Based Rehabilitation of Athletes with Glenohumeral Instability." *Knee Surgery, Sports Traumatology, Arthroscopy: Official Journal of the ESSKA* 24 (2): 382–89.

Cools, Ann M., Fredrik R. Johansson, Dorien Borms, and Annelies Maenhout. 2015. "Prevention of Shoulder Injuries in Overhead Athletes: A Science-Based Approach." *Brazilian Journal of Physical Therapy* 19 (5): 331–39.

Ellenbecker, T. S., and E. P. Roetert. 1999. "Testing Isokinetic Muscular Fatigue of Shoulder Internal and External Rotation in Elite Junior Tennis Players." *The Journal of Orthopaedic and Sports Physical Therapy* 29 (5): 275–81.

Fazarale, Joseph J., Robert A. Magnussen, Angela D. Pedroza, Christopher C. Kaeding, Thomas M. Best, and Justin Classie. 2012. "Knowledge of and Compliance with Pitch Count Recommendations: A Survey of Youth Baseball Coaches." *Sports Health* 4 (3): 202–4.

Fleisig, Glenn S., and James R. Andrews. 2012. "Prevention of Elbow Injuries in Youth Baseball Pitchers." *Sports Health* 4 (5): 419–24.

Fleisig, Glenn S., Becky Bolt, Dave Fortenbaugh, Kevin E. Wilk, and James R. Andrews. 2011. "Biomechanical Comparison of Baseball Pitching and Long-Toss: Implications for Training and Rehabilitation." *The Journal of Orthopaedic and Sports Physical Therapy* 41 (5): 296–303.

Fleisig, Glenn S., Alek Z. Diffendaffer, Kyle T. Aune, Brett Ivey, and Walter A. Laughlin. 2017. "Biomechanical Analysis of Weighted-Ball Exercises for Baseball Pitchers." *Sports Health* 9 (3): 210–15.

Fleisig, Glenn S., Adam Weber, Nina Hassell, and James R. Andrews. 2009. "Prevention of Elbow Injuries in Youth Baseball Pitchers." *Current Sports Medicine Reports*. https://doi.org/10.1249/jsr. 0b013e3181b7ee5f.

Gabbett, Tim. 2018. "Infographic: The Training-Injury Prevention Paradox: Should Athletes Be Training Smarter and Harder?" *British Journal of Sports Medicine* 52 (3): 203.

Garrison, J. Craig, Chris Johnston, and John E. Conway. 2015. "Baseball Players With Ulnar Collateral Ligament Tears Demonstrate Decreased Rotator Cuff Strength Compared to Healthy Controls." *International Journal of Sports Physical Therapy* 10 (4): 476–81.

Gregory, Bonnie, and John Nyland. 2013. "Medial Elbow Injury in Young Throwing Athletes." *Muscles, Ligaments and Tendons Journal* 3 (2): 91–100.

Han, Kyung-Jin, Yong-Kweon Kim, Seung-Kil Lim, Jin-Young Park, and Kyung-Soo Oh. 2009. "The Effect of Physical Characteristics and Field Position on the Shoulder and Elbow Injuries of 490 Baseball Players:

Confirmation of Diagnosis by Magnetic Resonance Imaging." *Clinical Journal of Sport Medicine: Official Journal of the Canadian Academy of Sport Medicine* 19 (4): 271–76.

Harada, Mikio, Masatoshi Takahara, Nariyuki Mura, Junya Sasaki, Tomokazu Ito, and Toshihiko Ogino. 2010. "Risk Factors for Elbow Injuries among Young Baseball Players." *Journal of Shoulder and Elbow Surgery / American Shoulder and Elbow Surgeons ... [et al.]* 19 (4): 502–7.

Harding, Josie L., Kelsey J. Picha, and Kellie C. Huxel Bliven. 2018. "Pitch Volume and Glenohumeral and Hip Motion and Strength in Youth Baseball Pitchers." *Journal of Athletic Training* 53 (1): 60–65.

Hatem, Stephen F., Michael P. Recht, and Brad Profitt. 2006. "MRI of Little Leaguer's Shoulder." *Skeletal Radiology*. https://doi.org/10.1007/s00256-005-0015-y.

Hurd, Wendy J., Kevin M. Kaplan, Neal S. ElAttrache, Frank W. Jobe, Bernard F. Morrey, and Kenton R. Kaufman. 2011. "A Profile of Glenohumeral Internal and External Rotation Motion in the Uninjured High School Baseball Pitcher, Part II: Strength." *Journal of Athletic Training* 46 (3): 289–95.

Hurd, Wendy J., and Kenton R. Kaufman. 2012. "Glenohumeral Rotational Motion and Strength and Baseball Pitching Biomechanics." *Journal of Athletic Training* 47 (3): 247–56.

Kibler, W. Ben, and W. Ben Kibler. 1998. "The Role of the Scapula in Athletic Shoulder Function." *The American Journal of Sports Medicine*. https://doi.org/10.1177/03635465980260022801.

Kovacic, Jeffrey, and John Bergfeld. 2005. "Return to Play Issues in Upper Extremity Injuries." *Clinical Journal of Sport Medicine: Official Journal of the Canadian Academy of Sport Medicine* 15 (6): 448–52.

Krajnik, Stephanie, Kieran J. Fogarty, Ellen E. Yard, and R. Dawn Comstock. 2010. "Shoulder Injuries in US High School Baseball and Softball Athletes, 2005-2008." *Pediatrics* 125 (3): 497–501.

Lane-Fall, Meghan B., Geoffrey M. Curran, and Rinad S. Beidas. 2019. "Scoping Implementation Science for the Beginner: Locating Yourself on the 'Subway Line' of Translational Research." *BMC Medical Research Methodology* 19 (1): 133.

Laudner, Kevin G., James T. Wilson, and Keith Meister. 2012. "Elbow Isokinetic Strength Characteristics among Collegiate Baseball Players." *Physical Therapy in Sport: Official Journal of the Association of Chartered Physiotherapists in Sports Medicine* 13 (2): 97–100.

Leong, Hio Teng, Sammi Sin Mei Tsui, Gabriel Yin-Fat Ng, and Siu Ngor Fu. 2016. "Reduction of the Subacromial Space in Athletes with and without Rotator Cuff Tendinopathy and Its Association with the Strength of Scapular Muscles." *Journal of Science and Medicine in Sport/Sports Medicine Australia* 19 (12): 970–74.

Lin, Hwai-Ting, Hsing-Tsen Ko, Kung-Che Lee, Ying-Cheng Chen, and Dean-Chuan Wang. 2015. "The Changes in Shoulder Rotation Strength Ratio for Various Shoulder Positions and Speeds in the Scapular Plane between Baseball Players and Non-Players." *Journal of Physical Therapy Science* 27 (5): 1559–63.

Lyman, S., G. S. Fleisig, J. W. Waterbor, E. M. Funkhouser, L. Pulley, J. R. Andrews, E. D. Osinski, and J. M. Roseman. 2001. "Longitudinal Study of Elbow and Shoulder Pain in Youth Baseball Pitchers." *Medicine and Science in Sports and Exercise* 33 (11): 1803–10.

Lyman, Stephen, Glenn S. Fleisig, James R. Andrews, and E. David Osinski. 2002. "Effect of Pitch Type, Pitch Count, and Pitching Mechanics on Risk of Elbow and Shoulder Pain in Youth Baseball Pitchers." *The American Journal of Sports Medicine* 30 (4): 463–68.

Malerba, J. L., M. L. Adam, B. A. Harris, and D. E. Krebs. 1993. "Reliability of Dynamic and Isometric Testing of Shoulder External and Internal Rotators." *The Journal of Orthopaedic and Sports Physical Therapy* 18 (4): 543–52.

Merolla, Giovanni, Elisa De Santis, Fabrizio Campi, Paolo Paladini, and Giuseppe Porcellini. 2010. "Supraspinatus and Infraspinatus Weakness in Overhead Athletes with Scapular Dyskinesis: Strength Assessment before and after Restoration of Scapular Musculature Balance." *Musculoskeletal Surgery* 94 (3): 119–25.

Moore, Stephanie D., Tim L. Uhl, and W. Ben Kibler. 2013. "Improvements in Shoulder Endurance Following a Baseball-Specific Strengthening Program in High School Baseball Players." *Sports Health* 5 (3): 233–38.

Myers, Joseph B., Sakiko Oyama, and Elizabeth E. Hibberd. 2013. "Scapular Dysfunction in High School Baseball Players Sustaining Throwing-Related Upper Extremity Injury: A Prospective Study." *Journal of Shoulder and Elbow Surgery/American Shoulder and Elbow Surgeons ... [et al.]* 22 (9): 1154–59.

Noffal, Guillermo J. 2003. "Isokinetic Eccentric-to-Concentric Strength Ratios of the Shoulder Rotator Muscles in Throwers and Nonthrowers." *The American Journal of Sports Medicine* 31 (4): 537–41.

Okoroha, Kelechi R., Jason E. Meldau, Toufic R. Jildeh, Jeffrey P. Stephens, Vasilios Moutzouros, and Eric C. Makhni. 2019. "Impact of Ball Weight on Medial Elbow Torque in Youth Baseball Pitchers." *Journal of Shoulder and Elbow Surgery/American Shoulder and Elbow Surgeons ... [et al.]*, April. https://doi.org/10.1016/j.jse.2019.01.025.

Oyama, Sakiko. 2012. "Baseball Pitching Kinematics, Joint Loads, and Injury Prevention." *Journal of Sport and Health Science.* https://doi.org/10.1016/j.jshs.2012.06.004.

Papotto, Brianna M., Thomas Rice, Terry Malone, Timothy Butterfield, and Tim L. Uhl. 2016. "Reliability of Isometric and Eccentric Isokinetic Shoulder External Rotation." *Journal of Sport Rehabilitation* 25 (2). https://doi.org/10.1123/jsr.2015-0046.

Popchak, Adam, Thomas Burnett, Nicholas Weber, and Michael Boninger. 2015. "Factors Related to Injury in Youth and Adolescent Baseball Pitching, with an Eye toward Prevention." *American Journal of Physical Medicine & Rehabilitation/Association of Academic Physiatrists* 94 (5): 395–409.

Provencher, Cdr Matthew T., Amun Makani, John W. McNeil, M. Lucius Pomerantz, Petar Golijanin, and Daniel Gross. 2014. "The Role of the Scapula in Throwing Disorders." *Sports Medicine and Arthroscopy Review* 22 (2): 80–87.

Reinold, Michael M., Leonard C. Macrina, Glenn S. Fleisig, Kyle Aune, and James R. Andrews. 2018. "Effect of a 6-Week Weighted Baseball Throwing Program on Pitch Velocity, Pitching Arm Biomechanics, Passive Range of Motion, and Injury Rates." *Sports Health: A Multidisciplinary Approach.* https://doi.org/10.1177/1941738118877 9909.

Reinold, Michael M., Kevin E. Wilk, Jamie Reed, Ken Crenshaw, and James R. Andrews. 2002. "Interval Sport Programs: Guidelines for Baseball, Tennis, and Golf." *The Journal of Orthopaedic and Sports Physical Therapy* 32 (6): 293–98.

Sabick, Michelle B., Young-Kyu Kim, Michael R. Torry, Michael A. Keirns, and Richard J. Hawkins. 2005. "Biomechanics of the Shoulder in Youth Baseball Pitchers: Implications for the Development of Proximal Humeral Epiphysiolysis and Humeral Retrotorsion." *The American Journal of Sports Medicine* 33 (11): 1716–22.

Sakata, Jun, Emi Nakamura, Makoto Suzukawa, Atsushi Akaike, and Kuniaki Shimizu. 2017. "Physical Risk Factors for a Medial Elbow Injury in Junior Baseball Players: A Prospective Cohort Study of 353 Players." *The American Journal of Sports Medicine* 45 (1): 135–43.

Sakata, Jun, Emi Nakamura, Tatsuhiro Suzuki, Makoto Suzukawa, Atsushi Akaike, Kuniaki Shimizu, and Norikazu Hirose. 2018. "Efficacy of a Prevention Program for Medial Elbow Injuries in Youth Baseball Players." *The American Journal of Sports Medicine* 46 (2): 460–69.

Saper, Michael G., Lauren A. Pierpoint, Wei Liu, R. Dawn Comstock, John D. Polousky, and James R. Andrews. 2018. "Epidemiology of Shoulder and Elbow Injuries among United States High School Baseball Players: School Years 2005-2006 through 2014-2015." *The American Journal of Sports Medicine* 46 (1): 37–43.

Scoville, Charles R., Robert A. Arciero, Dean C. Taylor, and Paul D. Stoneman. 1997. "End Range Eccentric Antagonist/Concentric Agonist Strength Ratios: A New Perspective in Shoulder Strength Assessment." *Journal of Orthopaedic & Sports Physical Therapy.* https://doi.org/10.2519/jospt.1997.25.3.203.

Seroyer, Shane T., Shane J. Nho, Bernard R. Bach, Charles A. Bush-Joseph, Gregory P. Nicholson, and Anthony A. Romeo. 2010. "The Kinetic Chain in Overhand Pitching: Its Potential Role for Performance Enhancement and Injury Prevention." *Sports Health* 2 (2): 135–46.

Sgroi, Terrance A., and John M. Zajac. 2018. "Return to Throwing after Shoulder or Elbow Injury." *Current Reviews in Musculoskeletal Medicine* 11 (1): 12–18.

Shanley, Ellen, Mitchell J. Rauh, Lori A. Michener, and Todd S. Ellenbecker. 2011. "Incidence of Injuries in High School Softball and Baseball Players." *Journal of Athletic Training*. https://doi.org/10.4085/1062-6050-46.6.648.

Shitara, Hitoshi, Atsushi Yamamoto, Daisuke Shimoyama, Tsuyoshi Ichinose, Tsuyoshi Sasaki, Noritaka Hamano, Akira Ueno, et al. 2017. "Shoulder Stretching Intervention Reduces the Incidence of Shoulder and Elbow Injuries in High School Baseball Players: A Time-to-Event Analysis." *Scientific Reports* 7 (March): 45304.

Slenker, Nicholas R., Orr Limpisvasti, Karen Mohr, Arnel Aguinaldo, and Neal S. Elattrache. 2014. "Biomechanical Comparison of the Interval Throwing Program and Baseball Pitching: Upper Extremity Loads in Training and Rehabilitation." *The American Journal of Sports Medicine* 42 (5): 1226–32.

Stickley, Christopher D., Ronald K. Hetzler, Bret G. Freemyer, and Iris F. Kimura. 2008. "Isokinetic Peak Torque Ratios and Shoulder Injury History in Adolescent Female Volleyball Athletes." *Journal of Athletic Training* 43 (6): 571–77.

Stratford, P. W., and B. E. Balsor. 1994. "A Comparison of Make and Break Tests Using a Hand-Held Dynamometer and the Kin-Com." *The Journal of Orthopaedic and Sports Physical Therapy* 19 (1): 28–32.

Trakis, James E., Malachy P. McHugh, Philip A. Caracciolo, Lisa Busciacco, Michael Mullaney, and Stephen J. Nicholas. 2008. "Muscle Strength and Range of Motion in Adolescent Pitchers with Throwing-Related Pain." *The American Journal of Sports Medicine*. https://doi.org/10.1177/0363546508319049.

Tyler, Timothy F., Michael J. Mullaney, Michael R. Mirabella, Stephen J. Nicholas, and Malachy P. McHugh. 2014. "Risk Factors for Shoulder and Elbow Injuries in High School Baseball Pitchers." *The American Journal of Sports Medicine.* https://doi.org/10.1177/0363546514535070.

Van Harlinger, Wanda, Lori Blalock, and John L. Merritt. 2015. "Upper Limb Strength: Study Providing Normative Data for a Clinical Handheld Dynamometer." *PM & R: The Journal of Injury, Function, and Rehabilitation* 7 (2): 135–40.

Wasylynko, David. 2015. "Chronic Pain due to Little Leaguer's Shoulder in an Adolescent Baseball Pitcher: A Case Report." *The Journal of the Canadian Chiropractic Association* 59 (4): 383–89.

Weiss, Jennifer M., Alexandre Arkader, Lawrence M. Wells, and Theodore J. Ganley. 2013. "Rotator Cuff Injuries in Adolescent Athletes." *Journal of Pediatric Orthopedics. Part B* 22 (2): 133–37.

Westrick, Richard B., Michele L. Duffey, Kenneth L. Cameron, J. Parry Gerber, and Brett D. Owens. 2013. "Isometric Shoulder Strength Reference Values for Physically Active Collegiate Males and Females." *Sports Health* 5 (1): 17–21.

Wilk, Kevin E., Christopher A. Arrigo, Todd R. Hooks, and James R. Andrews. 2016. "Rehabilitation of the Overhead Throwing Athlete: There Is More to It Than Just External Rotation/Internal Rotation Strengthening." *PM & R: The Journal of Injury, Function, and Rehabilitation* 8 (3 Suppl): S78–90.

Wilk, Kevin E., Keith Meister, and James R. Andrews. 2002. "Current Concepts in the Rehabilitation of the Overhead Throwing Athlete." *The American Journal of Sports Medicine.* https://doi.org/10.1177/0363546502030001201.

Zaremski, Jason L., and Brian J. Krabak. 2012. "Shoulder Injuries in the Skeletally Immature Baseball Pitcher and Recommendations for the Prevention of Injury." *PM & R: The Journal of Injury, Function, and Rehabilitation* 4 (7): 509–16.

In: Essential Topics in Baseball
Editor: Erik Welch

ISBN: 978-1-53616-533-3
© 2019 Nova Science Publishers, Inc.

Chapter 4

BATTER'S MENTAL REPRESENTATION OF THE STRIKE ZONE: AN EXAMINATION OF PRACTICE BAT SWINGING AND ITS DEVIATION FROM THE REAL IMPACT WITH THE BALL

Hiromu Katsumata, Fukutaro Kuroda and Fumiya Yamakuchi*

Department of Sports and Health Science,
Daito-Bunka University, Tokyo, Japan

ABSTRACT

Baseball batters practice swinging their bat to assess their movements, build a mechanically effective swing style, and improve the consistency of swing trajectory. To achieve this aim, they swing the bat to different locations in the air by imagining the flights of different pitches. These different trajectories of the bat pass through different locations in the strike

---

* Corresponding Author's E-mail: hiromu@xd6.so-net.ne.jp.

zone, and are considered to be a mental representation of the movements of the bat and ball. If this mental representation deviates from the actual strike zone (defined by the rule of baseball), the pitch may be missed, or the ball-bat impact may be inaccurate. Therefore, we investigated the difference between striking a real ball at various heights and lateral positions, and swinging a bat to imaginary locations in the strike zone. If the trajectory of the bat to an imaginary location (e.g., an inside-high pitch) deviates from the trajectory of the actual ball, the possibility of failing to correctly estimating the pitch will increase. Through the identification and correction of such a deviance the chance of failure can be reduced. Therefore, the aim of this study was to explore the association between mental representation and the actual event. Ten right-handed college baseball batters participated in the experiment. They swung a bat to five imaginary impact locations of different heights and lateral positions in the strike zone. They also hit a ball mounted on a tee stand placed in the strike zone which corresponded to the same five locations. The process was repeated seven times for each location, all of which were randomly assigned. Movements of the bat and ball were captured by an optical motion capture system at 250 Hz and 3-dimensional coordinates of the bat and ball were calculated. The focus of analysis was the difference between the bat top positions at the moment of the imaginary impact in the bat swinging task, and at the moment of impact in the tee-batting. When the batter swung a bat toward the imaginary impact location, the bat top position deviated from the location of the ball in the tee-batting task (i.e., by shifting to the outer edge in the lateral direction). In the pitcher-catcher orientation, the bat top position shifted forward when swinging the bat to the inside impact location, while the swing trajectories to the outside and middle lateral positions were consistent with the impact location in the tee-batting task. The vertical deviation was either upward or downward, depending on the participant. However, variability relative to mean bat top position in the swinging tasks was consistent with the tee-batting. These results suggest that the mental representation of swinging a bat to each location in the strike zone did not correspond to the actual strike zone, but was consistent for the bat swing movement to be reproducible across trials. In summary, using this method to assess the mental representation of bat movements to the strike zone will facilitate the identification of inaccurate practice swings and thereby lead to improvements in batting performance.

Keywords: baseball, mental representation, bat-swinging practice

INTRODUCTION

Baseball batters swing their bat in the air to warm up and confirm their hitting movements as they wait to bat. They also practice swinging the bat to shape their hitting style by focusing on body movement, without paying attention to the ball. During these practices and warm ups, they swing the bat by imaging the flight of the pitch, moving the bat toward the oncoming (imaginary) ball, and then visualizing striking it. Therefore, effective and accurate swing practice is achieved when batters correctly imagine the flight of pitch. This pitch visualization is influenced by their spatial sense of the strike zone. The pitch's trajectory to a specific location in the strike zone (e.g., an inside-high pitch) depends on the batter's ability to imagine the strike zone location and size relative to their body position. If the batter's imaginary strike zone is distorted relative to the real strike zone (determined by the batter's body size and position relative to the position of the home plate) their judgment on whether an oncoming pitch will be a strike or hit will have failed.

According to cognitive sport psychologists, implicit changes in cognitive responses are accompanied by explicit improvements in performance and skill acquisition [1]. In such a cognitive mechanism of skill execution, mental representation plays a key role in leaning and controlling motor skills. For instance, distinct differences in mental representation between the tennis serves of experts and novices have been reported [2]. This supports a contention such that an improvement in performance level to expertise is accompanied by the development of representation in the long-term memory [3]. Based on this cognitive mechanism, mental representation of the batter regarding spatial awareness (in terms of the imagined flight of the pitch to the strike zone) plays an important role in effective swing practice. Such spatial representation is stronger in superior batters and those showing improvements in batting skill. Mental practice or motor imagery rehearsal is a technique of repeatedly imagining a motor action without actual movement [4, 5], and is an important method used to develop motor skill representation and thereby improve performance. Combined physical and mental practice has been shown to be more effective than physical practice alone [6-8], attributed to the more elaborated representations obtained through the mental process [8]. Swing practice should not be regarded as mental practice since it involves actual movement, although it is executed with respect to an imaginary ball. In this sense, swing practice is used to reinforce the swing movement of the imaginary bat through an actual swing action, and to check if the swing corresponds to their visualization of a good contact. The evidence supporting the value of mental practice in performance improvement highlights the ability of swing practice to improve batting skills. Batters may question whether their swing practice is effective and their representation of the strike zone corresponds with the actual strike zone.

This study investigates the accuracy with which batters are able to imagine the strike zone. This was achieved by asking batters to swing a bat at imaginary pitches passing through different locations in the strike zone, and then examining the locations through which the bat passes in the actual strike zone. If the location of the bat differs from the impact location, the representation is deemed to be inaccurate; the imagined strike zone is incorrect and/or the imagined flight trajectory of the pitch does not match with the location of the real strike zone (through which the bat should pass). Batters will then be unable to effectively imagine different pitches that cover the entire strike zone. In essence, the imagined pitches will be outside the zone, and the batter will be blind to pitches that pass though certain zone locations. As a result of this poor representation, batting performance will be sub-standard and lead to missing the ball or making a poor contact.

The examination of bat swing movement from the viewpoint of mental representation demonstrates the way in which batters visualize a specific flight of a pitch and the spatial representation of the strike zone. Such information is invaluable for batters and coaches to identify inconsistencies between the trajectories of the visualized and actual pitches to the strike zone. As these inconsistencies can reduce the ability to judge pitches traveling to different locations in the strike zone (and modulating their bat swing accordingly), their removal will lead to improvements in batting skills. From this viewpoint, swing practice is useful not only for increasing the power for a batting movement, but for simulating hits of different pitches. This will facilitate the adjustment and organization of batting movements to render them suitable for different pitch trajectories. As the mental representation of swing movements in baseball have not yet been investigated, the results of our study will add to the current body of knowledge, and provide a method by which players can improve their batting skills.

METHOD

Participants

Ten male college baseball batters participated in our experiment (age: 21 ± 1.1 years; height: 1.72 ± 0.03 m; weight: 70.2 ± 8.2 kg). All were right-handed batters with experience of playing baseball for 11.7 ± 1.2 years. They were all regular members of a college baseball team which belonged to a Division I baseball conference. They practiced regularly four or five times a week, and play a competitive game on the weekend during the regular season. Therefore, their athletic level is representative of most college-level baseball players. After explaining the purpose and procedure of the experiment, each participant signed an informed consent form. The study was conducted according to the principles stated in the Helsinki Declaration and was approved by the appropriate ethics committee.

Task Description and Conditions

The participants were required to perform two tasks. The first was to swing a bat to five locations in the air which corresponded to imagined flights of pitches that pass through five different locations in the strike zone (swinging task). These five locations were combinations of the outside or inside edge and the highest or lowest height of the strike zone. These dimensions were determined by the width of the home plate (inside or outside pitch) and the height of batter's knee (low pitch) and underarm position (high pitch) (Figure 1-A). The second task (tee-batting task) was to hit a ball on a batting tee, which was positioned at one of the five locations in the strike zone. These five locations were the same as those used for the swinging task.

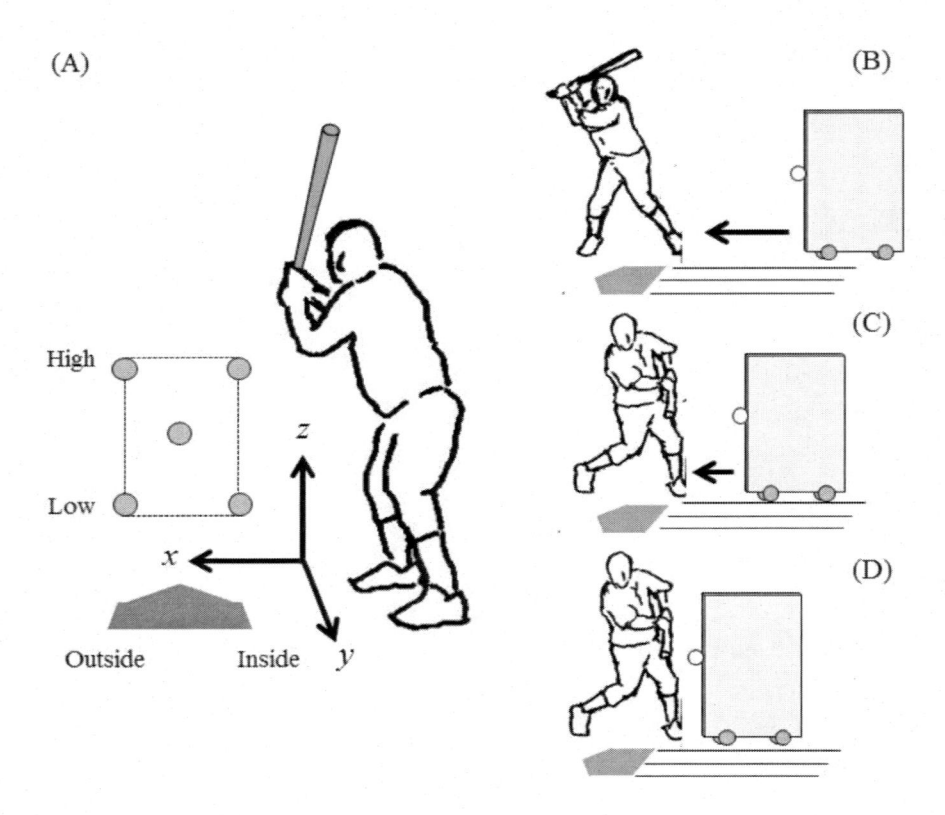

Figure 1. (A) Definition and impact locations of the strike zone used in the experiment. The global coordinate system was used: the x-axis was parallel to the front edge of a home plate; the y-axis was perpendicular to the x-axis (in the pitcher-catcher direction); and the z-axis was perpendicular to the x-y plane.
(B) to (D) Procedure to determine the ball position in the pitcher-catcher direction for height (high, middle, and low) and lateral position (in, middle, and out) in the strike zone.

Experimental Setup

All the participants used the same baseball bat (length: 84 cm; weight: 740 g; MIZUNO, Tokyo, Japan). In the tee-batting task, a plastic ball designed for indoor batting practice (weight: 18 g; diameter: 7 cm) was used, and the participants had to hit the ball placed on a tee stand (MIZUNO, Tokyo, Japan). For ball placement, the height of the ball from the ground was determined (based on the definition of the strike zone by official baseball rules) as follows: The height of the acromion (shoulder) and iliac point (hip) were measured and the midpoint was defined as the highest level of the strike zone. The inferior part of the patella (knee) was defined as the lowest level of the strike zone. The midpoint between these highest and lowest levels was defined as the middle level of the strike zone. Three tee stands were used to achieve the above three heights (high, low, and middle). A home plate was placed on the ground to define the outside and inside edges of the strike zone.

The participants' movements were recorded by a motion capture system consisting of 14 high-speed cameras using optical marker-based technology (Vicon MX, Oxford Metrics, USA) to record each movement at 250 Hz. The camera positions and angles were set up to record the entire bat and body movement. To record each limb and trunk movement, reflective markers were fixed on the following 9 anatomical parts of the body: the vertex (head); the right and left acromion (left and right shoulders) and iliac point (hip) to capture trunk movements; bone head of the fifth metatarsal (toe) to capture the address position and the step movement. Markers were also fixed at the top and bottom of the bat, and the ball was covered with reflective tape. For the purpose of study analysis, only data from the marker at the top of the bat was used.

Experimental Procedure

Before starting the experiment, each participant positioned themselves relative to the home plate (similar to their position in the batter's box during a game), and the position of the tip of the right toe was marked on the floor. In the swing and tee-batting tasks, the participant re-positioned according to this mark to achieve consistency relative to the home plate throughout the trial.

In the swinging task, the participants were asked to swing a bat to one of the five locations in the strike zone, through which they expected the ball to pass. At the start of each trial, the researcher gave an oral indication of which location the participant should swing the bat toward. The participants each performed seven trials for each of the five locations (35 in total). The order of the swing locations across the 35 trials was randomized.

Before starting the tee-batting task, the participants determined the location of the ball on the tee for a given lateral position (inside or outside) and height (high or low) in the strike zone, using the method described in a previous study [9]. The target height and course were indicated by the researcher via a reference frame, as illustrated in the inset of Figure 1-B. A plastic ball was attached at one of the three heights (high, middle, or low) along the vertical edge of the reference frame. These heights were based on the definition of the strike zone as described above. The reference frame was placed on one of three lines drawn on the floor approximately 3 m from the participant, indicating the direction of pitches toward the inside, middle, or outside edge of the strike zone. As such, these combinations define the specific height and course of a particular pitch in the strike zone. The researcher then moved the frame slowly along the line to the home base to help the participant to imagine the trajectory of each pitch and target it (Figures 1-B, C). The participant indicated an expected impact location with his bat by maintaining a posture at the moment of the ball-bat impact (Figure 1-D). The ball position projected on the line drawn in the direction of the pitcher-catcher (i.e., the y-component of the x-y plane) was measured and used as the position of the tee stand. For each of the five ball locations, the above procedure was repeated three times, and the ball location at which the participant felt most confident of a contact was used. The participants performed seven trials for each location (35 trials in total), and the order of the tee locations across the 35 trials was randomized.

Analysis

We obtained the three-dimensional positions of the reflective markers and the ball within a global coordinate system using software of the motion capture system (Vicon Workstation, Vicon Peak, USA). This coordinate system was defined as shown in Figure 1-A. The position data was smoothed by a second-order Butterworth filter with a cutoff frequency of 20-Hz.

The focus of analysis was the position of the bat at the moment (i) of ball-bat impact in the tee-batting task, and (ii) when the bat was estimated to hit the ball in the swinging task. For this analysis of bat position, the marker attached to the bat top was used. To this end, the moment of ball impact in the tee-batting task was identified as follows: As the bat approaches the ball on the tee, the ball-bat distance diminishes until it reaches a minimum value at the time of impact. As such, the ball-bat distance was calculated according to equation (1)

$$ball - bat\ distance = \sqrt{(x_{ball} - x_{bat})^2 + (y_{ball} - y_{bat})^2 + (z_{ball} - z_{bat})^2} \tag{1}$$

where x, y, and z are the components of three-dimensional coordinates, the subscripted ball and bat refer to the markers on the ball and bat top, and the moment of impact occurs when the minimum value is observed.

In the swinging task, the participants were asked to swing the bat to the locations through which they estimated the pitch would pass. The definition of the height and lateral position of these locations corresponded to the five ball locations used in the tee-batting task. If the participant's mental representation of the strike zone is consistent with the actual strike zone, their estimation and the actual location (of the ball in the tee-batting task) will be consistent. Therefore, the five locations of the imagined impact were defined as the fictitious impact location. The distance between the bat top and the fictitious impact location was calculated, and the moment of minimum value was defined as the assumed impact.

The position of the bat top at the moment of impact in the tee-batting task, and the time of the assumed impact in the bat swinging task, were used for the following analysis. In the tee-batting task, the participants were asked to imagine the flight of a pitch that passes through a given lateral position and height in the strike zone, and to determine the location of the ball on the tee along the pitcher-catcher line. Therefore, the position of the bat at the moment of assumed impact in the swinging task will correspond to that observed in the tee-batting task; the participant's mental representation of the strike zone is considered consistent with the actual strike zone. Moreover, they can correctly visualize the flight of a pitch, according to the fictitious impact location. Thus, we compared the bat top position at the moment of assumed impact with the position at the moment of impact in the tee-batting task. The comparison was performed while taking the following terms into consideration: the mean bat top position relative to the location of the ball (constant error; CE), the variability of the bat top position relative to the ball location (total variability; TV), and the variability of the bat top position relative to its mean position (variable error; VE), with reference to the established analysis of performance accuracy and variability [10].

CE values were calculated as shown below:

$$CE_x = \frac{\Sigma(x_{ball} - x_{bat\ top})}{n} \tag{2-1}$$

$$CE_y = \frac{\Sigma(y_{ball} - y_{bat\ top})}{n} \tag{2-2}$$

$$CE_z = \frac{\Sigma(z_{ball} - z_{bat\ top})}{n} \tag{2-3}$$

where subscripts of x, y, and z refer to the x, y, and z components of the positions of the bat top and ball at the moment of actual or assumed impact. The denominator n refers to the number of trials performed in each task. The fictitious impact locations were used to position the balls in the swinging task. This error measure indicates the extent to which the bat top position in the tee-batting task and the assumed impact deviate relative to the location of the ball or the fictitious impact location. In the tee-batting task, the difference between the position of the ball and bat top indicates the distance between the position of the bat top and the center of percussion (where the bat hits the ball (Figure 2)). The CE obtained in the tee-batting task is therefore used as a reference so a CE value in the swinging task larger than the tee-batting task indicates a greater discrepancy of bat top position between the swing and tee-batting tasks. This means that, for a given height-lateral position of impact, the location to which they swung the bat is different to the location of the ball in the tee-batting task.

TV values were calculated as shown below.

$$TV_x = \sqrt{\frac{\Sigma(x_{bat\ top} - x_{ball})^2}{n}} \tag{3-1}$$

$$TV_y = \sqrt{\frac{\Sigma(y_{bat\ top} - y_{ball})^2}{n}} \tag{3-2}$$

$$TV_z = \sqrt{\frac{\Sigma(z_{bat\ top} - z_{ball})^2}{n}} \tag{3-3}$$

where the subscripted text corresponds to those in the equation of CE. Equation (3) indicates the variability of the bat top position relative to the ball location in the tee-batting task and fictitious impact location in the swing task. If the trajectory of the bat in the swinging task passes through the fictitious impact location and is consistent through trial replicates, the TV value will become smaller. If there is no significant difference in the TV value between the tee-batting and swinging tasks, the imagined impact location (to which the participant swung the bat in the swinging task) is consistent with the impact location in the tee-batting task.

VE values were calculated as shown below.

$$VE_x = \sqrt{\frac{\Sigma(x_{bat\ top} - Mean(x_{bat\ top}))^2}{n}} \tag{4-1}$$

$$VE_y = \sqrt{\frac{\Sigma(y_{bat\ top} - Mean(y_{bat\ top}))^2}{n}} \tag{4-2}$$

$$VE_z = \sqrt{\frac{\Sigma(z_{bat\ top} - Mean(z_{bat\ top}))^2}{n}} \tag{4-3}$$

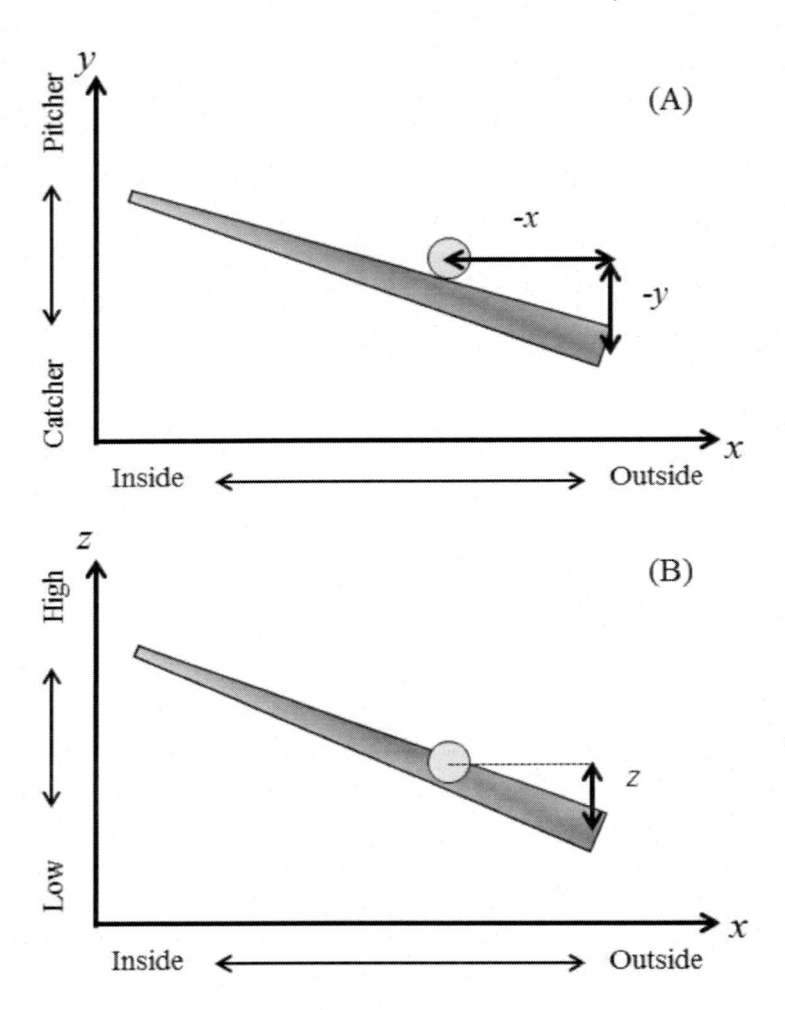

Figure 2. (A) Representations of $x_{ball}-x_{bat\ top}$ and $y_{ball}-y_{bat\ top}$, as measured using the top view of the ball-bat impact: Illustrates that $x_{ball}-x_{bat\ top}$ is a negative value when the bat strikes the ball at the center of percussion. The value becomes more negative when the bat top position moves further from the ball location. $y_{ball}-y_{bat\ top}$ becomes negative when the bat strikes the ball before reaching the point parallel to the x-axis. $y_{ball}-y_{bat\ top}$ becomes positive as the bat moves forward in the pitcher's direction
(B) Representations of $z_{ball}-z_{bat\ top}$, as measured using the rear view (the catcher side) of the impact: The incline of the bat at the moment of impact dictates whether $z_{ball}-z_{bat\ top}$ becomes negative (upwards) or positive (downwards).

where subscripted text corresponds to those in equations of CE and TV. The VE equation calculates the variability of the bat top position relative to the mean position of the bat top positions across trial replicates. As such, VE indicates the magnitude of consistency in the bat trajectories (i.e., the reproducibility of the procedure). If no difference in VE is observed between the swing and tee-batting tasks, it can be surmised that the bat has repeatedly moved to a consistent location, even when the participant has swung the bat to an imagined location. Therefore, a low value of VE in the swinging task indicates that the participant is able to estimate the impact location consistently and effectively.

Means and standard deviations of these variables were obtained for each participant, and a repeated-measures ANOVA was conducted on the effects of the two tasks and five impact locations (in-high, in-low, middle, out-high, and out-low). For the ANOVA, we conducted Mauchly's test of sphericity, then adjusted the degrees of freedom by applying the Greenhouse-Geisser correction for violations of circularity. If a significant effect of the impact locations was identified, paired t-tests between the swing and tee-batting task results were conducted for each of the five impact locations. A statistical significance was determined by $p < 0.05$.

RESULTS

Figure 3 shows representative trajectories of a bat top at the moment of impact with the ball in the tee-batting task and the assumed impact in the swinging task. The position of the bat top at the beginning of the movement and the trajectories of the participant's head and front foot as they swing the bat did not appear to differ between the tee-batting and swinging tasks. However, the trajectories of the bat top, and the bat position at the time of the impact, differed between the two tasks. Therefore, the locations to which the bat was swung in each of the different height-lateral position tasks were different from those observed in the tee-batting task.

Constant Error

The means and standard errors of CE for all the participants are shown in the left column of Figure 4. CE is a measure of the deviation of the bat top and ball positions in the tee-batting task. As the participants hit the ball with the bat's center of percussion, the CE in the tee-batting task does not indicate the magnitude of error in hitting the ball, but rather the position of the bat top relative to the ball's position. Therefore, the CE in the tee-batting task can be used as a reference to examine the location to which the bat was swung. If the bat trajectory approached the fictitious impact location, the CEs in the two tasks should not differ.

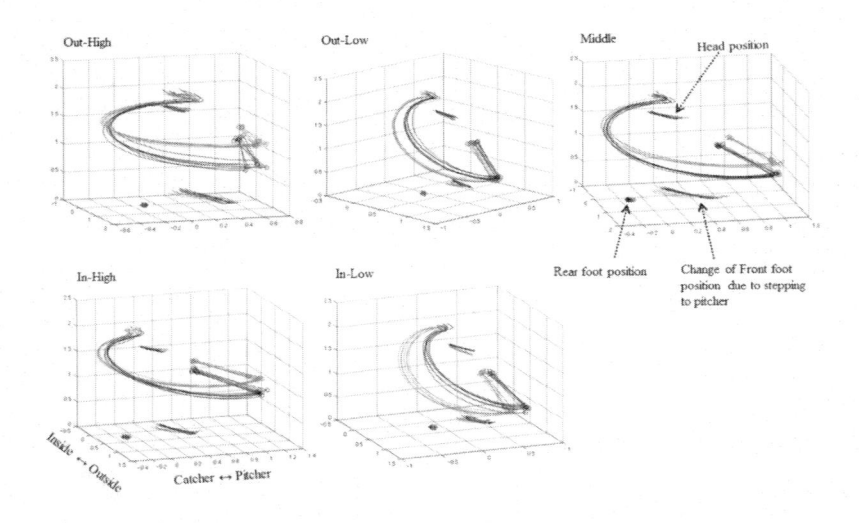

Figure 3. Superposed representative trajectories of the bat top for one exemplary participant. Curved lines refer to the trajectory of the bat top. Circles connected by a line indicate the top and bottom positions of the bat at the moment of impact in the tee-batting task and the assumed impact in the swinging task. Gray and black colors refer to the tee-batting and swinging tasks, respectively.

The x component of CE showed a negative value (Figure 4, left column), which indicates that the bat top position was the outside that of the ball (refer to Figure 2-A). A greater x component of CE signifies that the bat top has passed further outside the zone, relative to the ball. Figure 4 shows that the relatively consistent value of the x component of CE in the tee-batting task is due to the participant hitting the ball at the center of percussion. Figure 4 (top of left column) shows that the x component of CE was more negative in the swinging task than the tee-batting task. A repeated ANOVA revealed a significant main effect of task ($F(1, 9) = 28.321$, $p < 0.001$) without significant main effect of the impact location ($F(4, 36) = 1.927$, $p = 0.127$) and the interaction between the task and the impact location ($F(4, 36) = 1.051$, $p = 0.395$). A t-test post-hoc comparison of the impact location of the tee-batting and swinging tasks indicated significant differences in out-high, out-low, middle, and in-high positions. These differences suggest that the bat top position was further from the fictitious impact location than the actual point of impact. Therefore, when the participants swung the bat toward the imagined impact location, the position to which the bat moved was different from that observed in the tee-batting task. This result was more prominent in the out-high and in-high conditions. In contrast, the t-test did not detect a significant difference between the tee-batting and swinging tasks in regard to the swing of the bat to the in-low position. However, this may be due to inter-participant variability as shown by the large error bar.

The negative value of the y component of CE (Figure 4, middle of left column), indicates that the bat top position was in front of the ball location (refer to Figure 2-A). A repeated ANOVA revealed significant main effects of the task ($F(1, 9) = 18.778$, $p = 0.002$) and the impact location ($F(4, 36) = 9.106$, $p < 0.001$) with a significant association between the task and the impact location ($F(4, 36) = 3.620$, $p = 0.014$). In the tee-batting task, impact occurred after the bat had passed through the position (parallel to the x-axis) when hitting in-high and in-low balls. This tendency was prominent in the swinging task (Figure 4, middle of the left column). A post-hoc comparison of the impact locations of the tee-batting and swinging tasks confirmed a significant difference between in-high and in-low balls. As such, the bat top position was further ahead of the fictitious impact location in the swinging task compared to the tee-batting procedure. Therefore, when swinging the bat to in-high and in-low positions, the imagined location of impact in the two tasks was different. In contrast, the CE value of swinging a bat to out-high, out-low and middle positions did not show a significant difference from that of the tee-batting task. This result supports the contention that the imagined impact locations to which participants swung the bat (out-high, out-low and middle) were consistent with the fictitious impact locations (i.e., the ball location in the tee-batting task).

The bottom graph in Figure 4 (left column) shows the z component CE. A positive or negative CE value indicates that the bat top position was higher or lower than the position of the ball in the tee-batting task and the fictitious impact location in the swinging task, respectively (refer to Figure 2-B). Repeated-measures ANOVA did not reveal any significant differences between the tasks ($F(1, 9) = 0.100$, $p = 0.759$), the impact locations ($F(4, 36) = 0.512$, $p = 0.727$), or the task and the impact location ($F(4, 36) = 0.819$, $p = 0.522$). Therefore, the height of the bat as it was swung toward the ball did not differ between the tee-batting and swinging tasks. However, this result should be interpreted carefully due to large inter-participant variability in the swinging task, as indicated by the large error bars (Figure 4, bottom panel of the left column).

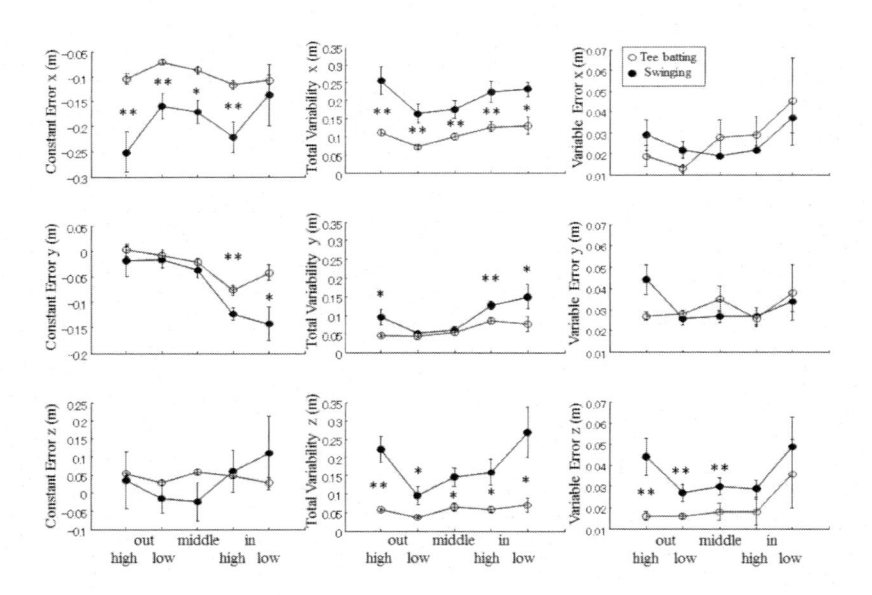

Figure 4. Overall mean and standard error of the mean of constant error (CE), total variability (TV), and variable error (VE) of all the participants (*: $p < 0.05$; **: $p < 0.01$).

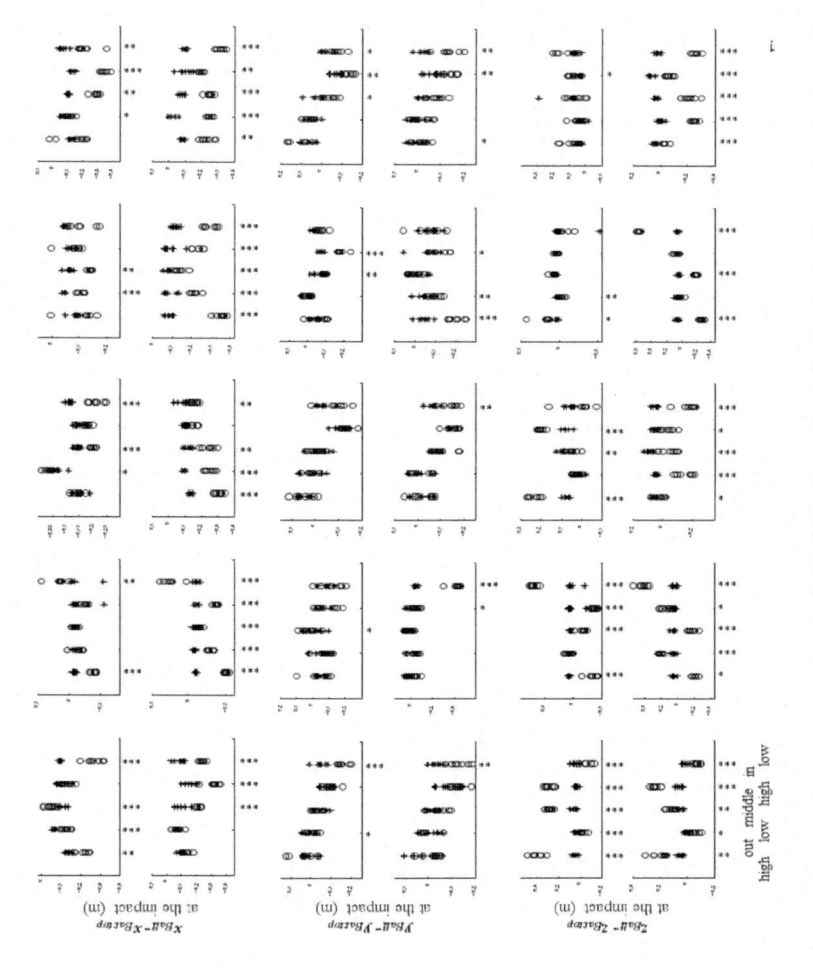

Figure 5. x_{ball}–$x_{bat\ top}$, y_{ball}–$y_{bat\ top}$, and z_{ball}–$z_{bat\ top}$ values of all trials, shown by * for the tee-batting and ○ for the swinging task. Each graph shows the results of each participant. The top two rows show x_{ball}–$x_{bat\ top}$, the two middle rows show y_{ball}–$y_{bat\ top}$, and the bottom two rows show z_{ball}–$z_{bat\ top}$.

Total Variability

TV indicates the variability of the bat top position relative to the location of the ball in the tee-batting task and the fictitious impact locations in the swinging task. As shown in Figure 4 (middle column), the x, y, and z components of TV in the tee-batting task were smaller than those of the swinging task for most of the impact positions. This tendency was confirmed by repeated measure ANOVA as follows. x component TV: the task ($F(1, 9)$ = 23.299, p = 0.001), the impact location ($F(4, 36) = 4.196$, p = 0.007), and the interaction ($F(4, 36) = 0.962$, p = 0.440); y component TV: the task ($F(1, 9) = 28.564$, p < 0.001), the impact location ($F(4, 36) = 6.839$, p < 0.001), and the interaction ($F(4, 36) = 1.849$, p = 0.141); z component TV: the task ($F(1, 9) = 23.530$, p = 0.001), the impact location ($F(4, 36) = 3.949$, p = 0.009), and the interaction ($F(4, 36) = 2.130$, p = 0.097). These ANOVA results demonstrate a significant difference among the impact positions. However, these differences were not analyzed further as the differences due to height and lateral position of the impact was not the aim of this study. Post-hoc t-tests revealed that the TVs of the swinging task were significantly larger than those of the tee-batting task in all locations except for the y component of the out-low and middle positions. The TV in the tee-batting task should be smaller than that of the swinging task, because the bat moves to a visible target (ball), while the bat moves to a visualized location in the swinging task. In the out-low and middle positions, the y component CE in the swinging task was also small and did not differ from the CE of the tee-batting task. These results support the contention that the mental representation of swinging a bat and the actual movement of the bat to these locations was consistent.

Variable Error

VE indicates the variability of the bat top position relative to the mean of the bat top position across trials, and is therefore a measure of the consistency of bat trajectories. Repeated-measures ANOVA was conducted for each of the x, y, and z component VEs, and only the main effect of task in the z component in the swinging task was significantly larger than that of the tee-batting task (F(1, 9) = 8.909, p = 0.015) with no significant effect of the impact location (F(4, 36) = 2.384, p = 0.069) and the interaction (F(4, 36) = 0.522, p = 0.720). Post-hoc t-test comparisons revealed a significantly larger VE in the swinging task than the tee-batting task in out-high, out-low, and middle positions (Figure 4, bottom of right column). ANOVA assessment of the x and y components did not show any significant differences (i) in the x component VE; the task (F(1, 9) = 0.092, p = 0.769), the impact location (F(4, 36) = 2.084, p = 0.103), and the interaction (F(4, 36) = 0.717, p = 0.586), and (ii) in the y component VE; the task (F(1, 9) = 0.058, p = 0.816), the impact location (F(4, 36) = 1.223, p = 0.318), and the interaction (F(4, 36) = 1.573, p = 0.202).

VEs in the x and y components (i.e., the inside-outside and pitcher-catcher directions, respectively) of the two tasks were not found to differ. These results indicate that the level of consistency of the bat position after being swung toward the imagined location was similar to that of the position of the bat top at the moment of impact with the tee. This supports the contention that mental representation (based on the participant's estimation of impact location) is consistent and effective. As such, the swing movements toward these fictitious impact locations were reproducible. However, such consistency was not observed in the z component (i.e., the vertical direction of the swing movement), especially in the movement to out-high, out-low, and middle positions. Therefore, the participants were unable to imagine the impact location in the air consistently, which may indicate less effective mental representations regarding the height of the strike zone.

Individual Differences

In the comparison of CE between the tee-batting and swinging tasks, significant differences were not observed in some of the impact locations. These results support the hypothesis that the location through which the bat passed in the two tasks was consistent. It can therefore be argued that the mental representation of the impact location is effective and consistent with the actual strike zone. However, as the lack of significant difference could be attributed to the large inter-participant variability in CE, we conducted post-hoc analysis for each participant to compare $x_{ball}-x_{bat\,top}$, $y_{ball}-y_{bat\,top}$, and $z_{ball}-z_{bat\,top}$ (used for calculating CE) values of the two tasks for each of the impact locations. In this way, we were able to examine the differences in the ball and bat top positions for individual participants.

Figure 5 shows individual differences between the x, y, and z components of the bat top position and the impact and fictitious impact location in the tee-batting and swinging tasks, respectively. Significant differences between the two tasks as judged by t-test analysis are presented within each graph. For $x_{ball}-x_{bat\,top}$ values (the top and second rows in Figure 5), six out of ten participants showed a significant difference in out-high, eight out of ten in out-low, nine out of ten in middle, five out of ten in in-high, and nine out of ten in in-low positions. For $y_{ball}-y_{bat\,top}$ values (the two middle rows in Figure 5), two out of ten participants showed a significant difference in out-high, two out of ten in out-low, three out of ten in middle, five out of ten in in-high, and six out of ten in in-low positions. For $z_{ball}-z_{bat\,top}$ values (the two bottom rows in Figure 5), nine out of ten participants showed a significant difference in out-high, six out of ten in out-low, eight out of ten in middle, eight out of ten in in-high, and seven out of ten in in-low positions. These findings confirm that the lack of significant differences in the z component of CE, based on ANOVA analysis (refer to the bottom of the left column in Figure 4), was due to the large variability of CE values among the participants. Likewise, the lack of significant differences in the x component of CE in in-low positions (refer to the top of the left column in Figure 4) was also attributed to this large variability. This conclusion is strengthened by the significant difference obtained in nine out of ten participants in the within-participant comparison. Conversely, a lack of significant differences in the y component of CE in out-high, out-low, and middle (refer to the middle of the left column in Figure 4) was associated with a lack of significant differences in the within-participant comparison (obtained in 8 to 7 out of 10 participants). Based on these results, significant differences are not evident between the tee-batting and swinging tasks in out-high, out-low and middle positions of the y component CEs.

Recapitulation of Results

Significant differences in CE values between the swing and tee-batting tasks indicated that the location to which the participants swung the bat differed from the impact location of a real hit in the strike zone. This result is supported by the significantly larger TV of the swinging task than the tee-batting task. Specifically, in swinging the bat to a specific location in the strike zone (i.e., out-high, out-low, middle, in-high, and in-low), the bat reached a position further to the outer edge, relative to the tee-batting task. In addition, when the bat was swung toward the imaginary in-high and in-low pitches, the impact was in front of that observed in the tee-batting task. Even though the imagined impact locations differed from the actual strike zone in the tee-batting task, these swing locations were consistent across trials, relative to those in the tee batting, given the no significant difference in VE between the tee-batting and swing conditions. These results indicate that mental representation of the strike zone for swinging a bat to specific courses is not correspondent with the actual strike zone but elaborated enough to swing a bat repeatedly to a specific location.

As opposed to it, significant difference in the y component of CE was not obtained between the tee-batting and swing conditions, for the impact locations of out-high, out-low, and middle. In addition to it, as for out-low and middle, TV (i.e., the variability of the bat top position relative to the assumed impact location) and VE (i.e., the consistency of the bat top position across trials) did not show significant differences between the tee-batting and swing conditions. Therefore, the above depth locations in the bat swing, especially for out-low and middle, were consistent with the ball-bat impact locations in the tee batting.

Regarding the height that the bat moved through at the time of the assumed impact in the swing condition, a significant difference in the z component of CE was not obtained. However, this was attributed to the large inter-participant variability in the bat swing movement, given the significantly larger TV and the significant difference in the bat top position between the swing and tee-batting condition by the within-participant post-hoc comparisons. Therefore, in swinging a bat in the air, the level of height, at which the participants swung a bat, was not consistent with the level of height in the actual strike zone. Furthermore, the result of significantly larger TV in out-high, out-low and middle in the swing condition than the tee-batting condition indicate the low level of reproducibility in the swing movement at the heights of these impact locations.

DISCUSSION

This study investigated the mental representation of swinging a bat in baseball. Our hypothesis stated that as the batter swings the bat to specific locations, they imagine the flight of the pitch to the impact location. The estimation of this location is based on a mental representation of the strike zone. These mental representations can be studied by asking batters to swing the bat to imaginary aerial locations (i.e., specific heights and lateral positions in the imaginary strike zone): this action is improved by practice and match experience. The specific question of this investigation was whether the location to which the bat is swung (based on the imaginary flight of the pitch) is different from the real impact location in the strike zone. To address this question, the position of the bat top at the moment of assumed impact in the swinging task, and moment of impact in the tee-batting task, were compared in terms of CE, TV, and VE. In summing up our findings, the imagined impact location of the swinging bat was shifted to the outer edge and forward (toward the pitcher) when the batter targeted in-high and in-low positions. With regard to the height of the swinging bat, inter-personal differences and large variability across trials were observed. Therefore, the results reveal not only a difference between imagined and actual impact, but also the relative ability of each participant to imagine these impact positions of varying heights and lateral positions.

This study is the first to focus on the batter's mental representation of the strike zone. The methodology of examining mental representation by analyzing the movement of the bat to the impact location (estimated by the batter) is a unique idea. However, several issues need to be addressed in further studies, and are discussed below. If a batter's mental representation can be elicited using this method, the procedure can be extended to investigate the level of effectiveness and consistency of imaging the strike zone. Our results indicate that the magnitude of CE, TV, and VE were different, depending on the height and lateral position of the strike zone. From this viewpoint, we expect that the effectiveness of batters in imagining specific locations in the strike zone is variable. It would be interesting to investigate whether differences in the effectiveness and consistency of swinging a bat to imaginary locations is correlated with the level of batting expertise. Likewise, there is merit in examining the association between the effectiveness and consistency of imaging specific locations and batting performance (e.g., in terms of batting averages for pitches delivered to specific locations). If effective mental representation is associated with a high level of batting skill, improvements in skill can be assessed using the methods outlined in this study. Moreover, improvements in mental representation should promote a higher level of bat swing skill.

To expand the focus of this study, further parameters should be included in the assessments of bat swing. In the present study, we used the bat top position at the time of impact as an analytical variable, because it is considered the simplest measure to describe the location of impact. The aim of the study was to examine the difference between the imaginary and actual strike zone, which underlines the importance of identifying a difference in the impact location of the two tasks. We regard this comparison as the first step toward elucidating the association between the mental representation of the strike zone and the actual strike zone. This is essential as differences in the bat position at the moment of impact varied between the tasks, so specific movement parameters will also be variable. However, based on the findings of this study, the analysis can be extended to include kinematic parameters that describe the movement of the bat and various regions of the body (e.g., bat angle at the moment of impact, trajectory of bat movement, direction of the front foot's forward step, head movement, and the direction of gaze).

The motivation for this study arose from practical aspects of performance development in baseball. Therefore, the implications of our findings will be of significant interest to coaches and players. The way in which batters imagine the location of the impact, relative to the locations in the actual strike zone, provides useful information to identify discrepancies between mental representation and actual batting movements. Since inaccuracies in mental representation can reduce batting performance (e.g., missing a strike pitch or failing to hit a ball), correcting the discrepancy will ultimately lead to less batting mistakes. Given the inter-participant variability in the impact locations, the methods described in this study can be used to assess the mental representation of individual batters. The information obtained is a useful way of evaluating batting skill levels and weaknesses in the ability of players to hit pitches flying to different locations.

CONCLUSION

This study investigated the mental representation of the strike zone by focusing on the deviation of the bat top position at the imaginary impact location in the bat swing from the bat top position at the ball-bat impact in the tee batting. The movement of the swinging bat deviated from the batting movement produced for the actual strike zone: the bat top position shifted to outside in the lateral direction, and shifted forward in the pitcher's direction in the bat swing to the inside impact locations, and the upward or downward deviation in the vertical direction was different depending on the participants. However, the variability relative to the mean bat top position across trials in the bat swing was consistent with the tee batting. The results of this study suggest that the batters' mental representation of swinging the bat at several locations in the strike zone did not correspond to the actual strike zone, although bat movements to specific locations were reproducible through repeated trials. As these deviations are thought to be the cause of an inaccurate impact, we conclude that the use of the methods developed in this study will facilitate the correction of mental representation and thereby improve batting performance.

REFERENCES

[1]   Magill, RA. *Motor learning and control: concepts and applications.*, 2011, New York, NY: McGraw-Hill.

[2]   Schack, T; Mechsner, F. Representation of motor skills in human long-term memory. *Neuroscience Letters*, 2006, 391, p. 77-81.

[3]   Ericsson, KA. Deliberate practice and the modifiability of body and mind: Toward a science of structure and acquisition of expert and elite performance. *International Journal of Sport Psychology*, 2007, 38, p. 4-34.

[4]   Jeannerod, M. Actions from within. *International Journal of Sport and Exercise Psychology*, 2004, 2, p. 376-402.

[5]   Jeannerod, M. Mental imagery in the motor context. *Neuropsychologia*, 1995, 33, p. 1419-1432.

[6]   Hall, C; Buckolz, E; Fishburne, G. Imagery and the acquisition of motor skills. *Canadian Journal of Sport Sciences*, 1992, 17, p. 19-27.

[7]   Stebbins, RJA. Compariosn of the effects of physical and mental practice in learning a motor skill. *Research Quarterly*, 1968, 39, p. 714-720.

[8]   Frank, C; et al., Mental representation and mental practice: Experimental investigation on the functional links between motor memory and motor imagery *PLoS One*, 2014, 9(14), p. 1-12.

[9]   Katsumata, H; et al., Coordination of hitting movement revealed in baseball tee-batting. *Journal of Sports Sciences*, 2017, 35(24), p. 2468-2480.

[10]   Schmidt, RA; Lee, TD. *Motor Control and Learning: A Behavioral Emphasis*. 5th ed. 2011, Champaign, IL, USA: Human Kinetics.

BIOGRAPHICAL SKETCH

Hiromu Katsumata, PhD

Affiliation: Department of Sports and Health Science, Daito-Bunka University

Education: PhD from the Graduate school in the Department of Kinesiology at The Pennsylvania State University

Business Address: Department of Sports and Health Science, Daito-Bunka University, 560 Iwadono, Higashi-Matsuyama City, Saitama Prefecture, 355-8501

Research and Professional Experience:

Studying motor control and learning as a doctorate student in the Graduate school in the Department of Kinesiology at The Pennsylvania State University (1997 - 2002)

Teaching motor control and learning to graduate and under-graduate students as a full-time faculty of the Department of Sports and Health Science at Daito-Bunka University (2005 - in the present)

Professional Appointments:

Professor in the Department of Sports and Health Science at Daito-Bunka University,

Publications from the Last 3 Years:

Katsumata, H. (2019). Attenuation of Size Illusion Effect in Dual-Task Condition. *Human Movement Science*, On-line publication.

Katsumata, H., Sasaki, J. & Kawai, T. (2017). A Preliminary Study to Capture the Characteristics of Backswing Movement in Baseball Throwing. *Journal of Ergonomics*, 7, 201.

Katsumata, H., Himi, K., Ino, T., Ogawa, K. & Matsumoto, T. (2017). Coordination of hitting movement revealed in baseball tee-batting. *Journal of Sports Sciences*, Jan 6, 1-13.

In: Essential Topics in Baseball
Editor: Erik Welch

ISBN: 978-1-53616-533-3
© 2019 Nova Science Publishers, Inc.

Chapter 5

USING GEOSTATISTICAL TECHNIQUES TO IMPROVE HEAT MAPS OF BATTING AABILITY

Dana Sylvan[1]*and Jared Cross*[2]
[1] Hunter College of the City University of New York,
New York, NY, US
[2] Saint Ann's School, Brooklyn, NY, US

Abstract

Baseball is a game of stats, more so in recent years with the advent of "big data" and the emerging field of data science. Extensive statistical literature has been devoted to baseball data, see the most recent text Marchi, Albert and Baumer (2019) and the references therein. However, comparatively less is known about the utility of geostatistical techniques to produce accurate and comprehensive heat maps. The freely available Statcast Trackman data provides continuous location coordinates for individual pitches using Doppler radar. This detailed spatial information can be employed to visualize a batter's ability across regions in and around the strike zone.

This chapter summarizes classical geostatistical methodology, shows how it can be applied to real data, and presents comprehensive heat maps based on Major League Baseball pitches from 2006 to 2018.

*Corresponding Author's Email: dsylvan@hunter.cuny.edu

The stochastic process underlying batting ability is assumed to be a spatial Gaussian field with isotropic covariance that is estimated from the aforementioned data. We then use the Kriging Residuals approach introduced in Cross and Sylvan (2015) to obtain best estimates of heat maps of batting ability for individual players. We also assess uncertainty in these estimates by using Monte Carlo simulations and resampling and show confidence regions for visualization. For a detailed description of classic geostatistical methods including an overview of R packages we refer to Zimmerman and Stein (2010).

1. Introduction

In baseball, heat maps are commonly used visuals for a batter's ability in and around the strike zone. The main interest is to identify hot and cold zones for each player. In the era of data science and motivated by the abundance of freely available data, extensive statistical literature has been devoted to baseball data. For a recent and comprehensive literature review see Marchi, Albert and Baumer (2019) and the references therein. However, comparatively less is known about the utility of geostatistical techniques to produce accurate and comprehensive heat maps. Moreover, several shortcomings have been identified by Baumer and Draghicescu (2010) and Cross and Sylvan (2015) concerning traditional heat maps. For instance, Cross and Sylvan (2015) show that traditional heat maps often produce inaccurate spatial estimates by not accounting for the distribution of batting abilities at each location and the covariance in batting ability between pairs of locations. Fast (2011) proved that hitters indeed have hot and cold zone but no rigorous assessment of heat maps' accuracy was made. In what follows we show that by using classic geostatistical tools based on first and second order moments we can achieve improved heat maps and quantify their uncertainty. We employ spatial interpolation (kriging) based on the league batting average and a two-parameter exponential decay model for the covariance in batting ability. This is a realistic model, it is straightforward to estimate and interpret by using existing tools and open source software, and adds uncertainty assessment. The rest of the chapter is organized as follows. Section 2 presents the data followed by a brief description of the theory of kriging (spatial interpolation) in Section 3. A geostatistical model for batting ability is described in Section 4 and its applications to real data follow in Section 5.

Concluding remarks are given in the last section.

2. Data

Sportvision has tracked Major League Baseball pitches from 2006 through 2014 using a system entitled PITCHf/x. Using two cameras, one behind home plate and the other behind first base, Sportvision captured roughly 20 images of each pitch on its path to the plate and from these images estimated the entire path of the ball. Using this path, Sportvision determined, among other things, the height and horizontal location of each pitch as it crossed the plate. Major League Baseball Advanced Media (MLBAM), recorded the results of each pitch in real time, classified each pitch based on its velocity and movement (for example as a Four-seam Fastball or as a Slider) and makes this data publicly available (http://gd2.mlb.com/components/game/mlb). For a detailed description of PITCHf/x and MLBAM see Fast (2010) and Baumer and Draghicescu (2010). From 2015 through the present, MLBAM has used Statcast to track pitches. "Statcast uses a combination of two different tracking systems – a Trackman Doppler radar and high definition Chyron Hego cameras. The radar, installed in each ballpark in an elevated position behind home plate, is responsible for tracking everything related to the baseball at 20,000 frames per second. This radar captures pitch speed, spin rate, pitch movement, exit velocity, launch angle, batted ball distance, arm strength, and more." (http://m.mlb.com/glossary/statcast) Throughout this chapter we use PITCHf/x, Statcast and MLBAM data provided by Fangraphs.com. A sample of PITCHf/x data is displayed in Table 1. In keeping with traditional heat maps (see for example espn.com) we consider final pitches of at bats and base our analysis on pitches identified as fastballs.

3. Spatial Interpolation

In geostatistics, an important problem of interest is to map a random field on a fixed spatial domain based on observed values of the process at a fixed number of random locations in the respective domain. Specifically, let $Z(s)$ be a random function defined for $s \in D \subset \mathbb{R}^d$. In order to map the random field Z we need to determine $Z(s_0)$ for any point $s_0 \in D$. In this study the spatial dimension is $d = 2$ and each spatial point is represented by the two coordinates px and

Table 1. A sample of 10 pitches; px is the distance to the center of the plate measured horizontally (feet); pz is the distance from the ground measured vertically (feet)

Batter	Pitcher Throws	px	pz	Pitcher Type	Outcome	At Bat	Hit
Judge, A.	R	0.54	1.89	FC	Groundout	1	0
Trout, M.	L	-1.38	2.1	SI	Pop out	1	0
Stanton, G.	R	0.5	2.17	FF	Strikeout	1	0
Trout, M.	R	1.76	1.9	SL	Strikeout	1	0
Judge, A.	R	-0.46	2.04	KC	Single	1	1
Stanton G.	R	0.58	2.89	KN	Strikeout	1	0
Betts, M.	R	-0.34	2	FT	Single	1	1
Trout, M.	L	-1.28	0.28	CH	Field Error	1	0
Trout, M.	R	-2.13	3.68	FT	Hit By Pitch	0	0

pz shown for each pitch in Table 1. The field of interest Z is batter ability viewed as a collection of spatially-indexed random variables. The domain D is the area in and around the strike zone, specifically the 40 inch by 40 inch area that extends vertically from 10 inches to 50 inches above the ground and 20 inches horizontally in either direction from the center of the plate. Assume that $\{s_1, s_2, \ldots, s_n\}$ is the set of points where the process is observed. The data is thus the collection $\{Z(s_1), Z(s_2), \ldots, Z(s_n)\}$. To keep notation simple and without confusion we will refer to the sampled values as $Z_i = Z(s_i), i = 1, 2, \ldots, n$. Regarding theoretical assumptions, in what follows we focus on second-order isotropic fields, where the following three conditions hold.

1. Invariance: $E[Z(s)] = \mu$ for all $s \in D$.

2. Stationarity: $\text{Cov}(Z_i, Z_j) := C(s_1, s_2) = C(s_1 - s_2)$ for all $s_1, s_2 \in D$. This means that meaning that the covariance function C depends on the spatial locations s_1, s_2 only through the spatial lag $s_1 - s_2$.

3. Isotropy: The covariance function C is a function of $||s_1 - s_2||$ alone, where $|| \cdot ||$ denotes the Euclidean distance.

The field of interest $Z(s)$ is represented as

$$Z(s) = \mu(s) + \varepsilon(s), \tag{1}$$

where $\mu(s)$ is the spatial mean function and the residual field $\varepsilon(s)$ is assumed to be zero-mean and isotropic. Then, for any point $s_0 \in D$, the Best Linear Unbiased Predictor (BLUP) of $Z(s_0)$ is determined as $Z^*(s_0) = \sum_{i=1}^{n} \lambda_i Z_i$ with $\sum_{i=1}^{n} \lambda_i = 1$. The weights λ_i are completely specified by the covariance function C. In matrix notation, if we write the covariance matrix $C_{ij} := C(s_i, s_j)$ with the vector $c_0 := C(s_i, s_0)$ and the vector of weights Λ, it can be shown that $\Lambda = C^{-1} c_0$ and the prediction variance is $\sigma^2(s_0) = C(0)\lambda(s_0)c_0$. This procedure is known as ordinary kriging. For computational details we refer to Chapter 3 in Chilès and Delfiner (1999). As in classic modeling, the problem is then to estimate the spatial mean $\mu(s)$ and the isotropic covariance function of the residuals for further use in statistical inference. What is different in this geostatistical setting is that it is not clear in general which needs to be estimated first, the mean or the covariance. Depending on the problem of interest, there are valid arguments for both approaches. This is in fact a circular problem and depending on data predictions may vary significantly. For an elaborate discussion on this topic we refer to Zimmerman and Stein (2010). In our study we model the isotropic covariance first, then use an overall league batting average estimate and conditional simulation to produce heat maps of percentile estimates for batting ability.

4. A Geostatistical Model for Batting Ability

As indicated in the previous section, the spatial covariance plays a crucial role in geostatistical modeling. In order to estimate the covariance in batting ability between pairs of locations in and around the strike zone we split the central 24 inch by 24 inch area with most frequent pitches into a six by six grid and fit the exponential decay model in equation (2) below to the empirical covariance, assumed isotropic.

$$C(i, j) := C(\|s_i - s_j\|) = \phi e^{-\theta \|s_i - s_j\|}. \tag{2}$$

The best fit is showed in Figure 1 (left) with $\hat{\phi} = 0.00286$ and $\hat{\theta} = 1.38$. The value $\sqrt{\hat{\phi}} = 0.053$ indicates the standard deviation in batting average ability at each location in the strike zone, while $\frac{\log 2}{\theta}$ indicates the half life of batting ability which is approximately 0.5 feet here. We also show the league average batting ability across locations within a 40 inch by 40 inch two dimensional area as seen by the catcher. The two visuals in Figure 1 should be interpreted in the context of equation (1). The dotted line in the batting average map outlines the square area within which pitches are called strikes. It should be noted that this average map is not very informative. Our goal is to identify batters' spatial peculiarities and produce accurate heat maps indicating the specific hot and cold zones for individual batters. Moreover, while it is true that the kriging predictors $Z^*(s_0)$, $s_0 \in D$ used to create the heat maps are unbiased and have minimum variance (and thus best), they are obtained by using an estimated covariance since the true covariance is unknown. Thus we are only able to produce Estimated BLUPs rather than the true BLUPs and we need to account for the added uncertainty associated with $\hat{\phi}$ and $\hat{\theta}$. To overcome these shortcomings we further use conditional simulations for more accurate uncertainty assessment, see next subsection. The league average map in Figure 1 (right) is based on all end-of-the-at-bat fastballs to right-handed batters, specifically 543,760 pitches.

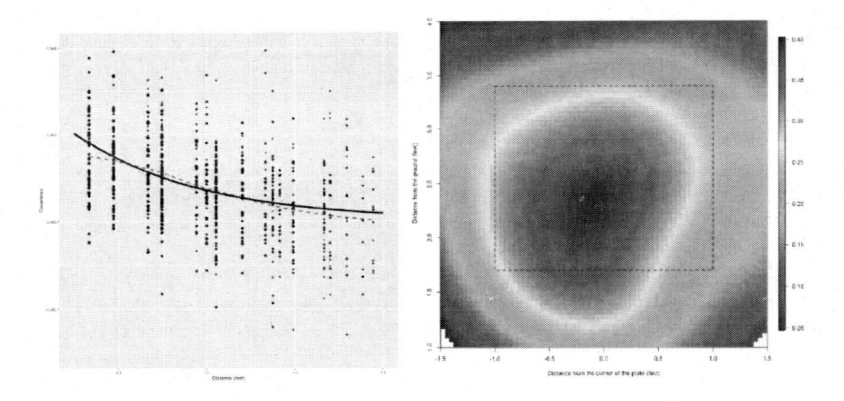

Figure 1. Covariance in batting average as a function of distance (left). The points are sized by the number of batters in each pair of zone. Solid line shows exponential best fit line; blue dashed line is based on locally weighted regression. League batting average by location for right-handed batters against fastballs (right).

4.1. Simulating Batter Outcomes

Since we do not know the true spatial batting ability of real batters we simulate idealized batters. The reasoning behind this conditional simulation technique is to view such an idealized batter as a realization of a multivariate normal distribution having the league batting average as mean and the exponential decay as covariance function. Thus each batter was given a batting ability at each location on a 20 by 20 grid covering the two dimensional 40 inch by 40 inch area in and around the strike zone. Then each idealized batter was used as a parameter to generate batter outcomes. In each simulation we use a number of pitches with the location of the pitches randomly sampled from the locations of the actual fastballs thrown within our predefined area. Each pitch result is simulated as a Bernoulli random variable with probability of a hit determined by the idealized batter's ability at the given location, see Figure 2 for an illustration. For the simulated seasons (for the imaginary batter with a known heat map), each season was 400 fastballs. A comprehensive discussion on kriging with estimated parameters is given in Stein (1999) Chapter 6. Cross and Sylvan (2015) discuss several algorithms that use spatial information to produce heat maps and show through extensive simulations that, while many were comparable, the method named "Kriging Residuals" performed best and also has solid theoretical justification. We use this method in next section to show applications to real data. In essence, the method places the hitter's observations within the context of the league average ability at every location and the spatial covariance structure previously estimated. For each player we compute their individual spatial residuals reflecting how much better or worse he performed at locations where he saw pitches than would be expected based on his overall success rate. Thus each batter's spatial residual is obtained as the difference between his observed results at each location and the adjusted league map (Figure 1 right). Finally, this map is added to the adjusted league map. The extensive Monte Carlo simulation study in Cross and Sylvan (2015) provides empirical proof about the improved accuracy of these heat maps.

4.2. Applications to Real Data

We used the methodology previously described to obtain heat maps of batting ability for several players. For illustration we show in Figure 3 heat maps for

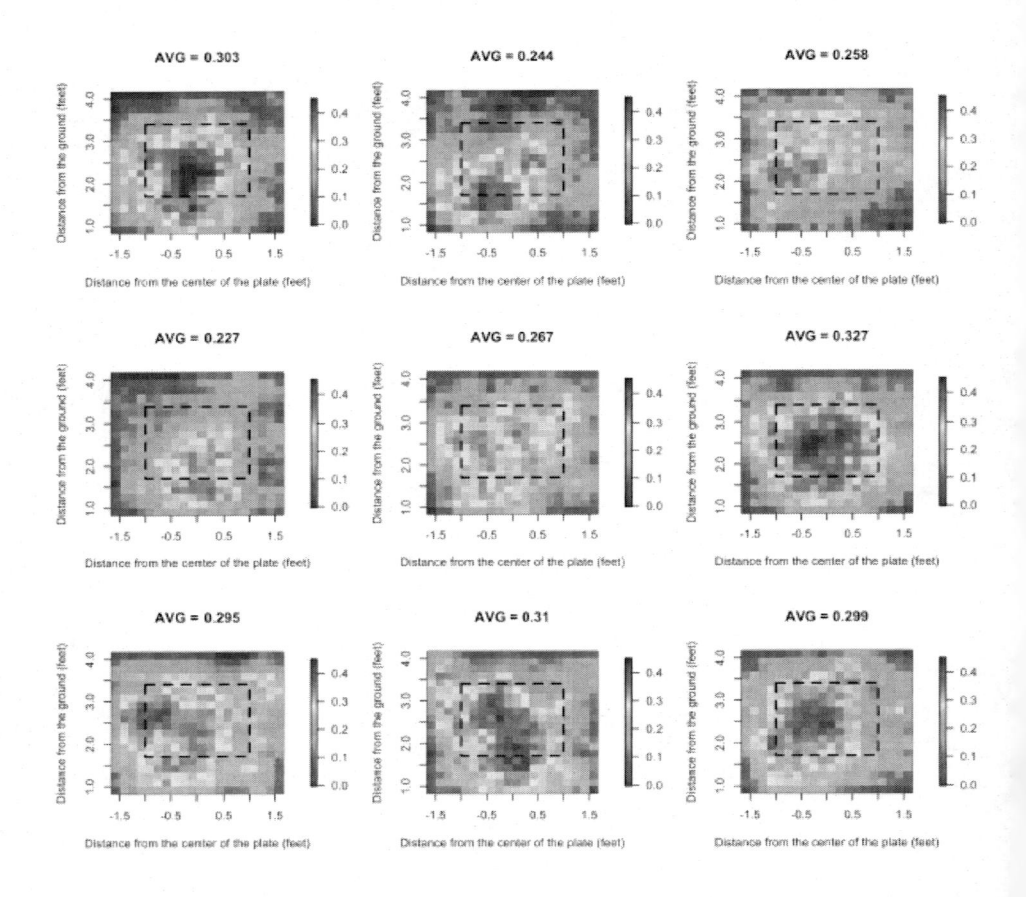

Figure 2. Nine realizations of a multivariate normal distribution with a mean determined by the league average and the fitted covariance (exponential decay model). The number **AVG** shown on top of each graph is the batter's overall batting ability given a typical distribution of pitches.

Mike Trout, Aaron Judge, Giancarlo Stanton, and Mookie Betts, respectively. Specifically, these figures show estimates of the 25th, 50th, 75th percentiles of players' actual ability in each location above or below his adjusted league map. The 50th percentile is centered at zero. They were based on 2259 pitches for

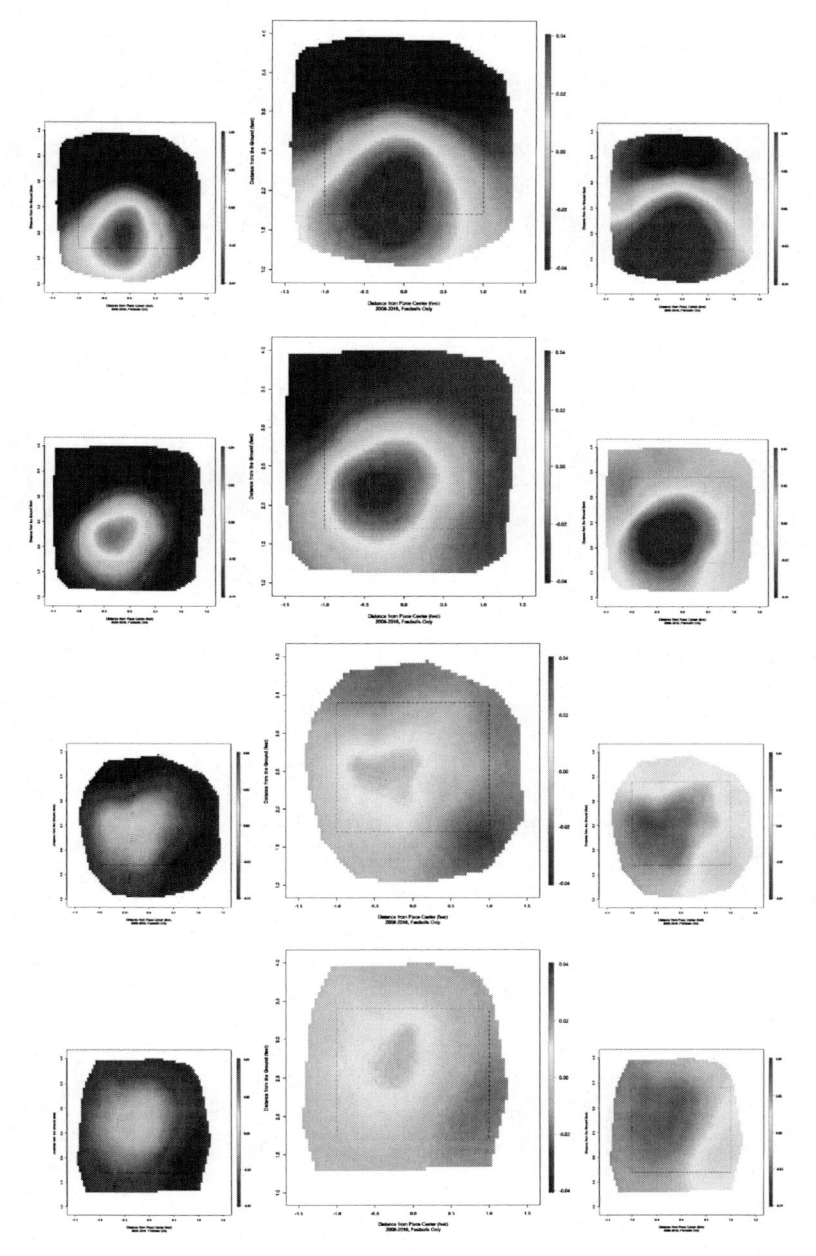

Figure 3. Heat maps for the spatial residuals based on fastballs only: 25th percentile estimates (left), 50th percentile estimates (middle), 75th percentile estimates (right) for the following players from top down: Mike Trout, Giancarlo Stanton, Mookie Betts, Aaron Judge.

Trout, 1941 pitches for Stanton, 1539 pitches for Betts and 560 for Judge, respectively. In Figure 3 you can see Trout's strength at the bottom of the strike zone and Stanton's excellence on pitches low and inside. We also see that that Betts' and Judges maps show predicted residuals closer to zero due to their shorter histories. We believe that these maps provide a more accurate and reliable rendering of the true batting ability of these players than traditional heat maps.

Discussion

Having a good understanding of a batter's strengths and weaknesses is a decisive factor in winning contests between pitchers and batters which are at the core of the game of baseball. For this reason quantifying correctly batting ability is of prime importance. The abundance of freely available baseball data, increased computing capabilities and fast data-driven algorithms make it possible to combine tools in classic geostatistics with simulation-based inferential techniques to improve estimation of the heat maps of batting ability. By displaying several percentile heat maps we can get a comprehensive view of the hot and cold zone for each batter. Cross and Sylvan (2015) make a case for "spatial boxplots" as visualization tools by displaying five maps corresponding to the 25th, 40th, 50th, 60th and 75th percentiles for each batter (a spatial analog to the five-number summary). In this report we are only showing the 25th and 75th percentile maps to accompany the median heat map. We believe that the maps in Figure 3 can be interpreted as confidence regions and that displaying more percentiles does not add significant new information or help interpreting the patterns carried in the middle maps. Computations were done in R using the package `fields`.

References

Baumer, B. and Draghicescu, D. (2010). Mapping batter ability in baseball using spatial statistics techniques. *JSM*, American Statistical Association, 3811–3822.

Chilès, J. and Delfiner, P. (1999). *Geostatistics. Modeling Spatial Uncertainty.* Hoboken, New Jersey: John Wiley & Sons, Inc

Cross, J. and Sylvan, D. (2015). Modeling spatial batting ability using a known covariance matrix. *Journal for Quantitative Analysis of Sports,* Volume 11 (3), 155–167. DOI 10.1515/jqas-2014-0089

Fast, M. (2010). What the heck is PITCHf/x? *The Hardball Times Baseball Annual 2010.*

Fast, M. (2011). Can we predict hot and cold zones for hitters? *Baseball Prospectus.*

Marchi, M., Albert, J. and Baumer, B. (2019). *Analyzing baseball data with R. Chapman & Hall.*

Stein, M.L. (1999). *Interpolation of spatial data: some theory of Kriging.* Springer.

Zimmerman, D. L. and Stein, M. L. (2010). Classical geostatistical methods. Chapter 3, *Handbook of spatial statistics*, edited by A. E. Gelfand, P.J. Diggle, M. Fuentes and P. Guttorp, 29–44. Chapman & Hall/CRC.

In: Essential Topics in Baseball
Editor: Erik Welch

ISBN: 978-1-53616-533-3
© 2019 Nova Science Publishers, Inc.

Chapter 6

EFFECT OF VISUAL OCCLUSION ON THE ACCURACY OF BATTING A STATIONARY BALL

Hiromu Katsumata*, Taketomo Hagiwara and Kento Nebashi

Department of Sports and Health Science,
Daito-Bunka University, Tokyo, Japan

ABSTRACT

Visual information on the trajectory of an oncoming pitch is critically important for a successful baseball hitting. However, the time available for batters to process this information and make a decision about swinging the bat is very limited, given the pitch's flight time of approximately 450 ms, as opposed to a batter's reaction time of 200 ms and bat-swinging movement time of 200 ms. Furthermore, the time available for the vision to be utilized is limited, given the time required for the visual feedback mechanism to work. Within this limited time window for baseball hitting, how long a batter can use the visual information, before the ball arrives to

---

* Corresponding Author's E-mail: hiromu@xd6.so-net.ne.jp.

the home plate, to predict the time and location of the pitch's arrival and prepare and produce a bat-swinging movement? To address this issue, we investigated the effect of occluding the vision of the batter during the bat-swinging movement on the accuracy of the ball–bat impact to obtain evidence regarding the utilization of visual information for accurate hitting. We examined hitting a stable ball mounted on a tee stand rather than hitting a flying ball to focus on the importance of vision in executing a batter's prepared or preplanned hitting movement for an impact location (predetermined by the tee position) by eliminating the necessity of processing visual information regarding the ball's flight to predict the time and location of the pitch's arrival and modulate the movement with respect to the flight of the pitch. For this purpose, 10 college baseball batters performed tee stand-batting with five different ball locations, which were set within the strike zone. They wore liquid crystal shutter goggles, and their vision was occluded approximately at the moment of different movement phases: initiation of stepping with a front foot toward the pitcher, the stepped foot touching the ground, initiation of the bat swing, and right before the moment of the ball–bat contact. Batting performance under these vision conditions was compared with that observed in the absence of visual occlusion. Movements of hitting motion and batted ball were recorded using an optical motion capture system at 250 Hz, and three-dimensional coordinates of the body landmarks and ball were calculated. The duration of the bat-swinging movement did not differ between the full-vision and occlusion conditions immediately prior to the ball–bat contact. However, when the vision was occluded at the step foot touchdown and swing initiation phases, the duration was significantly longer than that reported under the full-vision condition. The velocity of the bat movement did not differ between the full-vision and occlusion conditions. However, the velocity of the batted ball decreased when the full-visual occlusion was initiated at approximately 250 ms prior to the ball–bat impact. These velocity results indicate the reduced accuracy of the ball–bat contact due to the occluded vision. This finding suggests that the hitting movement is modulated for an accurate ball–bat contact on the basis of the visual information available until approximately 150 ms prior to impact.

Keywords: baseball, hitting, visuomotor control, vision for action

INTRODUCTION

Vision is critical for baseball hitting, such that a bat-swinging movement is organized on the basis of visual information regarding an oncoming pitch.

However, time constraint makes baseball hitting challenging, under which a batter must execute a hitting movement, as described below. For instance, a pitch flying at a velocity of 140 km/h arrives at the home plate, which is 18.44 m away from the pitcher's plate, in approximately 450 ms. The reaction time of the batter after he decides to swing a bat in response to the pitch requires approximately 200 ms [1, 2], and a bat-swinging movement requires another 200 ms [3-5]. Thus, the batter's time for utilizing visual processing to judge the flight of an oncoming pitch and organize an accurate and timely bat-swinging movement is limited. The available time is further reduced as the velocity of the pitch increases. In baseball games and exercises, "keep your eye on the ball" is a common phrase used by coaches and batters to ensure effective batting performance. However, the utilization of visual information to produce a bat-swinging movement with respect to an approaching ball has a limitation, given the visuomotor delay due to the time required for the visual-feedback control mechanism to function [6-9]. Therefore, batters organize and modulate the bat-swinging movement by relying on visual information, which is available until a certain moment of time before the ball arrives at the home plate or the ball–bat impact occurs. These facts lead to the following question. Until which moment of time before an oncoming pitch arrives at the home plate do batters need visual information for hitting the ball accurately? If sufficient time for obtaining visual information can be ensured, then the accuracy of the ball–bat impact will be increased; otherwise, the accuracy will be reduced. In this study, we address this question by examining the effect of occluding a batter's vision during a batting movement on the accuracy of the ball–bat impact.

For this purpose, we asked experienced college baseball batters to hit a stationary ball placed on a tee stand. During this process, we occluded their vision using liquid crystal shutter goggles at different time points of the batting movement and examined the effect of the visual occlusion on the accuracy of the ball–bat impact. It is expected that early visual occlusion would result in reduced accuracy of the ball–bat impact due to the limited time in utilizing the visual information and executing the batting movement. However, as the batting movement progresses to the ball–bat impact, batters will not be able to react to visual information due to the visuomotor delay inherent in producing a movement via visual processing. Therefore, even when the batter's vision is not occluded, the batting movement is executed without relying on the visual information at the last certain moment before the ball–bat impact. The accuracy of the impact is determined by this limitation. Thus, we attempted to identify the duration of the visual occlusion prior to the ball–bat impact, within which the magnitude of the impact accuracy is consistent with the impact accuracy without occlusion. This duration indicates the last moment, after which the batter will not be able to utilize the visual information in controlling the movement (i.e., the visuomotor delay in the batting movement).

A rationale for examining the batting movement for a stationary ball rather than an oncoming pitch is as follows. In tee stand-batting, the ball is placed at the batter's preferred location, so the batter can prepare his bat-swinging movement toward the impact location. If the batter can preprogram the bat-swinging movement and this programmed movement can be executed as planned, then visual information after the bat-swinging movement is initiated will not be necessary to accurately hit the ball. However, a movement may not be perfectly preprogrammed with respect to given movement conditions, and there is also noise inherent in producing human movements [10, 11]. Therefore, the correction of movement error and modulation of movement to improve the accuracy of performance are required. By examining the difference in the accuracy of movement (i.e., the accuracy of the ball–bat impact) depending on the availability of vision, we expect to obtain information regarding the last moment, until which batters can use visual information for the correction or modulation of the movement. From this viewpoint, this study may reveal the necessity of vision-based movement modulation to execute a preplanned bat-swinging movement toward an impact position. As opposed to that, the accuracy of the ball–bat impact in hitting an oncoming ball is influenced by visual processing regarding the kinematics of the pitch and spatial and temporal prediction regarding the upcoming impact (i.e., when and where the bat should meet the pitch). This study focuses on the role of vision in executing a bat-swinging movement by avoiding the aforementioned effect of visual processing of the oncoming pitch and spatial–temporal modulation of movement to react to the flight of the pitch. Data on the time window within which the vision will not play a role in executing a movement toward the moment of the ball–bat impact is important in exploring the batter's reaction and modulation of movement with respect to an approaching ball. Thus, we expect that the experimental paradigm used in this study may be extended to the investigation of the role of vision in hitting an oncoming pitch.

METHODS

Task Description and Conditions

The participants wore liquid crystal shutter goggles (TKK2275; Takei, Tokyo, Japan) and hit a ball placed on the tee stand (MIZUNO, Tokyo, Japan) in five different locations in the strike zone. The five locations were determined based on the width of the home plate (i.e., the inside edge, outside edge, and middle of the home plate) and the participant's body size (i.e., the height of batter's knee, underarm position, and midpoint of high and low pitches) following the strike zone defined by the rules of baseball (Figure 1). At the beginning of the batting trial, the liquid crystal shutter goggles were transparent; thus, the participants could see the ball. However, in some of the trials, the experimenter shut the goggles to be opaque after they initiated the batting movement. Therefore, they could no longer see the ball but continued to swing the bat toward the ball. The experimenter manually shut the goggles at one of the following movement phases, which were visually detected by the experimenter: 1) start of stepping (the initiation of the front foot striding movement to the pitcher); 2) step foot landing (the moment of the stride foot landing on the ground); 3) start of the bat swing (the initiation of the bat swing, which is determined by the start of the hand movement to swing the bat toward the ball); and 4) prior to impact (immediately before the ball–bat impact). A total of 20 trials for each of these occlusion conditions were included in the task performance. In addition, 20 trials were performed under the full-vision condition, in which the goggles were not shut during the execution of the movement. The order of the 100 trials (20 trials for each of the five vision conditions) was randomized, and the five locations of the ball were also randomized to prevent the participants from simply repeating the same movement to the same impact location, which could be executed without relying on vision.

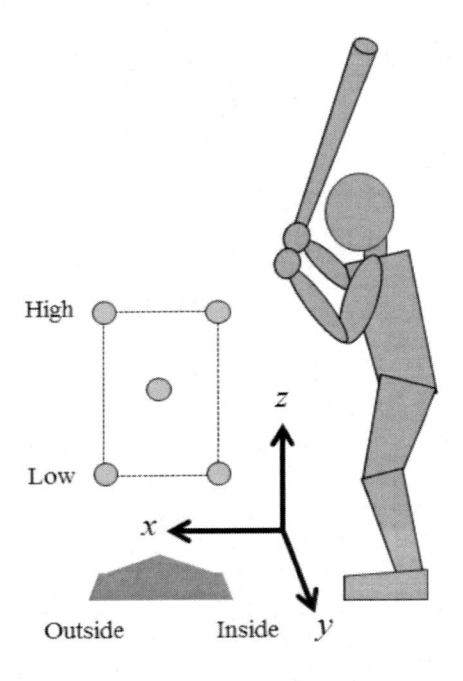

Figure 1. Definition of the global coordinate system and five ball locations determined according to the strike zone.

Experimental Setup

The participants used the bat (MIZUNO, Tokyo, Japan) with the same length (0.84 m) and weight (0.74 kg) and hit a ball, which was made of plastic for indoor batting practice (weight: 18 g; diameter: 7 cm). A net (height: 2 m; width: 2 m; MIZUNO, Tokyo, Japan) for batting practice was placed at approximately 1.5 m away from the participants' direction to the batting position (the pitcher's orientation). To prepare for the three different conditions of ball height (i.e., high, low, and middle), three tee stands with adjustable height were used. The participant's bat-swinging movement and the movement of the ball and bat were recorded by a motion capture system consisting of 14 high-speed cameras using optical marker-based technology (Vicon MX; Oxford Metrics, Oxfordshire, USA) at a sampling frequency of 250 Hz. The cameras were placed to record the entire bat and body movements. The switch to make the liquid crystal shutter goggles transparent or opaque was connected to the motion capture system, and the moment when the goggles became opaque was recorded. To capture the body movements, reflective markers were fixed on 19 anatomical landmarks of the body: the vertex (head), the right and left acromion (left and right shoulders) and iliac point (hip) to capture trunk movements, and the bone head of the fifth metatarsal (toe) to capture the address position and step movement. Reflective markers were also attached to the top and bottom of the bat, and the ball was covered with reflective tape.

Experimental Procedure

Prior to the experiment, the participants addressed with respect to the home plate placed on the floor as they address in a game, and the position of the rear foot toe was marked on the floor to make the address position consistent across the trials. With respect to this address position, the depth locations of the ball (the pitch–catcher direction) were determined for each of the five courses and height (inside-high, inside-low, middle, outside-high, and outside-low) by the location, in which each participant felt comfortable to hit the ball. For this procedure, the experimenter showed the ball, which was attached on the reference frame that shows the course and height of the ball location, and the participant indicated, using a bat, where he felt comfortable to hit the ball [12]. The depth locations for each of the five impact locations were recorded and used to place the tee stand in the experiment.

In the tee stand-batting trials, the experimenter placed the ball on the tee stand, and batters addressed with respect to the home plate's position based on the mark of the position of the rear foot toe on the floor. Following the experimenter's verbal cue to start the batting movement, the participant initiated the movement and hit the ball. In the visual occlusion trials, the experimenter switched the liquid crystal shutter goggles to make them opaque. The instruction to the participants for executing the task performance was to hit the ball as hard and accurately as possible in the orientation of the pitcher and center field with the bat-swinging movement and continue the swinging movement even after the vision was occluded. If necessary, each participant could take a short break between trials to avoid fatigue. The duration of the data collection process was approximately 60 minutes per participant.

Analysis

The three-dimensional positions of the reflective markers and the ball were defined in a global coordinate system via the motion capture system (refer to Figure 1 for the definition of the coordinate system). The position data were smoothed by a second-order low-pass filter with a cutoff frequency of 20 Hz. The velocity of marker movements was subsequently calculated using numerical differentiation.

We identified the following movement events.

Start of the bat swing: The moment when the top of the bat reached the most pitcher-side position during the rotation of the bat was defined as the start of the bat movement.

Ball–bat impact: The moment at which the ball–bat distance reached its minimum value during the approach of the bat to the ball was defined as the moment of the ball–bat impact. The ball–bat distance was calculated in accordance with the following equation.

$$ball - bat\ distance$$
$$= \sqrt{(x_{ball} - x_{bat})^2 + (y_{ball} - y_{bat})^2 + (z_{ball} - z_{bat})^2}$$

In the equation, x, y, and z are the components of the three-dimensional coordinates and the subscripts ball and bat refer to the markers of the ball and bat top, respectively.

On the basis of these movement events, the following variables were calculated for analysis.

Duration of the occlusion: The time from the moment the liquid crystal shutter goggles became opaque to the moment of the ball–bat impact was calculated. This calculation was used to confirm that the duration of visual occlusion differed depending on the timing of the experimenter switching off the shutter goggles following the visual detection of different movement phases in the batting movement.

Duration of the bat swing: The time from the start of the bat swing to the ball–bat impact was calculated.

Velocity of the bat immediately before the ball–bat impact: The y component (i.e., the direction of the ball to be hit) of the velocity of the bat top's marker immediately before the ball–bat impact was used as a measure indicating the force with which they could swing a bat to hit the ball to the net.

Velocity of the ball immediately after the ball–bat impact: The y component of the velocity of the ball movement immediately after the ball–bat impact was used as a measure indicating the results of the impact.

When the participants could hit the ball at the center of the percussion of the bat at the correct orientation of the bat with respect to the ball location (central collision), the velocity of the batted ball increases. By contrast, failure to hit the ball (eccentric collision) reduces the resultant ball velocity in the hitting orientation. If the occlusion of vision influences the accuracy of bat swinging toward the location of the ball, then a less successful ball–bat impact will be observed compared with the ball–bat impact reported under the full-vision condition.

Bat vertical angle of incidence (y-z plane): The angle of incidence of the bat on the sagittal plane was calculated by projecting a regression line obtained using the last three data points of the bat top's marker immediately prior to the ball–bat impact and calculating the angle between the vector and z axis (Figure 2A).

Ball vertical projection angle (y-z plane): The ball projection angle in the vertical direction was calculated by projecting a regression line obtained using the last 8–10 data points of the ball immediately after the ball–bat impact on the sagittal plane and calculating the angle between the vector and z axis (Figure 2A).

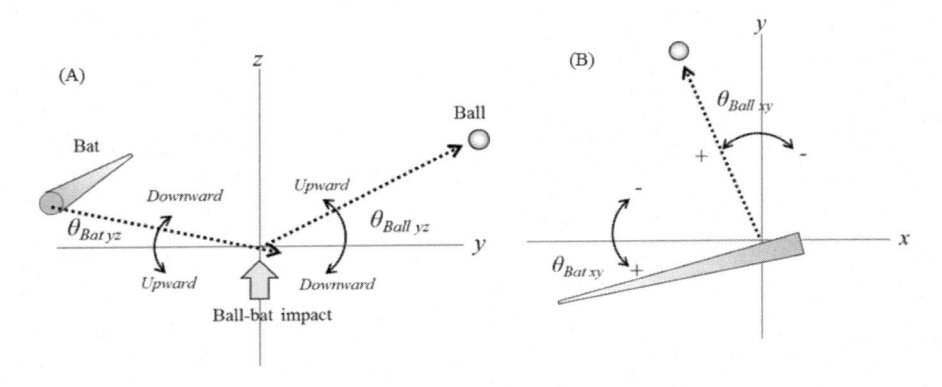

Figure 2. Definition of the ball and bat angles. (A) Bat incidence angle before the ball–bat impact and ball vertical projection angle after the impact. (B) Bat lateral orientation angle before the ball–bat impact and ball lateral projection angle after the impact.

Bat lateral orientation angle (x-y plane): The orientation angle of the bat on the horizontal plane was calculated by projecting a vector consisting of the bat top and bottom markers on the horizontal plane and calculating the angle between the vector and x axis (Figure 2B).

Ball lateral projection angle (x-y plane): The ball projection angle in the lateral direction was calculated by projecting a regression line obtained using the last 8–10 data points of the ball immediately after the ball–bat impact on the horizontal plane and calculating the angle between the vector and y axis (Figure 2B).

We conducted analysis of variance (ANOVA) with repeated-measures designs focused on the main effects of the five vision conditions (i.e., full vision, start of stepping, step foot landing, start of the bat swing, and prior to impact) to statistically compare the results. For the ANOVA, we conducted Mauchly's test of sphericity and subsequently adjusted the degrees of freedom by applying the Greenhouse–Geisser correction for violations of circularity. Any significant main effect was further evaluated through Sidak's multiple comparison tests. A $p < 0.05$ denotes statistical significance.

RESULTS

Duration of the Occlusion

Figure 3A shows the mean value of the duration of the occlusion, which indicates the time from the moment when the liquid crystal shutter goggles became opaque to the moment of the ball–bat impact. As shown in the figure, the duration appeared to be longer and shorter when the experimenter shut the goggles following the visual detection of the start of the batter's striding movement and the moment before the ball–bat impact. A repeated-measures ANOVA revealed a significant main effect of the vision condition ($F[3, 27] = 198.804$; $p < 0.001$). Subsequently, post-hoc multiple comparisons reveal the following results. The duration of occlusion at the start of stepping was significantly longer than that reported under any of the occlusion conditions (i.e., step foot landing, the start of the bat swing, and prior to impact; $p < 0.001$). The duration did not differ between the step foot landing and start of the bat swing ($p = 0.707$); however, these measurements were significantly longer than those observed prior to impact ($p < 0.001$). Therefore, the duration of occlusion prior to impact was significantly shorter than that recorded for any of the other occlusion conditions. In a post-hoc analysis, the time difference between the step foot landing and start of the bat swing was calculated by identifying the moment of the step foot landing using the marker of movement of the left foot toe. The mean and standard deviation of the time difference was -22 ± 78 ms. A negative value indicates that the start of the bat swing occurred earlier than the step foot landing. This result means that the timing of the step foot landing and start of the bat swing occurred at almost the same time. Accordingly, the timing of shutting the goggles for these occlusion conditions was not distinct. Considering this result, we regarded the duration of visual occlusion to be differentiated for investigating the effect of differences in the duration of the occlusion on the accuracy of the ball–bat impact.

Duration of the Bat Swing

Figure 3B shows the duration of the bat swing (i.e., the time from the start of the bat swing to the ball–bat impact). The mean of the duration across all vision conditions and participants was 275 ± 18 ms. A representative bat trajectory from 250 ms prior to impact to the moment of the impact is shown in Figure 4 to visually capture the timing of the start of the bat swing and vision occlusion. In the figure, the stick picture of 250 and 150 ms prior to impact was highlighted using a bolded stick. This is approximately the timing of occlusion in the vision occlusion condition at the start of the bat swing or the step foot landing and the occlusion prior to impact. Visual occlusion at the start of stepping, step foot landing, and start of the bat swing appeared to exert an effect on the duration of the bat swing.

A repeated-measures ANOVA revealed a significant main effect of the occlusion ($F[4, 36] = 6.923$; $p < 0.001$), and post-hoc multiple comparisons reveal the following results. The duration of the bat swing in the full-vision condition was significantly shorter than that reported at the start of stepping ($p < 0.005$), step foot landing ($p < 0.01$), and start of the bat swing ($p < 0.05$). By contrast, the duration of the swing did not differ between the full-vision and occlusion conditions prior to impact ($p = 0.781$). The duration of the bat swing under the occlusion condition prior to impact was significantly shorter than that reported at the start of stepping ($p < 0.05$) and step foot landing ($p < 0.01$). The duration of the bat swing did not differ between the start of stepping and step foot landing ($p = 0.724$). Therefore, following vision occlusion, the duration of the bat swing was affected by the time of the start of the bat swing. However, after the start of the bat swing (159 ms prior to impact on average), the effect of visual occlusion was not observed.

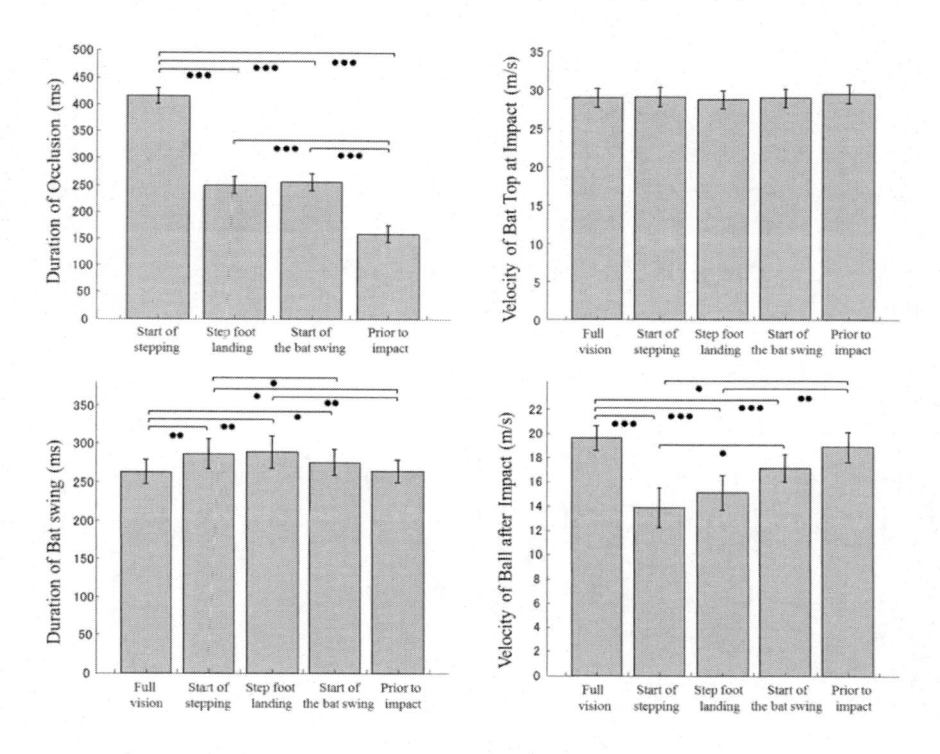

Figure 3. Mean values of the parameters for each vision condition. (A) Duration of occlusion, (B) duration of the bat swing, (C) velocity of the bat top before the ball–bat impact, (D) velocity of the ball after the impact. Each bar graph indicates the mean value obtained for each vision condition. Error bars refer to the standard error of the mean. Significant difference detected by the post-hoc multiple comparisons was superposed (● $p < 0.05$, ●● $p < 0.01$, ●●● $p < 0.001$).

Velocity of the Bat Immediately Before the Ball–Bat Impact

Figure 3C shows the velocity of the bat immediately prior to the ball–bat impact, which did not appear to be associated with the vision condition. Furthermore, a repeated-measures ANOVA did not reveal a significant effect ($F[4, 36] = 1.776$; $p = 0.155$). We used the measured bat velocity to examine the force with which the batters could swing a bat to hit the ball; however, the force was not affected by the visual occlusion.

Velocity of the Ball Immediately After the Ball–Bat Impact

Figure 3D shows the velocity of the ball immediately after the ball–bat impact. As shown in the figure, the velocity of the ball was associated with the visual occlusion. Early occlusion (i.e., at the start of stepping) was linked to a great decrease in the velocity of the ball. The repeated-measures ANOVA revealed a significant effect of the occlusion ($F[4, 36] = 16.759$; $p < 0.001$). Post-hoc multiple comparisons revealed the following results,

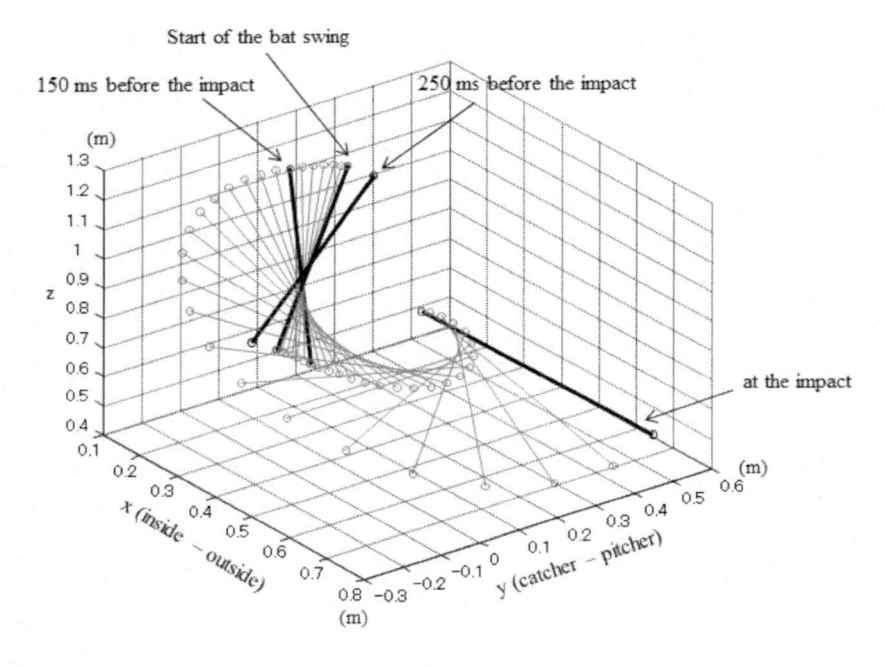

Figure 4. Stick images of representative bat trajectories were superposed from the start of the bat swing to the ball–bat impact. A stick image of the bat at the start of the bat swing, 250 ms before the impact, which occurred before the start of the bat swing, 150 ms before the impact, and the ball–bat impact was highlighted by the bolded stick. The timing of initiation of the visual occlusion was approximately 250 and 150 ms before the impact. This corresponded to the occlusion condition of the step foot landing or the start of the bat swing and the occlusion before the impact (Figure 3A). The start of the bat movement was defined as the moment when the top of the bat reached the most pitcher-side position during the rotation of the bat.

which support the aforementioned feature. The velocity of the ball under the full-vision condition was significantly greater than that measured at the start of stepping ($p < 0.005$), step foot landing ($p < 0.005$), and start of the bat swing ($p < 0.005$). By contrast, the velocity of the ball under the occlusion condition before the impact did not differ from that measured under the full-vision condition ($p = 0.184$). By contrast, it was significantly greater than that measured at the start of stepping ($p < 0.005$) and step foot landing ($p < 0.01$). In addition, the velocity of the ball under the occlusion condition at the start of the bat swing was significantly greater than that recorded at the start of stepping ($p < 0.005$) and step foot landing($p < 0.005$). Therefore, the velocity of the ball was associated with the timing of the visual occlusion. That is, the timing of the visual occlusion, which was earlier than the timing before the impact, affected the velocity of the ball. Early occlusion was associated with decreased ball velocity. However, this effect was not observed under the occlusion condition before the impact.

Bat Vertical Angle of Incidence

In Figure 5A, the bat vertical angle of incidence before the moment of the ball–bat impact was superposed. The angle of incidence ($90°$) indicates that the bat top's trajectory toward the positin of the ball was horizontal. Values larger or smaller than $90°$ indicate the bat top moved downward or upward toward the ball, respectively (Figure 2A). Therefore, the angle of incidence under the full-vision condition indicates the downward movement of the bat (mean: $93.3 \pm 5.9°$), whereas the bat top under the visual occlusion condition at the step foot landing moved upward (mean: $88.3 \pm 5.9°$). Regarding the other vision conditions, the mean value of the angle was $89.8 \pm 6.1°$ at the start of stepping, $90.0 \pm 5.4°$ at the start of the bat swing, and $93.1 \pm 5.9°$ under occlusion prior to impact. A repeated-measures ANOVA revealed a significant main effect of the vision condition ($F[4, 36] = 33.462$; $p < 0.001$). Post-hoc multiple comparisons confirmed this tendency. The angle of incidence under the full-vision condition was significantly larger than that measured at the start of stepping ($p < 0.005$), step foot landing (p

< 0.001), and start of the bat swing (p < 0.01). The angle under occlusion prior to impact was significantly larger than that recorded at the start of stepping (p < 0.005), step foot landing (p < 0.001), and start of the bat swing (p < 0.01); however, it did not differ from that observed under the full-vision condition (p = 1.000). Therefore, the downward bat movement toward the ball under the full-vision condition shifted to the upward movement due to the visual occlusion.

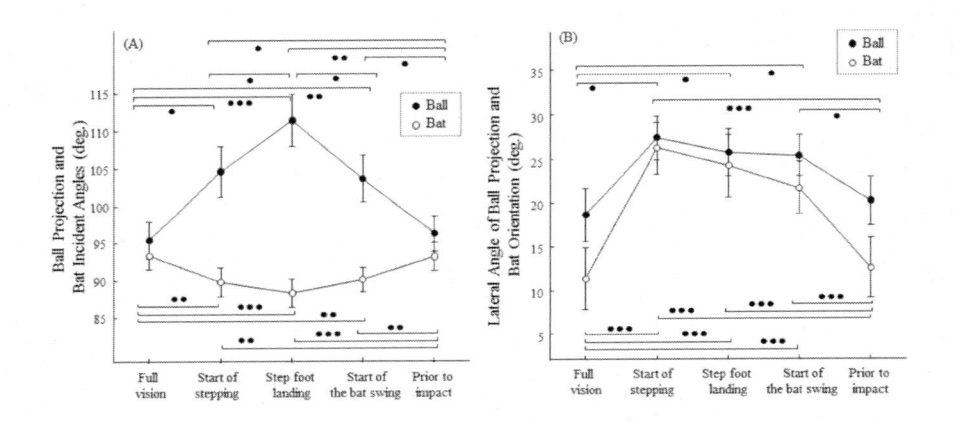

Figure 5. Mean values of the bat and ball angles for each vision condition. (A) Bat incident angle before the ball–bat impact and ball vertical projection angle after the impact. (B) Bat lateral orientation angle before the ball–bat impact and ball lateral projection angle after the impact. Error bars refer to the standard error of the mean. Significant difference detected by the post-hoc multiple comparisons was superposed (● p < 0.05, ●● p < 0.01, ●●● p < 0.001).

Ball Vertical Projection Angle

In Figure 5A, the ball projection angle after the ball–bat impact was superposed. Values larger or smaller than 90° indicate that, following the impact, the ball was projected in the air upward and downward, respectively. The figure shows that the movement of the ball was further upward due to the visual occlusion, and this feature was most prominent in the occlusion at the step foot landing. A repeated-measures ANOVA revealed a significant effect of the vision condition (F[4, 36] = 21.073; p < 0.001). Post-hoc multiple comparisons revealed the following results. The angle under the occlusion condition at the start of stepping, step foot landing, and start of the bat swing was significantly upward compared with that measured under the full-vision condition ($p < 0.05$) and under occlusion prior to impact ($p < 0.05$). No significant difference was observed between the full-vision and occlusion conditions prior to impact ($p = 1.000$). Regarding the comparison between the start of stepping, step foot landing, and start of the bat swing, the angle at the step foot landing was significantly larger than that measured under the other two conditions ($p < 0.05$) (Figure 5A). These results indicate that the visual occlusion affected the projection angle of the ball to be further upward, except for the occlusion prior to impact.

Bat Lateral Orientation Angle

In Figure 5B, the bat lateral orientation angle before the ball–bat impact was superposed. As shown in Figure 2B, the angle $0°$ means that the orientation of the bat was a right angle with respect to the pitcher–catcher line. Moreover, the positive or negative values indicate that the orientation of the bat faced to the left or right field, respectively. A repeated-measures ANOVA revealed a significant effect of the vision condition ($F[4, 36] = 53.547$; $p < 0.001$). Post-hoc multiple comparisons revealed the following results. The lateral orientation angle under the full-vision condition was significantly smaller than that measured at the start of stepping ($p < 0.001$), step foot landing ($p < 0.001$), and start of the bat swing ($p < 0.05$). This was also the case for the visual occlusion condition prior to impact, with the angle being significantly smaller than that recorded under occlusion at the start of stepping ($p < 0.001$), step foot landing ($p < 0.001$), and start of the bat swing ($p < 0.05$). A significant difference was observed between the full-vision and occlusion conditions prior to impact conditions ($p = 0.986$). These results indicate that visual occlusion affected the lateral orientation angle of the bat immediately before the ball–bat impact in the direction of the left field. However, this effect was not observed under the occlusion prior to impact condition.

Ball Lateral Projection Angle

In Figure 5B, the ball lateral projection angle after the ball–bat impact was superposed. The positive or negative values indicate that the movement of the ball was inclined to the left or right field, respectively. A repeated-measures ANOVA revealed a significant effect of the visual occlusion ($F[4, 36] = 10.374$; $p < 0.001$). Post-hoc multiple comparisons revealed that the lateral projection angle under the full-vision condition was significantly smaller than that measured under occlusion at the start of stepping, step foot landing, and start of the bat swing ($p < 0.05$). Regarding occlusion prior to impact, the angle was significantly smaller than that measured at the start of stepping ($p < 0.001$) and start of the bat swing ($p < 0.05$). Such a significant difference was not observed under the full-vision condition ($p = 0.994$). These results indicate that the visual occlusion further shifted the lateral projection angle of the ball toward the direction of the left field. However, such an effect was not observed under the occlusion prior to impact condition.

DISCUSSION

Visual occlusion affected the duration of the bat swing, velocity of the ball after the impact, and angles of ball projection and bat movement when the shutter goggles became opaque by proximately 250 ms prior to the ball–bat impact (refer to "step foot landing" and "start of the bat swing" in Figure 3A). However, these effects were not observed and the parameter values were consistent with those reported under the full-vision condition when the vision was occluded after the start of the bat swing, which was approximately 150 ms prior to impact (refer to "before impact" in Figure 3A). These results demonstrate that, after the initiation of the bat rotational movement toward the ball (refer to "start of the bat swing" in Figure 4), the batting movement required visual information until approximately 150 ms prior to the ball–bat impact. However, the movement was completed at the moment of the impact without use of visual information.

In this study, the experimenter applied visual occlusion by switching off the shutter goggles based on his visual detection of the batting motion phase. Although the timing of the occlusion at the different motion phases was consistent throughout the trials and reliable for the comparison analysis, a limitation of this occlusion method did not allow us to examine in further detail the approximately 100 ms time window between the start of the bat swing and occlusion prior to impact (Figure 3A). By examining this time window, the critical time point beyond which the visual occlusion cannot be used for executing the movement may be investigated. Nevertheless, the findings of this study contribute important information to understanding the visuomotor process for producing and controlling the bat-swinging movement. The study demonstrated that the visuomotor mechanism requires visual information for the accurate ball–bat impact even at around the moment of the initiation of the bat swing. This finding suggests that the bat-swinging movement is not executed in a way that programing the whole–body movement with respect to the given ball position is completed before initiating the bat rotation and the movement is produced according to the program. Instead, even after the bat swing is initiated, the vision-based modulation of movement occurs at least until approximately 150 ms prior to impact. In other words, the visuomotor mechanism will not be able to utilize or react to visual information approximately 150 ms before the impact onward, which is in line with the visuomotor delay reported in previous studies [6-9, 13].

The duration of the bat-swinging movement was longer when the vision was occluded by the time of approximately 250 ms before the impact (refer to "step foot landing" and "start of the bat swing" in Figure 3A). Due to the visual occlusion, visual information required to organize the bat movement with respect to the ball position was deprived. Thus, the visuomotor mechanism appeared not to function in a similar manner to that observed under the full-vision condition. According to a study investigating the effect of visual occlusion at the moment of movement initiation on the accuracy of reaching to an object on a table and grasping it, the duration of the movement time was increased due to the occlusion [14]. The investigators of the study advocated that the movement was executed by a control mechanism based on memory regarding the position of the target. Applying this finding to the present study, the batter may have swung a bat with respect to the memory of the ball position by switching to a control mechanism, which is different from the vision-based control. The prolonged duration of the bat swing due to the visual occlusion may be attributed to the reduced velocity of the movement by groping in the air to overcome the blindfolded situation. However, the velocity of the bat prior to impact under the visual occlusion condition was consistent with that recorded under the full-vision condition. Therefore, even when the vision was occluded, the batters could swing the bat to hit a ball as hard as possible as they did under the full-vision condition.

While the velocity of the bat before the impact was consistent under the full-vision and visual occlusion conditions (Figure 3C), the velocity of the ball after the impact decreased due to the occlusion. Furthermore, this tendency was more prominent at the earlier timing of the occlusion (Figure 3D). As the velocity of the bat before the impact was consistent regardless of the vision condition, the velocity of the ball after the impact should be consistent if the bat could meet the ball as effectively as under the full-vision condition. Therefore, the decrease in the velocity of the ball under visual occlusion was due to the failure to accurately hit the ball on the center of the percussion. This result supports a contention that the vision-based modulation of the bat movement operated during the batting action even after the bat rotation was initiated up until approximately 150 ms prior to impact. After this moment, modulation of the bat movement by the vision will not be possible, given the visuomotor delay (i.e., the minimum time required to modulate an ongoing movement in response to visual information) of approximately 100 ms [6-9]. The reduction in the velocity of the ball was prominent under the visual occlusion at the start of stepping and the step foot landing (Figure 3D). An explanation for this effect is that the memory of the ball position obtained through these motion phases did not correspond to the actual ball position relative to the body by the shift or sway of the body position induced during the stepping action. In other words, the visual detection of the ball position relative to the body is important for organizing the swinging movement relative to the ball position. This finding suggests that the coordination of the bat-swinging movement is unfolding by continuously attuning to the information regarding the position of the ball [15-17].

As shown in Figure 5, the incidence of the bat angle toward the moment of the ball–bat impact was affected by the visual occlusion, such that the angle changed from the downward to the upward direction due to the vision. This effect was prominent in the occlusion at the step foot landing (Figure 5A). This effect was accompanied by the ball vertical projection angle, in which the change in the upward projection angle increased relative to the change in the bat incidence angle. This finding indicates the less successful ball–bat impact due to the eccentric collision, which is ineffective to produce the ball velocity after the impact (Figure 3D). During the bat-swinging movement, the gravitational force is applied to the bat and, thereby, the downward torque around the wrist of the batter occurs, resulting in the bat top to move downward. Batters modulate the trajectory of the bat top to move toward the position of the ball by counteracting against this gravitational effect. Visual information regarding the position of the ball plays a role in such modulation. Therefore, insufficient modulation due to the loss of visual information induced by the occlusion resulted in improper impact. Regarding the association between the bat lateral orientation angle and ball lateral projection angle, following the occlusion of vision, the ball–bat impact occurred by the bat angle oriented more toward the left field compared with that observed under the full-vision condition. This resulted in a shift of the ball projection angle to the corresponding direction in the left field. Given the bat rotational trajectory as shown in Figure 4, when the timing of the ball–bat impact was relatively late, the bat angle at the impact is oriented more toward the left field. Therefore, in the memory-based execution of the bat swing under visual occlusion, the timing of the ball–bat impact was delayed probably due to the inconsistency between the actual and memorized positions of the ball. If the effect of the visual occlusion simply increased the variability of the bat-swinging movement, then the error in the ball–bat impact is expected to be bidirectional (i.e., impacting the ball upward and downward or to the left and right fields). However, the results of the ball projection angle showed a consistent tendency, that is, more upward and to the left field. We also examined the standard deviation of these angle measurements based on the expectation that a larger error in the impact will induce larger variability. Nevertheless, the results did not show a significant difference between the full-vision and visual occlusion conditions. These results suggest that the deprivation of vision did not result in the loss of control. However, the movement was organized toward the moment of the impact.

The present study addressed the question: until what moment of time before a pitch arriving at the home plate, do batters use visual information for hitting the ball accurately? We found that batter can modulate the bat swing movement until approximately 150 ms before the ball–bat impact, after which the vision-based control cannot be operated. What is the importance of the 150 ms time window to baseball batting performance? According to the bat trajectory shown in Figure 4, the movement of the bat at 150 ms prior to impact was not accelerated sufficiently. The modulation of vision-based movement will not come into play to bring the bat to the position of the ball after this moment. Therefore, the swinging of the bat toward the ball should be prepared at this moment. In baseball games, we observed batters modulating their movement in response to flights of pitch approaching to different locations in the strike zone or to different kinds of pitches (e.g., breaking ball and change of pace) delivered by a pitcher aiming to upset the timing of the bat-swinging. The results of this study suggest that these reactive modulations are induced based on visual information, which is available by approximately 150 ms prior to the ball arriving at the home plate. In a previous study that investigated the response of batters to high- and low-velocity pitches [18], the timing of bat swing initiation was modulated depending on the velocity of the pitch by controlling the timing of thrust on the ground by a step foot at the motion phase of landing a step foot on the ground. Based on the aforementioned evidence, the time window from the step foot landing to the moment 150 ms prior to the ball–bat impact is an important motion phase that may determine the success or failure of the impact.

CONCLUSION

The role of vision in baseball batting performance was investigated by examining the effect of visual occlusion during batting of a stationary ball placed on a tee stand. The visual occlusion at the stepping movement phase and the start of the bat swing induced the deterioration of the ball–bat impact, as revealed by the decrease in the velocity of the batted ball and off-center collision. However, under the occlusion condition after the initiation of the bat swing (approximately 150 ms before the ball–bat impact), the accuracy of the impact was consistent with that observed under the full-vision condition. These results indicate that batters utilize visual information approximately 150 ms prior to the ball–bat impact. After this time window, the modulation of vision-based movement cannot come into play to enhance the accuracy of the impact. Therefore, the movement phase from landing the step foot to the initiation of the bat swing is essential in preparing the bat-swinging movement toward the position of the ball.

REFERENCES

[1]   Slater-Hammel, A. T. and R. L. Stumpner, Batting reaction-time. *Research Quarterly*, 1950. 21: p. 353-356.

[2]   Slater-Hammel, A. T. and R. L. Stumpner, Choice batting reaction-time. *Research Quarterly*, 1951. 22: p. 377-380.

[3]   Adair, R. K., The physics of baseball. *Physics Today*, 1995: p. 26–31.

[4]   Breen, J. L., What makes a good hitter? *Journal of Health, Physical Education, Recreation*, 1967. 38: p. 36–39.

[5]   Race, D. E., A cinematographic and mechanical analysis of the external movements involved in hitting a baseball effectively. *The Research Quarterly*, 1961. 32: p. 394–404.

[6]   Bootsma, R. J., & van Wieringen, P. C. W., Timing an attacking forehand drive in table tennis. *Journal of experimental psychology: Human Perception and Performance,* 1990. 16(1): p. 21-29.

[7] Brenner, E. and J. B. J. Smeets, Fast responses of the human hand to changes in target position. *Journal of Motor Behavior*, 1997. 29: p. 297-310.

[8] Carlton, L. G., Processing visual feedback information for movement control. Journal of Experimental Psychology: *Human Perception and Performance,* 1981. 7: p. 1019-1030.

[9] Savelsbergh, G. J. P., H. T. A. Whiting, and R. J. Bootsma, Grasping tau. *Journal of Experimental Psychology: Human Perception and Performance,* 1991. 17: p. 315-322.

[10] Schmidt, R., et al., Motor-output variability: a theory for the accuracy of rapid motor acts. *Psychological Review*, 1979. 47: p. 415–451.

[11] van Beers, R. J., P. Haggard, and D. M. Wolpert, 2004. *Journal of Neurophysiology,* 2004. The role of execution noise in movement variability (91): p. 1050 - 1063.

[12] Katsumata, H., et al., Coordination of hitting movement revealed in baseball tee-batting. *Journal of Sports Sciences*, 2017. 35(24): p. 2468-2480.

[13] Lee, D. N., et al., Visual timing in hitting an accelerating ball. *Quarterly Journal of Experimental Psychology*, 1983. 35(A): p. 333-346.

[14] Singhal, A., et al., Dual-task interference is greater in delayed grasping than in visually guided grasping. *Journal of Vision*, 2007. 7(5): p. 1-12.

[15] Fitch, H. L. and M. T. Turvey, On the control of activity: Some remarks from an ecological point of view, in *Psychology of motor behavior and sport* D. M. Landers and R. W. Christina, Editors. 1978, Human Kinetics: Champaign, ILL. p. 3-35.

[16] Warren, H. W., The perception-action coupling, in Sensory-motor organizations and development in infancy and early childhood, H. Bloch and B. I. Bertenthal, Editors. 1990, Kluwer: The Netherlands. p. 23–37.

[17] Whiting, H. T. A., Action is not reaction! A reply to McLeod and Jenkins. *International Journal of Sport Psychology*, 1991. 22: p. 296-303.

[18] Katsumata, H., A functional modulation for timing a movement: A coordinative structure in baseball hitting. *Human Movement Science*, 2007. 26: p. 27–47.

BIOGRAPHICAL SKETCH

Hiromu Katsumata, PhD

Affiliation: Department of Sports and Health Science, Daito-Bunka University

Education: PhD from the Graduate school in the Department of Kinesiology at The Pennsylvania State University

Business Address: Department of Sports and Health Science, Daito-Bunka University, 560 Iwadono, Higashi-Matsuyama City, Saitama Prefecture, 355-8501

Research and Professional Experience:
Studying motor control and learning as a doctorate student in the Graduate school in the Department of Kinesiology at The Pennsylvania State University (1997 - 2002)
Teaching motor control and learning to graduate and under-graduate students as a full-time faculty of the Department of Sports and Health Science at Daito-Bunka University (2005 - in the present)

Professional Appointments:
Professor in the Department of Sports and Health Science at Daito-Bunka University,

Publications from the Last 3 Years:
Katsumata, H. (2019) Attenuation of Size Illusion Effect in Dual-Task Condition. *Human Movement Science*, On-line publication.

Katsumata, H., Sasaki, J., & Kawai, T. (2017) A Preliminary Study to Capture the Characteristics of Backswing Movement in Baseball Throwing. *Journal of Ergonomics*, 7:201.

Katsumata, H., Himi, K., Ino, T., Ogawa, K., & Matsumoto, T. (2017) Coordination of hitting movement revealed in baseball tee-batting. *Journal of Sports Sciences*, Jan 6:1-13.

In: Essential Topics in Baseball
Editor: Erik Welch

ISBN: 978-1-53616-533-3
© 2019 Nova Science Publishers, Inc.

Chapter 7

SPIT TOBACCO USE IN BASEBALL

Ted Eaves, EdD*

Department of Health and Exercise Science,
Wake Forest University, Winston-Salem, NC, US

ABSTRACT

There is a long history of tobacco use in baseball that goes back to the 19th century and the creation of the sport. Athletes and coaches initially used spit tobacco (ST) as a way to both keep their mouths moist during dusty games and to alter the baseball to improve grip and break. However, there are significant health risks associated with the use of ST, including: oral diseases; systemic illnesses, such as cardiovascular disease; and various forms of cancer. The use of ST during games by collegiate and professional athletes and coaches, who are role models for the younger generations of baseball players, legitimizes the practice and relationship that ST has developed with the sport and enforces behavior that is detrimental to the health of all. It is important for baseball players and coaches to understand their role in the modeling of proper behaviors for younger athletes to protect their health and permanently sever the connection between baseball and ST.

* Corresponding Author's E-mail: eaveseh@wfu.edu.

INTRODUCTION

The use of Smokeless (Spit) Tobacco (ST) and baseball have been closely connected since the advent of the sport in the 1840s [1]. Tobacco use began initially as a way to keep the athletes' mouths moist while playing on dusty fields and has evolved and maintained its relationship and association with the sport in many ways ever since. In fact, the original baseball cards were produced by tobacco companies and sold in cigarette packs while numerous players have been paid spokesmen for tobacco products [1]. ST usage rates among baseball players in the high school, college, and professional ranks range from 34-52% in spite of partial or full bans at all levels of play [2-4]. While coaches have been found to have lower usage rates than players – ranging from 13-32% in various studies, their use of ST was still significantly higher than the general population in the US, which is approximately 3% [4-5]. Use rates for players and coaches have remained relatively consistent since the 1980s and have shown no sign of a decrease. The high prevalence rates in baseball have often been associated with a ritualistic and superstitious behavior among the athletes, and the attitude that ST use is acceptable and even 'mandated' by the sport and its participants [6-7].

The significant level of usage by players-especially professional players who compete with large audiences in person and through televised games-and coaches acts as an implicit product endorsement for the youth players who see these individuals as role models [2]. Sports, and its participants, have enormous influence in our culture, and it is viewed as the optimal arena for athletes and coaches to make a positive difference in the lives of children and adolescents while acting as a moral example for others [8-11]. When these moral examples act as negative role models by publicly and overtly using ST, it legitimizes that use as acceptable and even an integral part of being a successful athlete [2]. Prominent ST users also diminish the perceived health risks associated with tobacco in the minds of young baseball players, because if an elite athlete is doing it, then it must not be dangerous and may even provide some positive ergogenic benefit or enhance their athletic ability. Once ST use has begun, adolescents often are less likely to be realistic about the health risks that they may face and be overly optimistic about their ability to quit if they decide that they no longer want to use ST [12].

When discussing tobacco products, it is important to understand the health risks associated with use, the history that built the connection between ST use and baseball, and the significance of the opportunity for positive role modeling that athletes and coaches may provide to children and adolescents. Utilizing the prominent role that sports and athletes play in society to teach healthy behaviors to young athletes will allow professional players and coaches to be active partners in the effort to eliminate ST use in adolescent baseball players and delegitimize the relationship between tobacco and baseball [13].

SPIT (SMOKELESS) TOBACCO

Smokeless, or spit, tobacco consists of two primary varieties-oral moist snuff and chewing tobacco. Oral moist snuff is a finely ground or shredded tobacco leaf that is commonly sold in a small round tin. Snuff users place a pinch of snuff or 'dip' between their lower lip and gum where it stays until it is removed [14-15]. While the tobacco is between the lower lip and gum, the users suck on the dip and spit out a tobacco juice and saliva mixture, which is why it is often referred to as spit tobacco [15]. Chewing tobacco, on the other hand, is a more coarsely cut tobacco and is packaged in loose or plug form in pouches. Chewing tobacco users place a 'chew' or wad of tobacco in their cheek and chew it in a manner similar to gum or sunflower seeds until it is removed. Chewing tobacco also creates a juice/saliva mixture that must be spit out or swallowed. The resultant spit mixture separates ST from other oral products like snus-small packets or sachets of finely cut tobacco-and dissolvable tobacco products, such as orbs, sticks, or strips that do not induce a liquid discharge during use. These products do not have a significant prevalence in sports at this time.

The use of ST became widely recognized as a major public health problem in the mid-1980s [16-17]. The awareness and acknowledgement of the dangers of use came as a result of several factors, including: increased understanding of the cancer risk associated with the product, the changing demographics of users, the increasing number of users, and a wide-scale advertising and marketing campaign initiated by the smokeless tobacco industry [16, 18]. By 1986, Congress had enacted a legislative ban on television and radio advertising of ST products, as well as requiring a warning label be placed prominently on these products similar to the warning labels included on cigarette packs [18].

Also in 1986, the US Surgeon General concluded that ST was addictive and that it shared many characteristics with drugs such as cocaine, heroin, and alcohol [16]. The report concluded that there was sufficient scientific evidence that the use of smokeless tobacco was carcinogenic-it could cause cancer in humans-and was not a safe alternative to smoking [18-20]. A follow-up report in 1993 by the Surgeon General advocated the use of the term spit tobacco instead of smokeless tobacco--a term that was created by the tobacco industry--to prevent the erroneous belief in users that 'smokeless meant harmless' [7, 14]. The report also found that nicotine in cigarettes and smokeless tobacco was itself a drug and should fall under the review and regulation of the Food and Drug Administration, although Congress did not require that tobacco products be regulated by the government agency until 2009 [21].

The enhanced awareness and publicity garnered by the ST industry in the mid-1980s was far different from that seen in the previous decade. The smokeless tobacco industry was essentially near extinction in the 1970s, as the primary users of the product--adults aged 65 and older--were not being replaced with new users [16]. In 1970, adult males aged 65 and over had the highest prevalence of use (12.7%) and chewing tobacco was the primary form of ST. Since 1970, ST has gone from a product used mostly by older men to one that is predominantly used by young men and boys [22]. This trend occurred as a result of new product development (mainly the moist snuff products) and aggressive marketing campaigns geared toward this younger demographic [16, 22-23].

Currently, men aged 18-24 are more likely to use ST than older men (8.4% to 5.6%) with an even higher prevalence rate seen in high school boys

(9.2%) [15-16, 18, 22]. Of the 12-14 million ST users in the United States, one third are younger than 21 with more than half of them initiating their habit before the age of 13 [24]. In fact, the only demographic group nationwide that has shown a significant increase in prevalence of use since 2002 is males aged 12 to 17, who have increased their level of use from 3.4 to 4.4% [25]. This early initiation age and high level of prevalence is concerning because of the risk for sustained exposure and use throughout the lifetime of the ST user, and the increased risk for significant disease that is most often associated with prolonged use [26].

Adolescent ST users have helped to make moist snuff the only tobacco product in the United States with an increase in sales for almost every year since the early 1970s. ST sales have increased from 17.2 million pounds in 1972 to approximately 150 million pounds in 2017 [15, 16, 27-30]. For adolescents in the United States, ST use is seen most often in older teens, boys, Caucasians, Native Americans/Alaska Natives, and rural residents of the south, midwest, and west [17].

Despite recent reports of potential declines in use, ST remains a serious concern as tobacco companies promote new products, including flavored products and spit-less options such as pre-packaged sachets of powdery tobacco-commonly referred to as 'snus', which is the Swedish term for ST-and dissolvables [31]. These products are considered a viable alternative to cigarettes for smokers who are inconvenienced by increasingly restrictive bans on smoking in workplaces and public institutions such as restaurants and bars [19, 31]. While traditional ST, which generates excess saliva and requires either spitting or swallowing the generated mixture of saliva and tobacco juice, is not generally considered an appealing alternative by smokers, these new products, which produce less of the spit mixture are gaining popularity throughout the US [31].

In conjunction with the development of these new products, tobacco companies are emphasizing all types of ST as a healthy tobacco option for users. It is generally considered to be less dangerous and deadly than cigarettes and cigars because ST has considerably lower concentrations of the toxic substances and carcinogens that smoking creates from the combustion and smoke inhalation found with that habit [32]. The decreased levels of carcinogens (cancer-causing agents) in ST--as opposed to smoking--lead to lower risks for mortality and morbidity with use, which has led many tobacco companies, public health organizations, and other groups to recommend ST products as harm reduction or reduced exposure products that can be an alternative for smokers who are unable or unwilling to quit using tobacco [20, 32]. However, while ST may have fewer cancer-causing agents than cigarettes, it is far from a 'safe' alternative to smoking because there are still 28 identified carcinogens found in the product, including tobacco-specific *N*-nitrosamines, *N*-nitrosamino acids, and aldehydes. Many of these carcinogens are generated during the post-harvest processing of the tobacco and lead to the numerous health and mortality risks that are associated with ST use [19, 33-34].

The other concern with considering ST products as a reduced exposure or less risky product is the current limited regulation of the ST products that are produced and sold in the United States. Because of inconsistent regulation, there is nothing to prevent a tobacco company from altering the content of an ST product in ways that would make it more toxic, including altering the level of nitrosamines, pH, and moisture content, which all may affect the level of nicotine that is available to the user and the level of carcinogens in the product [19, 31]. The altering of tobacco products to make them more addictive to users has been confirmed as one of many techniques that tobacco companies have used both currently and in the past to keep users addicted and ensure a steady or increasing client base and profit margin.

HEALTH EFFECTS OF ST

Drawing conclusions about the health effects of ST use is complicated because of the wide range of products that fall into this category and by the variety of compounds, which may be mixed with the tobacco during production-some of which are harmful by themselves [33, 35]. However, studies have consistently found negative oral health effects, such as oral cancer, as well as harmful systemic health effects associated with continued use of ST, such as cardiovascular disease, sexual impotence, female reproductive issues, and several forms of cancer [34, 36-40].

Health effects associated with the mouth, such as oral leukoplakia-a premalignant lesion found in the inner lip, tooth stains, plaque, gingivitis, periodontitis, and tooth decay/loss are the most common effects found with ST use. These diseases are seen predominantly in users of moist snuff and associated with the amount of tobacco use, recency of use, and the consistency of the habit. Each of these oral health effects is progressively more damaging as a result of continued tobacco use [34, 36-40].

The most serious oral health effect that is correlated with ST use though is oral cancer. Oral cancer is a dangerous disease with a 54% mortality rate five years after diagnosis [20, 33]. Numerous research studies have found that there is a substantial risk for oral cancer associated with all types of ST use [20, 33-34]. In fact, 90% of all cases of oral cancer diagnosed worldwide are estimated to be caused by tobacco use [26]. The risk for developing oral cancer with ST use has been found to be 2 to 14 times more likely than the risk for non-users [33-34]. Oral cancer may be caused by any of the 28 known carcinogens found in spit tobacco. The most dangerous carcinogen found in ST is tobacco-specific nitrosamines because of the abundance of the substance that is present in ST products and the strong likelihood that cancerous tumors will develop with exposure to the nitrosamines [31]. Tobacco companies can limit the formation of nitrosamines during the tobacco-processing phase, and some-though not most-of the companies have even decreased nitrosamine levels significantly in their products. However, even the lower amounts of nitrosamines found in ST products are still 100 to 1,000 times higher than nitrosamine levels found in other products, such as food or beer [31, 41].

There are other types of cancer also found in ST users-including esophageal, pharyngeal, laryngeal, stomach, and pancreatic cancer [20, 31, 33-34, 36]. Studies have found that there is a fivefold increase in the risk of developing esophageal cancer in ST users as compared to non-users [34]. There was also an excess risk for pancreatic and stomach cancer in ST users. This association occurred even when the researchers controlled for smoking and alcohol consumption, habits that have also been associated with stomach and pancreatic cancer [14, 26, 31, 34]. While oral cancer is associated with the location of the dip in the mouth of an ST user, the other types of cancer are more closely associated with the juice that is generated while using the tobacco products, especially with ST users who either intentionally or unintentionally swallow the juice [42]. The higher risk seen in those users is believed to be because individuals who ingest the juice are primarily the most addicted to the product and swallow the tobacco juice for the increased nicotine buzz that occurs as a result.

The final, and arguably the most dangerous, health effect that is associated with ST use is nicotine addiction [16, 33, 40]. Nicotine is a highly addictive natural stimulant that is found in tobacco and causes a physical and psychological dependence in users. The levels of nicotine in ST are consistently higher than that found in cigarettes, sometimes as much as three times higher, and can be adjusted higher or lower by tobacco companies during production [16]. The use of ST leads to the development of a tolerance for nicotine, which causes the user to crave more, and stronger, tobacco products in order to generate the same effects that were felt early in their use, even as the addiction progresses [16]. The stronger products that are used by people who have built up a tolerance for nicotine tend to be the products that have higher levels of carcinogens and therefore a higher risk for disease. Tolerance is the capacity for a given dose of any drug to produce less of an effect after repeated doses, which then requires an increase in intake over time to achieve the desired effect. Tolerance is important to consider when discussing health effects because developing a tolerance to tobacco's properties and effects may lead to increased use and an increased level of toxin and carcinogen intake [16].

Some consider nicotine addiction the most hazardous health effect because it is the reason that ST users continue the habit in spite of knowing about the dangerous health effects associated with tobacco. However, there are other alternatives for the delivery of nicotine, such as prescription medications and over the counter patches or gums that can act as a healthier long-term alternative to ST products or during tobacco cessation attempts. These pharmaceutical options are FDA approved and regulated by the government during production to ensure that the products are safe and pure.

They allow the regulation of the amount of nicotine for current users or allow one to taper the amount of nicotine that is delivered to the body and decrease the intensity of any withdrawal symptoms for those trying to quit smoking or other tobacco use. Tobacco companies have long pitched ST use as a nicotine alternative or even as a smoking cessation tool because they argue that ST is a less harmful tobacco option when compared to cigarettes. But ST use as a tool to quit smoking should not be considered a viable option because of the lack of regulations in production and the serious health consequences associated with any tobacco use.

ST USE IN THE UNITED STATES

ST consumption in the United States has a current prevalence rate of 3.3% of adults nationally [15, 25]. Current ST users are defined as those people who state that they have used the product at least once in the past thirty days. The majority of users tend to be male (6% of the male adult population), Native American/Alaska Natives (9%), or Caucasian (4%) [15]. Many ST users also fall in the adolescent or young adult age ranges. Several studies conducted in this population have placed the prevalence rate of high school males between 8% and 14% and the prevalence rate in adults 18-24 between 5% and 8.7% [30-31, 43-45]. Numerous other sociocultural and psychosocial variables are associated with ST use other than age, race, and gender. Having one or no parent in the household, lower parental education, blue-collar parental or personal occupations, rural environment, lower academic performance, previous cigarette smoking, having friends who use ST, living with adults who use ST, and/or concurrent alcohol or marijuana use all have been associated with an increased risk for initiation and continuation of use [44, 46-48]. While not all variables leading to higher rates of ST use can be altered or corrected, studies have found that finding ways to decrease the rate and age of initiation can help to reduce the prevalence of ST use while also decreasing how long that tobacco use occurs in individuals before cessation. Decreasing these variables will lead to better health outcomes as a lower prevalence of ST use or a decreased time of use for an individual leads to less risk for the damaging health effects and possible mortality associated with tobacco [44, 46-48].

ST use, especially in adolescents, has become such an important topic nationally that intervention and cessation objectives have been included in *Healthy People 2000, Healthy People 2010*, and *Healthy People 2020* as a component of the tobacco use focus points [45, 47, 49, 50]. Decreasing the initiation and prevalence of use in males aged 12 through 24 by more than 4% was designated a significant objective in *Healthy People 2000*. This goal was not achieved and has been re-introduced in both updated versions for 2010 and 2020 [45, 47]. The goal in the most recent document is to reduce overall use to 0.4% and reduce adolescent use to 1% of the population, while also attempting to increase the average age of initiation for ST use [50]. The age of initiation is an important factor to consider because high school seniors who view themselves as regular users report that they tried ST for the first time by the sixth grade (23%), eighth grade (53%), or ninth grade (75%). Increasing the age of initiation would mean that adolescents considering first time use would have a higher level of maturity and understanding of the risks associated with tobacco. The older the individual, the less likely they would be to initiate the habit. This suggests that prevention and cessation programs need to be implemented at the middle school level if the goals and objectives of *Healthy People 2020* are to be met [19, 45, 51].

ST USE IN BASEBALL

One of the common variables associated with the use of ST is participation in athletics at all levels [7, 14, 41, 48, 49, 52-57]. Studies of high school athletes have found current use rates between 6 and 21% in all sports even though most high school athletes are too young to purchase tobacco products [56, 58]. A National Collegiate Athletic Association (NCAA) study conducted in 2017 reported that 13% of collegiate athletes in all sports used ST on a regular basis [6, 59]. This widespread use occurred in spite of an NCAA regulation, enacted in 1994, that bans the use of ST products in practice and competition [6, 27, 41]. In addition, studies of athletes in professional sports have found that ST usage can be as high as 50% on teams in select sports, such as ice hockey, wrestling, lacrosse, and baseball. Baseball, more so than any other sport, has shown consistently high levels of ST use, in spite of the NCAA ban and a similar ban on use enacted by minor league baseball in 1993 for all on-field personnel and players [53, 59-60]. Athletes in this sport, both professional and those at the amateur level, have shown a high prevalence rate for ST use ranging from 34-50% in high school, 44% in the NCAA, and 50% in the professional ranks [7, 14, 59, 60].

The sport of baseball has a long history and connection with the use of ST at all levels from as young as little league--where a bubble gum product called Big League Chew prepares young mouths for the use of chewing tobacco--to minor and major league teams [7, 14, 30, 41, 58, 61]. The custom of using ST in baseball began more than a century ago, almost as soon as the new sport emerged as an adult activity during the 1850s [1]. Tobacco use was initially popular because players on dusty baseball fields used the product to keep their mouths moist during games [53, 62]. ST was also used as a way to roughen the baseball itself in an attempt to alter the trajectory of the ball during a pitch. Players would saturate the ball with tobacco juice and then rub the ball in the dirt, which would make the ball easier to grip and cause it to break in different directions on its way from the pitcher's hand to the plate. Some players and managers would even use ST as a way to signal pitches and plays during the game. The intentional placement of ST in the mouth at certain times in a game or changing the location of the chew from cheek to cheek between pitches would often be a sign for the players in the field what would occur on the next pitch [1].

Tobacco use in general was a key ally in the effort to establish baseball as a manly, adult activity rather than placed in the same category as the childish games that had preceded it. The initial leaders of the sport went to great pains to enhance the masculine nature of the activity, including using a harder ball that made the game more painful and putting a new emphasis on the athletes' strength [1]. As the momentum of the sport grew in the late 1860s after the civil war, many of the initial professional teams were affiliated with local cigar stores. At a time when paying someone to play baseball was unheard of and bewildering to many, the especially talented athletes were enticed to join specific teams through offers of employment as proprietors of cigar and tobacco clubs [1]. These cigar stores/clubs also helped the sport by enhancing its image as an acceptable, nonthreatening, and even safe activity. Cigar stores, as the ultimate male enclave, were considered far less objectionable hangouts for young men than saloons or brothels. The popularity and propriety of the cigar stores helped to increase the exposure baseball received and eventually amplified its prestige and transformed it into the national pastime [1].

As baseball became a fixture around the country, tobacco cemented its relationship with the sport by introducing a new innovation to the game-photographic cards of the local players that could only be obtained at the cigar store that served as a team's headquarters [1]. This type of promotional campaign became especially effective once cigarette companies took over the concept and began to mass-produce cards that featured photographs of hundreds of major-league players and managers that were placed in tobacco packages. As cigarette use gained popularity in the US, so did the purchase of specific brands of cigarettes for the purpose of collecting the included baseball cards [1].

Initially, cigars, pipes, and ST were the most acceptable types of tobacco for use in America. Cigarettes, which were popular in Turkey and other eastern countries, did not have the same level of social respectability in the western countries, like the US, because they introduced a new form of use-inhalation smoking [1]. The other forms of tobacco and their smoke were too harsh to be inhaled, but as new types of tobacco were developed that were better suited for inhalation smoking, cigarette consumption rose significantly and became more accepted socially. By 1910, cigarette use had gained widespread approval and popularity, and the collection of the baseball cards that were included in the packs had become a nationwide craze with tobacco companies producing approximately seventy-five different series of cards. Boys who wanted to show their allegiance to the sport would beg their fathers to buy specific brands of cigarettes solely for the coveted cards that were included [1].

Ironically, it was the opposition to the tobacco sponsorship of baseball cards that perhaps sealed the association between tobacco use and the sport. Honus Wagner was considered one of the all-time great athletes in the sport as the shortstop for the Pittsburgh Pirates. Wagner expressed concern that the use of his image on baseball cards, which he felt implied his approval of tobacco use, would encourage boys who revered him for his play on the field to take up smoking [1]. The American Tobacco Company, which was producing the card, agreed to Wagner's request to not include his baseball card in their cigarette packs; however, several dozen cards had already been produced and were in circulation. Those cards, because of their scarcity, became the most valuable cards on the market at the time-a fact that has continued to be true to this day as confirmed by a recent sale of one of the cards for over $3 million-and significantly increased the awareness of and fascination with card collection through the purchase of tobacco [1]. Baseball card collection as a tobacco marketing tool had proven to be extremely successful for both the sport and the product.

Tobacco use, specifically cigarette smoking was popular in baseball throughout the first half of the twentieth century with numerous players serving as paid spokesmen for their selected brand of tobacco. It was not until the 1950s that cigarettes began to fall out of favor with ballplayers and endorsements began to decline because medical science started to produce irrefutable evidence that there was a link between cigarette smoking and cancer, emphysema, and heart disease. Yet, the relationship between tobacco use and baseball did not end there. ST use reemerged as an option and again became a staple on the baseball diamond after World War II [1].

It became more popular in the 1970s and 1980s in response to an aggressive marketing campaign targeted toward professional baseball players [58]. Tobacco companies saw advertising through baseball as a way to attract new, more active demographic groups who were not interested in cigarette use. They offered free samples and promotional materials to teams and players and used the sport in advertising campaigns as an example of how to use ST while being an active individual. ST use has been prevalent in baseball and continued throughout the years because it is an activity that allows ST use through unique practice/game situations, including the opportunity to use ST products during competition with less concern for hazardous conditions [6-7]. The fits-and-starts structure of the game, the lulls in activity, and a decreased risk of contact and/or collision allow for increased ST consumption during games that is not possible in other sports [1, 6].

There is also a social norm associated with baseball players that ST use is acceptable and even 'mandated' by ritualistic and superstitious manners [6, 7, 55]. Tobacco use has been such an integral part of the game and its culture that a ballplayer often wouldn't be considered 'one of the boys' without using ST. Players in the nineteenth century were considered oddities and given derisive nicknames if they refused to use tobacco [1]. Even today, baseball athletes, especially at the high school and collegiate level, experience intensive role modeling through the visible use of ST by professional players, coaches, and peers, sports-centered advertising, and promotional programs with free samples [6-7]. Sport-specific use and role modeling are evident with research reporting that more than 50% of high school, collegiate, and professional baseball players predominantly used ST during the competitive baseball season or used it dramatically more during the season than out of season [6-7, 30]. Many athletes report that there is a certain pull to use ST merely from stepping onto the field. They may not use tobacco products in everyday life, but when baseball season starts, the habit and the urges return immediately.

Given the prominent place that baseball has in the culture of the United States, the potential influence that athletes can have on young people, and the fact that sports are often the vehicle by which we pass on many of our treasured national ideals and values to the younger generations, it is important to continue the effort to help players at all levels avoid initiation of the habit or to quit their current use [53, 58]. It is also important to change the policy, environmental influences, and social norms that sanction and support ST use in baseball and make it a prominent cultural component of the game [14, 58]. Removing tobacco use as one of the traditions of the sport will help current and future baseball players lead healthier lives and avoid the risk of debilitating disease. Current players at the highest levels of the sport can lead the charge by acting as positive role models for the younger athletes.

ROLE MODELING IN BASEBALL

Role modeling is extremely important in the early stages of development for an adolescent who is forming the core standards and beliefs that will be the foundation for his/her future character [38, 63-66]. The individuals that adolescents admire are seen as possessing character traits that teens should learn in order to achieve similar success, such as playing professional baseball [67]. Role models are important aspects of an adolescent's life not just because of the particular role that they may play (i.e., parent, coach, or professional athlete), but also because they can demonstrate how to navigate through all sorts of situations in life [8]. Role models play a significant part in the socialization of young people by providing examples of behavior and values and reinforcing or validating those morals and actions [68].

Sports especially have an enormous influence in our culture and society because they are an optimal arena for personal development of an individual's moral judgment [8, 11]. Professional athletes in this arena, who are looked to as cultural icons for a variety of qualities from athletic prowess to personal character, have a heightened influence on the conduct of others and they should be sensitive to the additional moral obligations to behave well because children and adolescents will mimic the behavior-both good and bad-that is exhibited during games either live or on TV [8-9].

Professional baseball players are identified as the prototypical athletes and role models for their sport, and that role provides them with the opportunity to model either positive or negative behaviors regarding ST use. Adolescents are willing to engage in more risky behaviors, including ST use, when they associate that behavior with people that they admire [69-70]. The emulation of respected male figures has often been described as essential to the process of ST initiation for young males. Televised games that show ST use by the athletes and coaches broadcast an implicit product endorsement to millions of viewers worldwide, while youth playing fields can be ideal settings for ST experimentation because when elite players, coaches, and peers use tobacco, it normalizes the behavior within the environment, which then fosters initiation among younger players [2].

Continuous reinforcement of tobacco use as a societal norm--or a baseball norm--is precarious because it becomes common practice and is no longer considered dangerous or unhealthy. This positive norm and acceptance of tobacco use by adults and peers in the eyes of an adolescent will lead that teen to believe the social pressure to use tobacco is in their best interest and that significant others will not disapprove of tobacco use. If adolescents believe that ST use is acceptable or even expected of them by their friends and family, then they are more likely to ignore the health risks associated with tobacco, which will then lead to an inability or lack of desire to resist using ST and initiation of the habit [66].

Athletes at all levels of baseball are role models for young people, especially boys, and should take advantage of that role and act in a positive and healthy manner for fans through diminished or complete cessation of ST use and participation in public education campaigns against the use of ST [14, 53, 55]. Prevention programs created specifically for baseball athletes would be an excellent way to highlight the number of professional players that do not use ST and focus on creating effective strategies that convince student-athletes of their personal vulnerability to the health risks associated with ST use and override what they see as the positive aspects of use, including peer approval [14, 59].

One aspect of prevention programs that has not been utilized to this point with baseball teams and athletes is incorporating coaches as advocates for healthy behavior. Although there are many factors that support the use of ST among young baseball players, including: the sale of tobacco to minors, parental acceptance of ST use, ST use by family members, and perceptions of use by baseball-associated role models, it is the perception of use by those in a leadership position that may have the largest sway [14]. Coaches, especially at the high school level, have a rare opportunity to instill values, ethics, and sportsmanship in their athletes, which makes it incumbent upon them to present a wholesome and positive image to their athletes [63]. Coaches should understand that the impact that their attitudes, perceptions, indifferences, and personal use of ST can have a significant influence on the use of ST in young athletes [7, 41, 54, 55, 71].

Coaches rank as the #1 positive influence on today's youth, making them truly the guardians of youth sports and the protectors of the health of those athletes [72]. Personal tobacco use by a coach provides an implied consent to the team and reinforcement of the connection between baseball and ST [73]. For instance, research has demonstrated that ST use in baseball players was three times higher on a team where the coach also was a ST user [74]. Because of these concerns, it is essential that coaches reconsider any personal ST use and how it may be perceived by their athletes while also developing an awareness of which athletes on their team use ST and which ones may be at risk for initiation. This awareness would allow the coaches to have conversations with at-risk athletes to discuss the risks of tobacco use. Coaches should also be involved in implementing prevention or intervention techniques to decrease or eliminate use [6]. Developing an understanding in baseball coaches that they can be positive role models for their athletes is essential in the effort to rid the sport of ST addiction and the positive perception of use [6]. If the coaches would utilize clear and explicit efforts to guide the athletes on their team away from ST use, baseball would be better able to decrease adolescent and collegiate athlete addiction to this dangerous substance [6, 41].

Coaches spend a considerable amount of time with youth in sports and are responsible for enhancing their athletes' physical, mental, and tactical abilities at a significant point in adolescent development and play a critical role in that development [75-76]. Coaches are also able to establish a team climate and culture that will influence the social norms associated with that sport. If youth are constantly being told about positive influences and social norms, then coaches should be actively modeling those same behaviors now and into the future. If negative acts are not being modeled by social agents, then the likelihood that adolescents will perform those acts is decreased [76]. Therefore, if coaches want to have a positive influence on youth, then they need to uphold high standards for their personal behavior [77]. Because of the important role that sport plays in society and its potential for building character, promoting success, and creating lifelong healthy habits, it is essential that coaches and players be good role models and emphasize positive behaviors, while also intervening in negative behavior and discussing the potential consequences of that behavior [11, 76, 78]. Regarding ST use, it is vital that coaches and professional athletes, as significant social agents in the minds of adolescent athletes, avoid visible use of ST-especially during competition, eliminate product endorsement-either through direct advertisement or the use of promotional devices, and addressing ST use with the team and individual players to identify the health hazards associated with use and offer assistance in quitting [2, 71].

REGULATION OF ST USE IN BASEBALL

The NCAA and Minor League Baseball were at the forefront of regulating ST use when they both enacted bans on use in practices and competition in 1993 and 1994; however, Major League Baseball (MLB) did not follow suit initially because of player backlash [6, 27, 41]. Finally, in 2012 as part of the negotiations for a new five-year collective bargaining agreement between MLB and the Players Association (MLBPA), it was agreed that players, coaches, managers, and other team personnel would be banned from carrying ST products onto the field in their uniforms or to use ST products during team-sponsored appearances or interviews [79]. The new policy was due in large part to a dedicated promotional effort sponsored by the Campaign for Tobacco-Free Kids. Tobacco-Free Baseball was an initiative intended to set the right example for America's kids and to protect the health of the players [80].

The Tobacco-Free Baseball initiative has continued to work with MLB, as well as the city and state governments that host the professional teams to eliminate ST completely from the sport of baseball. In the most recent collective bargaining agreement between MLB and MLBPA (2016), all players who are entering the league for the first time starting in the 2017 season will be banned from using ST in games [70, 80]. And as of the beginning of the 2019 season, 16 of the 30 MLB stadiums are designated as tobacco-free as a result of state and local laws and ordinances [80]. These initiatives have gone a long way toward delegitimizing the long-standing relationship between ST use and baseball, but there is still a need for coaches and players to be actively involved to take the final steps in ensuring that future generations of athletes are tobacco free.

CONCLUSION

Spit tobacco consists primarily of two varieties-moist snuff and chewing tobacco. Moist snuff is a finely ground tobacco leaf sold in small cans and popular in sports such as baseball. Chewing tobacco is a more coarsely cut tobacco that is sold in pouches or plug form. All forms of ST cause serious health issues such as gingivitis, tooth decay, cardiovascular disease, sexual impotence, female reproductive issues, and several forms of cancer. Oral cancer is the most serious health effect linked to ST use with a 54% mortality rate five years after diagnosis.

The sport of baseball has a long history and connection with the use of ST. Baseball is an activity that allows ST use because of unique practice/game situations, including the opportunity to use ST products during competition with less concern for hazardous conditions. There are many factors that support the use of ST among young baseball players, including the sale of tobacco to minors, parental acceptance of ST use, ST use by family members, and perceptions of use by baseball-associated role models--specifically professional players and coaches at all levels. Coaches and professional athletes are role models for younger baseball players and need to exemplify positive behaviors and discourage negative actions on the field. Being a role model for healthy behaviors would help to break the connection between ST use and baseball now and into the future, while also protecting the adolescent athletes from the significant health effects that may occur as a result of ST use.

REFERENCES

[1] Morris, P. Personally, I Have Nothing against Smoking. *NINE: A journal of baseball history and culture.* 2009;18(1):37-62.

[2] Chaffee BW, Couch ET, Walsh MM. *Smokeless Tobacco in Sport and Use among Adolescents.* UCSF: Center for Tobacco Control and Education. 2015.

[3] Conrad AK, Hutton SB, Munnelly M, Bay RC. Screening for Smokeless Tobacco Use and Presence of Oral Lesions in Major League Baseball Athletes. *J Calif Dent Assoc.* 2015;43(1):14-20.

[4] Eaves T, Strack RW. Factors Affecting High School Baseball Coaches' Enforcement of School Tobacco Policy. *J Child Adolesc Sub Abuse.* 2014;24(2):125-130.

[5] *The NSDUH Report: Smokeless Tobacco Use, Initiation, and Relationship to Cigarette Smoking.* Substance Abuse and Mental Health Services Administration. 2017.

[6] Eaves T, Schmitz RJ, Siebel EJ. Prevalence of Spit Tobacco Use and Health Effects Awareness in Baseball Coaches. *J Calif Dent Assoc.* 2009;37(6):403-410.

[7] Walsh M, Hilton JF, Ernster VL, et al. Prevalence, Patterns, and Correlates of Spit Tobacco Use in a College Athlete Population. *Addict Behav.* 1994;19(4):411-427.

[8] Feezell R. Celebrated Athletes, Moral Exemplars, and Lusory Objects. *J Philosophy Sport.* 2005;32(1):20-35.

[9] Guest AM, Cox S. Using Athletes as Role Models? Conceptual and empirical perspectives from a sample of elite women soccer players. *Int J Sports Sci Coaching.* 2009;4(4):567-581.

[10] Martin EM, Ewing ME, Gould D. Social Agents' Influence on Self-Perceived Good and Bad Behavior of American Youth Involved in Sport: Developmental Level, Gender, and Competitive Level Effects. *Sport Psychologist.* 2014;28(2):111-123.

[11] Melin R. Are Sportspersons Good Moral Role Models? *Phys Culture Sports Stud Res.* 2014;64(1):5-17.

[12] Wackowski OA, DelnevoCD. Smokers' attitudes and support for e-cigarette policies and regulation in the USA. *Tob Cont.* 2015;24:543-546.

[13] Eaves T. The Relationship Between Spit Tobacco and Baseball. *J Sport Soc Issues.* 2014;437-442.

[14] Cooper J, Ellison JA, Walsh MM. Spit (Smokeless)-Tobacco Use by Baseball Players Entering the Professional Ranks. *J Athl Train.* 2003;38(2):126-132.

[15] *Smoking and Tobacco Use: Fact Sheet Smokeless Tobacco.* Centers for Disease Control. 2018.

[16] Henningfield J, Fant RV, Tomar SL. Smokeless Tobacco: An addicting drug. *Adv Dent Res.* 1997;11(3):330-335.

[17] Nelson D, Mowery P, Tomar, S, Marcus S, Giovino G, Zhao L. Trends in Smokeless Tobacco Use Among Adults and Adolescents in the United States. *Am J Public Health.* 2006;96(5):897-905.

[18] Wang TW, Asman K, Gentzke JS, Cullen KA, Holder-Hayes E, Reyes-Guzman C, Jamal A, Neff L, King BA. Tobacco Product Use Among Adults-United States, 2017. *Morbidity and Mortality Weekly Report.* 2018;67(44):1225-1232.

[19] Boonn A. *Smokeless Tobacco in the United States: An overview of the health risks and industry marketing aimed at children and the compelling need for effective regulation of all tobacco products by the FDA*: Campaign for Tobacco-Free Kids. 2007.

[20] Tomar S. Epidemiological Perspectives on Smokeless Tobacco Marketing and Population Harm. *Am J Prev Med.* 2007;33(6):S387-S397.

[21] *FDA Regulation of Tobacco Products: A common sense law to protect kids and save lives.* Campaign for Tobacco-Free Kids. 2010.

[22] Boonn, A. *United States Smokeless Tobacco Company: A real public health 'bandit':* Campaign for Tobacco-Free Kids. 2008.

[23] Masouredis C, Hilton JF, Grady D, Gee L, Chesney M, Hengl L, Ernster VL, Walsh MM. A Spit Tobacco Cessation Intervention for College Athletes: Three-month results. *Adv Dent Res.* 1997;11(3):354-359.

[24] Morrison M, Krugman DM, Park P. Under the Radar: Smokeless tobacco advertising in magazines with substantial youth readership. *Am J Public Health,* 2008;98(3):543-548.

[25] *The NSDUH Report: Smokeless Tobacco Use, Initiation, and Relationship to Cigarette Smoking: 2002 to 2007.* Substance Abuse and Mental Health Services Administration. 2009.

[26] *Tobacco Basics Handbook* (3rd ed.). Alberta Alcohol and Drug Abuse Commission. 2008.

[27] Burak L. Smokeless Tobacco Education for College Athletes. *J of Phys Educ, Recreation, and Dance.* 2001;72(1):37-38, 53.

[28] *Federal Trade Commission Smokeless Tobacco Report for the Year 2006.* Federal Trade Commission. 2009.

[29] Shopland D. US Consumption of Chewing Tobacco and Snuff, 1982-1997. *J Natl Cancer Inst.* 1997;89(21):1573.

[30] Siegel D, Benowitz N, Ernster VL, et al. Smokeless Tobacco, Cardiovascular Risk Factors, and Nicotine and Cotinine Levels in Professional Baseball Players. *Am J Pub Health.* 1992;82(3):417-421.

[31] Stepanov I, Jensen J, Hatsukami D, Hecht SS. New and Traditional Smokeless Tobacco: Comparison of toxicant and carcinogen levels. *Nicotine Tob Res.* 2008;10(12):1773-1782.

[32] Hecht S, Carmella SG, Murphy SE, Riley WT, Le C, Luo X, Mooney M, Hatsukami DK. Similar Exposure to a Tobacco-Specific Carcinogen in Smokeless Tobacco Users and Cigarette Smokers. *Cancer Epidemiol Biomarkers.* 2007;16(8):1567-1572.

[33] Boffetta P, Hecht S, Gray N, Gupta P, Straif K. Smokeless Tobacco and Cancer. *Lancet Onc.* 2008;9(7):667-675.

[34] *IARC Monograph on the Evaluation of Carcinogenic Risks to Humans: Smokeless tobacco and some tobacco-specific N-Nitrosamines*: International Agency for Research on Cancer 2007.

[35] McKee M, Gilmore A. Commentary: Smokeless tobacco: Seeing the whole picture. *Intl J Epidemiol,* 2007;36(4):805-808.

[36] Boonn A. *Health Harms from Smokeless Tobacco Use*: Campaign for Tobacco-Free Kids. 2008.

[37] Conrad AK, Hutton SB, Perry MM, Bay RC. Screening for Smokeless Tobacco Use and Presence of Oral Lesions in Major League Baseball Athletes. *J Calif Dent Assoc.* 2015;43(1):15-20.

[38] Gansky S, Ellison JA, Kavanagh C, et al. Patterns and Correlates of Spit Tobacco Use among High School Males in Rural California. *J Pub Health Dent.* 2009; 69(2):116-124.

[39] Gupta S, Gupta R, Sinha DN, Mehrotra R. Relationship Between Type of Smokeless Tobacco & Risk of Cancer: A systematic review. *Indian J Med Res.* 2018;148(7):56-76.

[40] Walsh M, Hilton JF, Ellison JA, Gee L, Chesney MA, Tomar SL, Ernster VL. Spit (Smokeless) Tobacco Intervention for High School Athletes: Results after 1 year. *Addict Behav.* 2003;28(6):1095-1113.

[41] Gansky S, Ellison JA, Rudy D, et al. Cluster-Randomized Controlled Trial of An Athletic Trainer-Directed Spit (Smokeless) Tobacco Intervention for Collegiate Baseball Athletes: Results after 1 year. *J of Athl Train.* 2005;40(2):76-87.

[42] Boyle RG, Jensen J, Hatsukami DK, Severson HH. Measuring dependence in smokeless tobacco users. *Addict Behav.* 1995;20(4):443–450.

[43] Boonn A. *Smokeless Tobacco in the United States*: Campaign for Tobacco-Free Kids. 2008.

[44] Ebbert J, Rowland LC, Montori VM, Vickers KS, Erwin PJ, Dale LC. Treatment for Spit Tobacco Use: A quantitative systematic review. *Addiction.* 2003;98(5):569-583.

[45] Lamkin L, Davis B, Kamen A. Rationale for Tobacco Cessation Interventions for Youth. *Preventive Medicine,* 1998;27(5):A3-A8.

[46] Morrell H, Cohen LM, Bacchi D, West J. Predictors of Smoking and Smokeless Tobacco Use in College Students: A preliminary study using web-based survey methodology. *J Am College Health.* 2005;54(2):108-115.

[47] *Healthy People 2020: Tobacco Use Data Details.* Office of Disease Prevention and Health Promotion. 2009.

[48] Tomar S, Giovino GA. Incidences and Predictors of Smokeless Tobacco Use among US Youth. *Am J Pub Health.* 1998;88(1):20-26.

[49] Hilton J, Walsh MM, Masouredis CM, et al. Planning a Spit Tobacco Cessation Intervention: Identification of beliefs associated with addiction. *Add Behav.* 1994;19(4):381-391.

[50] *Healthy People 2010: Understanding and Improving Health.* Office of Disease Prevention and Health Promotion. 2009.

[51] Newman I, Shell DF. Smokeless Tobacco Expectancies Among a Sample of Rural Adolescents. *Am J Health Behav.* 2005;29(2):127-136.

[52] Castrucci B, Gerlach KK, Kaufman NJ, Orleans CT. Tobacco Use and Cessation Behavior Among Adolescents Participating in Organized Sports. *Am J Health Behav.* 2004;28(1):63-71.

[53] Connolly G, Orleans CT, Blum A. Snuffing Tobacco out of Sport. *Am J Public Health.* 1992;82(3):351-353.

[54] Davis T, Arnold C, Nandy I, et al. Tobacco Use Among Male High School Athletes. *J Adolesc Health.* 1997;21(2):97-101.

[55] Gingiss P, Gottleib NH. A Comparison of Smokeless Tobacco and Smoking Practices of University Varsity and Intramural Baseball Players. *Addict Behav.* 1991;16(5):335-340.

[56] Horn K, Maniar SD, Dino GA, et al. Coaches' Attitudes Toward Smokeless Tobacco and Intentions to Intervene with Athletes. *J Sch Health,* 2000;70(3):89-94.

[57] Walsh M, Hilton JF, Masouredis CM, et al. Smokeless Tobacco Cessation Intervention for College Athletes: Results after 1 year. *Am J Pub Health.* 1999;89(2):228-234.

[58] Severson H, Klein K, Lichtenstein E, et al. Smokeless Tobacco Use among Professional Baseball Players: Survey results, 1998-2003. *Tob Control.* 2005;14(1):31-36.

[59] NCAA Research Staff. *NCAA Study of Substance Use Habits of College Student-Athletes.* Indianapolis: National Collegiate Athletic Association. 2018.

[60] Sinusas K, Coroso JG. A 10-year study of Smokeless Tobacco Use in a Professional Baseball Organization. *Med Sci Sports Exercise,* 2006;38(7):1204-1207.

[61] Chiamulera C, Leone R, Fumagalli G. Smokeless Tobacco Use in Sports: 'Legal doping'? *Addiction,* 2007;102(12):1847-1848.

[62] Ranalli D, Cianflone D. Spit Tobacco: Baseball's hidden health hazard. *Coach and Athletic Director,* 1996;65(9):8-9.

[63] *Target for Today: The abolition of chewing tobacco.* National Federation Interscholastic Coaches Association 1995.

[64] Flay BR, Hu F, Siddiqui O, et al. Differential Influence of Parental Smoking and Friends' Smoking on Adolescent Initiation and Escalation of Smoking. *J Health Social Behav.* 1994;35(3):248-265.

[65] Manning M. The Effects of Subjective Norms on Behaviour in the Theory of Planned Behaviour: A meta-analysis. *Br J Social Psychol.* 2009;48(4):649-705.

[66] Wiium N, Breivik K, Wold B. The Relationship between Smoker Role Models and Intentions to Smoke among Adolescents. *J Youth Adolesc.* 2006;35(4):551-562.

[67] Buford May, RA. The Good and Bad of it All: Professional black male basketball players as role models for young black male basketball players. *Sociology Sport J.* 2009;26(4):443-461.

[68] Lyle J. Role Models, Sporting Success and Participation: A review of sports coaching's ancillary roles. *Int J Coach Sci.* 2013;7(2):25-40.

[69] Winn, DM. Smokeless Tobacco: Impact on the health of our nation's youth and use in Major League Baseball. Testimony before the *Subcommittee on Health Committee on Energy and Commerce United States House of Representatives.* 2010.

[70] Chaffee, BW, Couch, ET, Gansky, SA. Adolescents' smokeless tobacco susceptibility by perceived professional baseball players' use. *J Public Health Dent.* 2018;78(1):5-8.

[71] Skinner JHC, Bobbili SJ. Coaches' Knowledge and Awareness of Spit Tobacco Use Among Youth Athletes: Results of a 2009 Ontario study. *Chronic Dis and Injuries in Canada.* 2012;32(3):149-155.

[72] *What Sport Means in America: A study of sport's role in society.* United States Anti-Doping Agency. 2011.

[73] Martinsen M, Sundgot-Borgen J. Adolescent elite athletes' cigarette smoking, use of snus, and alcohol. *Scandinavian J Med Sci Sports.* 2014;24(2):439-446.

[74] Walsh MM, Ellison J, Hilton JF, et al. Spit (Smokeless) Tobacco Use by High School Baseball Athletes in California. *Tob Control.* 2000;9(Supplement II):ii32-ii39.

[75] Becker AJ. It's not What They Do, It's How They Do It. *Int J Sports Sci Coaching.* 2009;4(1):93-119.

[76] Smith S. Tax-hike on Chewing Tobacco, Cheap Cigars expected to Reduce Use. *Maryland Reporter.* 2012.

[77] Shields DL, Bredemeier BL, LaVoi NM, Power FC. The sport behavior of youth, parents, and coaches: The good, the bad, and the ugly. *J Res Character Education.* 2005;3(1):43-59.

[78] Chaffee, BW, Couch, ET, Urata, J, Gansky, SA, Essex, G, Cheng, J. *Predictors of Smokeless Tobacco Susceptibility, Initiation, and Progression over Time among Adolescents in a Rural Cohort, Substance Use and Misuse.* 2019;54(7):1154-1166.

[79] Silverstein R. *The Relationship Between Spit Tobacco and Baseball.* National Summit on Smokeless Tobacco. 2013.

[80] *Knock Tobacco Out of the Park.* Tobacco-Free Baseball. 2019.

BIOGRAPHICAL SKETCH

Ted Eaves

Affiliation: Wake Forest University

Education: EdD, LAT, ATC, CSCS

Business Address: 1834 Wake Forest Rd, Winston-Salem, NC, US

Research and Professional Experience: Head Athletic Trainer for 7 years; spit tobacco researcher for 17 years

Professional Appointments: Member of Tobacco-Free Baseball Initiative

INDEX

Related Nova Publications

A QUICK GUIDE FOR CLINICAL BIOCHEMISTRY

AUTHORS: Buthainah Al Bulushi and Mohamed Essa, PhD

SERIES: Biochemistry Research Trends

BOOK DESCRIPTION: This book will be a useful reference for new students, non-native English medicine and life science students as it relies on figures and diagrams that explain the concepts and diagnosis of diseases in a simple way.

SOFTCOVER ISBN: 978-1-53614-860-2
RETAIL PRICE: $82

PROTEASES: FUNCTIONS, MECHANISMS AND USES

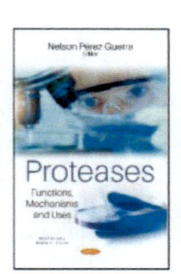

EDITOR: Nelson Pérez Guerra

SERIES: Biochemistry Research Trends

BOOK DESCRIPTION: The book provides an overview of the latest knowledge about the functions and action mechanisms of protease enzymes and their applications in different industrial fields.

HARDCOVER ISBN: 978-1-53615-854-0
RETAIL PRICE: $230

To see a complete list of Nova publications, please visit our website at www.novapublishers.com

Related Nova Publications

A Closer Look at the Comet Assay

Editor: Keith H. Harmon

Series: Biochemistry Research Trends

Book Description: *A Closer Look at the Comet Assay* opens with a discussion on the clinical applications of comet assay. Comet assay is rapid, simple method which able to assess DNA damage in different samples like blood, cells and tissues.

Hardcover ISBN: 978-1-53611-028-9
Retail Price: $160

MCQ in Clinical Biochemistry

Author: Pranav Kumar Prabhakar, PhD

Series: Biochemistry Research Trends

Book Description: Multiple Choice Questions (MCQs) are the backbone for all entrance examinations throughout the world. MCQs are used to evaluate student's cognitive acumen in all the fields and discipline.

Hardcover ISBN: 978-1-53616-174-8
Retail Price: $230

To see a complete list of Nova publications, please visit our website at www.novapublishers.com